ORIGINAL
ROLLS-ROYCE
& BENTLEY
1946-65

Other titles available in the *Original* series are:

Original AC Ace & Cobra
by Rinsey Mills
Original Aston Martin DB4/5/6
by Robert Edwards
Original Austin Seven
by Rinsey Mills
Original Austin-Healey (100 & 3000)
by Anders Ditlev Clausager
Original Citroën DS
by John Reynolds with Jan de Lange
Original Corvette 1953-1962
by Tom Falconer
Original Corvette 1963-1967
by Tom Falconer
Original Ferrari V8
by Keith Bluemel
Original Honda CB750
by John Wyatt
Original Jaguar E-Type
by Philip Porter
Original Jaguar Mark I/II
by Nigel Thorley
Original Jaguar XJ
by Nigel Thorley
Original Jaguar XK
by Philip Porter
Original Land-Rover Series I
by James Taylor
Original Mercedes SL
by Laurence Meredith
Original MG T Series
by Anders Ditlev Clausager
Original MGA
by Anders Ditlev Clausager
Original MGB
by Anders Ditlev Clausager
Original Mini Cooper and Cooper S
by John Parnell
Original Morgan
by John Worrall and Liz Turner
Original Morris Minor
by Ray Newell
Original Porsche 356
by Laurence Meredith
Original Porsche 911
by Peter Morgan
Original Porsche 924/944/968
by Peter Morgan
Original Sprite & Midget
by Terry Horler
Original Triumph TR2/3/3A
by Bill Piggott
Original Triumph TR4/4A/5/6
by Bill Piggott
Original Vincent
by J. P. Bickerstaff
Original VW Beetle
by Laurence Meredith
Original VW Bus
by Laurence Meredith

ORIGINAL
ROLLS-ROYCE
& BENTLEY
1946-65

by James Taylor

Photography by Mark Dixon
Edited by Warren Allport

The photographs on the jacket and preliminary
pages show examples of 1957 Bentley Continental
S-series Park Ward drophead coupé (front cover),
1955 Rolls-Royce Silver Dawn (back cover),
1947 Bentley MkVI (half title page),
1959 Rolls-Royce Silver Cloud (title page) and
1960 Bentley S2 (contents page).

Published 1999 by Bay View Books Ltd
The Red House, 25-26 Bridgeland Street
Bideford, Devon EX39 2PZ, UK

Series edited by Mark Hughes
Designed by Chris Fayers

ISBN 1 901432 18 1
Printed in China

Contents

Introduction

The Rolls-Royce and Bentley motor cars covered in this book were current when I was still at school, and for me they have always and will always represent the marques at their best. So I was delighted to be entrusted with the task of pulling together *Original Rolls-Royce and Bentley 1946-65*, as it enabled me to get to much closer grips with a favourite subject.

The number of contradictions in existing books on the subject made me suspect that it would not be an easy task, and I was proved right time and again. To my surprise, I even found contradictions within Rolls-Royce's own literature on some issues. I must, of course, acknowledge the editorial guidance, experience and wisdom of Warren Allport, who on several occasions was able to fill gaps in my knowledge and on several more encouraged me to go the extra mile to resolve questions of detail. There were times when that extra mile felt more like half-way round the world, and there were also times when it proved impossible to go the full distance; however, I hope

that the ultimate value of this book will not be diminished by the inevitable lacunae. Perhaps others will be able to resolve some of the outstanding questions. If so, then this book will at least have done a good job in highlighting them.

No serious researcher into this subject can get anywhere without consulting the incredibly detailed factory records, which are held by the Sir Henry Royce Memorial Foundation at The Hunt House in Paulerspury. My thanks therefore go to curator Philip Hall who guided me around the system and pointed me in the right direction for resolving most of the queries I had.

Pictures are known to be worth a thousand words, and I am convinced that there are many cases when Mark Dixon's pictures illustrate points of detail far better than my words ever could. So I am very grateful indeed to those owners and enthusiasts who made their cherished cars available for photography.

James Taylor
Oxfordshire

Owners of Featured Cars

John Gallagher (1947 Silver Sand Bentley MkVI 4¼-litre, B181BG); Tony Jenkin (1951 Black Bentley MkVI 4¼-litre, B207MB); Dermott Kydd (1951 Tudor Grey over Shell Grey Rolls-Royce Silver Dawn 4¼-litre, SDB134); Graham Pearce (1953 Midnight Blue over Cream Bentley R-type, B435SP); Brian Palmer (1954 Black over Shell Grey Rolls-Royce Silver Dawn, SOG90); David Clarke (1954 Velvet Green over Donegal Green Bentley R-type, B40ZY); Jack Henley (1955 Shell Grey Rolls-Royce Silver Dawn, SVJ75); Edward Thornton (1955 Tudor Grey Bentley S-series, B84AN); John McGlynn (1959 Mason's Black Rolls-Royce Silver Cloud, SNH118); Gerald Bonner (1959 Black Rolls-Royce Silver Cloud Long Wheelbase, CLC35); Frank Parkin (1960 Sage Green over Smoke Green Bentley S2, B395BR); Geoffrey Bates (1962 Dawn Blue Rolls-Royce Silver Cloud II, SAE473); Alfred Gooding (1962 Sage Green over Velvet Green Rolls-Royce Silver Cloud II Long Wheelbase, LLCC90); Max Brown (1963 Sand Rolls-Royce Silver Cloud III, SCX303); Peter Baines (1964 Sable over Sand Bentley S3, B56BG); Martin Sargeant of Goudhurst Service Station (on behalf of owner of 1965 Astral Blue Rolls-Royce Silver Cloud III H. J. Mulliner Flying Spur, CSC43B).

Especial thanks are due to Rolls-Royce and Bentley specialist dealer Peter J. Fischer and his staff at P. J. Fischer Classic Automobiles, Northumberland Garage, Dyers Lane, Upper Richmond Road, Putney, London SW15 6JR for providing coachbuilt models from their extensive stock for photography. These included: 1954 Bentley Continental (R-type) H. J. Mulliner saloon (BC45D); Bentley Continental S-series 1957 H. J. Mulliner (fastback) saloon (BC88BG), 1957 Park Ward drophead coupé (BC51CH), 1959 H. J. Mulliner two-door saloon (BC27GN) and 1959 H. J. Mulliner Flying Spur four-door saloon (BC44LFM); 1961 Rolls-Royce Silver Cloud II H. J. Mulliner convertible coupé (standard steel saloon conversion) (SZD43); 1961 Bentley Continental S2 Park Ward drophead coupé (BC58LCZ); 1964 Bentley Continental S3 Park Ward saloon (BC124XC) and 1964 Rolls-Royce Silver Cloud III James Young four-door saloon (SFU127).

Additional photographs: James Mann photographed the 1961 Rolls-Royce Silver Cloud II H. J Mulliner coupé convertible and 1964 Bentley Continental S3 Park Ward saloon, and Maurice Rowe the 1959 Rolls-Royce Silver Cloud Long Wheelbase. The 1953 Bentley Continental (R-type) H. J. Mulliner saloon (BC8C) is courtesy of *Classic & Sports Car* and the 1965 Bentley Continental S3 Park Ward drophead coupé (BC78XC) is from the library of Neill Bruce. Peter Fischer provided the pictures of the 1963 Bentley S3 Long Wheelbase saloon (BAL10) and Paul Wood, of Rolls-Royce distributors P & A Wood, supplied the picture of the 1965 Bentley Continental S3 James Young saloon (BC38XE) owned by Alec Norman.

Past, Present & Future

As the Second World War shuddered to an end in 1945, it was by no means certain that Rolls-Royce would ever resume the manufacture of motor cars. The company had maintained its reputation during the hostilities through the activities of its aero engine division, which had been separated from the chassis division (as the car side was called in the days when it made no bodies) in 1937. There had been no new Rolls-Royce motor cars since 1940, and the only designs which existed were those which had been under development when the war had broken out. Nevertheless, an enthusiastic committee within the company energetically promoted the cause of resuming chassis manufacture, and in due course a decision was taken at the highest level that car manufacture should be re-started – not at Derby but in the wartime aero-engine factory at Crewe.

The choice of Crewe for post-war manufacture was also to have a considerable influence on the components used in the cars, for although there was no foundry or forge there was a very extensive machine shop. Consequently the post-war cars differed from many other makes in that many of the parts were designed and machined in the factory, and that applied from specialist items such as the large diameter engine valves right down to mundane items such as nuts and bolts. Supplied castings and forgings were also purchased in a raw state for machining by Rolls-Royce. Other components, such as electrics, which were obtained from specialist suppliers were always checked to

The first post-war model from Crewe was the Bentley MkVI. This 1947 example (B181BG) in Silver Sand belongs to John Gallagher.

ensure that they met Rolls-Royce's high standards for both operation and finish, whilst many ostensibly proprietary parts were in fact specially made to a Rolls-Royce specification and differed in various ways. A typical example of this is the SU HD8 carburettor (fitted to the V8 Silver Clouds/ Bentley S-series), which had a modified float chamber with extra insulation, a stainless steel (instead of brass) throttle spindle, a stoved black enamel finish and cadmium-plated visible screws and levers. Since Crewe had its own plating facility many external fixings were cadmium-plated for corrosion resistance and chromium plating was to a superior thickness and standard too.

However, things were going to be very different from the way they had been in the 1930s. Most important of all was that there would have to be a reduction in the variety of different models in order to keep manufacturing costs under control. The principle of a 'rationalised range' of chassis and engines, which shared a high percentage of common components, had already been accepted before the war, and it was now put into effect. There would be a single basic chassis design, capable of being stretched by lengthening the wheelbase. Initially, this would form the basis of a short-wheelbase owner-driver saloon and a longer-wheelbase formal limousine. There would also be a single basic engine design, with overhead inlet valves and side exhaust valves. Known as the B range, this would be available with four, six or eight cylinders to power different models.

Perhaps even more important, because it represented a fundamental change for Rolls-Royce, was that the company would offer its new owner-driver saloon as a complete car and not only as a chassis for bodying by one of the specialist coachbuilders. The reasons were that the standardisation of a single body style would reduce

manufacturing costs and would make the task of the company's retailers easier in carrying out maintenance and repairs. So a 'standard steel' saloon body was designed and a supply agreement was reached with the Pressed Steel company. Of course, the chassis of the owner-driver saloon would also be available separately for special bodywork. The work done at the end of the 1930s on the rationalised range had been progressed by the use of experimental chassis throughout the war on essential work, and by 1946 the company was ready to introduce its first new post-war cars.

Political considerations also influenced the models that entered production in 1946, however. Under the Socialist government, which was elected in Britain early in 1946, it was clear that wealth and ostentation were going to be out of favour. So the plans for an owner-driver Rolls-Royce were not developed – although they would be picked up again later – and instead a decision was taken to market the volume model as a Bentley. There would of course be a Rolls-Royce as well, but this would be the larger formal limousine. The Bentley, described at the time as a sports saloon, was known logically as a MkVI because the last production model before the war had been called a MkV. The Rolls-Royce was named the Silver Wraith, the first part of that name coming from the popular name of Silver Ghost for the Edwardian 40/50hp model, and the second part coming from the rather staid owner-driver saloon chassis of the late 1930s.

Post-war economic conditions in Britain also shaped the destiny of Rolls-Royce to a large extent. Government policies favoured manufacturers who exported the larger percentage of what they made, and Rolls-Royce had every intention of complying. Only a small percentage of the cars built at Crewe was earmarked for sale on the home

Four years later, when Tony Jenkin's Black MkVI (B207MB) was built, the styling had changed only in small details, but the engine had been bored out from 4¼ to 4½ litres.

market, and so it was not surprising that the demands and tastes of export markets played a big part in influencing the development of Rolls-Royce and Bentley motor cars in this period.

When production of the MkVI Bentley began in 1946, it was made with right-hand drive only. However, there was a limited number of markets which would take cars with right-hand drive, and in particular the potentially massive North American market demanded cars with their steering wheels on the left. So, after selling a small number of right-hand-drive MkVI chassis across the Atlantic, Crewe bit the bullet and started to make its cars with left-hand drive as well during 1948. This involved not only moving the steering wheel, but also modifying several other items, such as the lighting arrangements, to comply with regulations in overseas markets.

It was the American market, and the need to exploit it, which influenced the next development at Crewe, too. Americans were less than happy at being asked to pay Rolls-Royce prices for a car badged as a Bentley, especially as the Bentley name meant very little in the USA. So Crewe obliged by developing a Rolls-Royce version of the MkVI, which it announced in 1949 as the Silver Dawn. There were in fact many more differences between MkVI and Silver Dawn than are generally realised, and not the least of them was that the Rolls-Royce was a rather more sedate

conveyance than the Bentley. Nevertheless, the new model sold well, and satisfied a good number of overseas customers.

The late 1940s and early 1950s were the days of shortages and of rationing, and it was quite commonplace for British car manufacturers to produce a car that was simply not available on the home market. So it was with the Rolls-Royce Silver Dawn, until a relaxation of Government policies enabled the model to be introduced to Britain in 1953. By this time, it had undergone two important changes.

The first one had been a switch from the original 4257cc engine to a more powerful big-bore 4566cc type in 1951. The second had been a substantial transformation at the rear of the body, as a result of customer dissatisfaction with the size of the boot. Developed initially as a Bentley MkVII, but rarely called by that name outside Crewe, the modified car had been extended by six inches at the rear and given a much more commodious boot, which also made for even better balanced styling. In Bentley form, it took over from the MkVI during 1952 and was known initially simply as a Bentley Sports Saloon, although latterly as the Bentley R-type. In Rolls-Royce guise, it remained a Silver Dawn when the bigger boot was introduced at the same time.

By the early 1950s, it was quite clear to Rolls-Royce that the American market represented a

Introduced mainly to meet American market demands, the Rolls-Royce Silver Dawn was a less powerful derivative of the contemporary Bentley MkVI. This 1951 example (SDB134) in Tudor Grey over Shell Grey is owned by Dermott Kydd.

From 1952, a longer boot was introduced on both the Bentley and Rolls-Royce models. This 1953 Bentley R-type (B435SP) in Midnight Blue over Cream has the two-tone colour styling associated with the earlier cars and is owned by Graham Pearce.

The longer boot of the later cars can be seen clearly on Brian Palmer's 1954 Silver Dawn (SOG90), which also has the standard two-tone colour split in Black over Shell Grey.

sales opportunity which it could not afford to ignore, and that it would therefore have to pander to American tastes without losing the essentially British character of its products. So it was that 1953 brought the option of two-pedal transmission, albeit for export only at first. The Bentley R-type and Rolls-Royce Silver Dawn were made available with the option of what Crewe considered to be the best automatic gearbox then on the market, which was the Hydra-Matic designed by General Motors in America. This four-speed epicyclic gearbox with fluid flywheel was consid-

erably modified to meet Rolls-Royce requirements, and was manufactured under licence at Crewe from 1954.

Meanwhile, demand from continental Europe had also influenced the shape of Rolls-Royce products. At the end of the 1930s, Rolls-Royce had been looking at a sporting model designed for high-speed work on the long continental roads, and had built a single prototype known as the Corniche. This was unfortunately damaged in an accident in France and the streamlined body was then destroyed in a bombing raid shortly after the war

The styling was dating rapidly by the time David Clarke's R-type Bentley (B40ZY), painted in Velvet Green over Donegal Green, was built in late 1954 although there was no denying its elegance. Jack Henley's 1955 Silver Dawn (SVJ75) finished in Shell Grey (right) is one of the final year's production, and has been discreetly fitted with turn signal lamps above the rear bumper to make it safer to use in modern traffic conditions.

began, but the idea of such a model did not go away. After the war, the major European coach-builders started looking for new chassis on which to exercise their craft, and of course turned to the Bentley MkVI among others. However, the MkVI had been conceived for very upright bodywork to suit British tastes, and its bonnet and scuttle were both too tall to suit the long and low styles preferred on the European continent.

So from 1948, a few MkVI chassis were specially modified to meet these requirements, and were sent abroad to receive coachwork. These cars

were known as Bentley Crestas, and the project lasted for some three years and around a dozen cars. Meanwhile, however, Rolls-Royce had started work on its own high-performance model with rakish lines, under the name of Corniche II. Based on the 4½-litre MkVI chassis, it had the lower bonnet line and more steeply raked steering column of the Cresta cars, allied to higher overall gearing and – the key to the whole project – new lightweight bodywork whose construction was based on principles introduced by H. J. Mulliner in 1948. The prototype appeared in 1951, and a

The Continental was the pinnacle of Bentley motoring in 1953 when this H. J. Mulliner-bodied fastback saloon (BC8C) was delivered. The long sloping tail was most distinctive and the body shape evolved after wind-tunnel testing by Rolls-Royce but still provided space for four adults and luggage. Note the single large tailpipe for the special exhaust system. The Continental name badge on the boot is a later addition as are the direction indicators.

year later the car went on sale as the Bentley Continental. It was the fastest four-seater saloon of its day, and became a legend in Britain, where examples were not sold before 1953.

From 1954, Rolls-Royce began to release small numbers of Continental chassis to other coach-builders, including its subsidiary Park Ward. This move allowed the customers to dictate more of the specification of the completed cars, and much of the original purity of the Continental was lost as extra equipment was added and the cars put on weight. To counter this, the six-cylinder engine was bored out yet again, this time to 4887cc.

This engine was available only for the Continental chassis, but it was also developed further to become the sole power unit available for the car which would replace the R-types and Silver Dawns in 1955. This was developed under the code-name of Bentley IX or Siam, beginning in 1951, and when it entered production it bore the name of Rolls-Royce Silver Cloud. For the Bentley equivalent – exactly the same except for the grille and for badging details – the name of S-series was chosen as a logical follow-on from the outgoing R-type.

The Silver Cloud and Bentley S-series were larger cars than those they replaced, and in both standard saloon and coachbuilt forms were much more modern in appearance. The Bentley proved the stronger seller, partly because the Rolls-Royce name was still primarily associated with formal limousines, whereas the MkVI and R-type models had made clear that the Bentley was an owner-driver saloon. However, from 1957 there were long-wheelbase limousine versions of both types,

intended partly to plug the gap between the owner-driver cars and the much more expensive and now rather old-fashioned Silver Wraith. This car had by then been stretched to an even longer (133in) wheelbase, and within two years would give way to the enormous Phantom V formal limousine, derived from the chassis and running-gear of the Silver Cloud.

The Silver Cloud and S-series Bentley brought some further important changes to the Crewe products. Both of them were available only with automatic transmission, and from 1956 they were made available with power-assisted steering. Electrically-operated windows followed soon afterwards, again pandering largely to the American market. Yet these new convenience gadgets proved so popular with the customers that they soon became expected on every car from Crewe. Even the Continental version of the S-series, introduced shortly after the saloons in 1955, gradually succumbed, although at this stage it retained a very distinct identity through a more powerful engine, higher gearing, and the lower bonnet-line associated with the earlier Continentals.

By the end of the 1950s, the six-cylinder engine had reached the end of its development life, and only increasing the output of the version in the standard chassis to that initially reserved for the Continentals kept it competitive into 1959. That year, Rolls-Royce unveiled a completely new all-alloy V8 engine, with a capacity of 6230cc and markedly more power and torque than the old six-cylinder. It was perhaps not quite as refined as the older engine, and in the early days of production it certainly suffered from a number of teething

Despite the (Irish) registration number, Professor Edward Thornton's Tudor Grey 1955 car is a Bentley (B84AN). The S-series cars had a considerably modified 4887cc version of the six-cylinder B60 engine.

The Bentleys outnumbered their Rolls-Royce Silver Cloud equivalents by about three to two during production of the six-cylinder chassis. This is one of the last six-cylinder Clouds, a 1959 model (SNH118) in Mason's Black belonging to John McGlynn.

troubles. However, the basic design was sound enough for the engine to survive in production for another three and a half decades, until the new Silver Seraph introduced a German-built BMW V12 into the Crewe model range in 1998.

It is worth reflecting on the reasons why the engine introduced in 1959 had a V8 configuration. Undoubtedly, it allowed a large swept volume to be fitted into a relatively short overall length, whereas the straight-eight version of the B-series engine had been enormously long and heavy. Probably equally influential in the decision to proceed with this type of engine, however, had been the need to sell Rolls-Royce and Bentley models in the USA, where V8 engines were the everyday norm and six-cylinder engines were associated with the entry-level model of domestic manufacturers' ranges. Once again, the expectations of overseas customers had influenced the direction that Rolls-Royce would take.

The cars which were powered by the new V8 engine were visually indistinguishable from those they replaced, and were simply known as the Rolls-Royce Silver Cloud II and the Bentley S2.

There were no immediately apparent external changes when the V8 engine replaced the six-cylinder type for the S2 and Silver Cloud II models. This 1960 Bentley (B395BR) in Sage Green over Smoke Green belongs to Frank Parkin.

With the arrival of the V8 engine, the Rolls-Royce badged car outsold its Bentley equivalent for the first time; the ratio was about four to three. This 1962 Silver Cloud II (SAE473) in Dawn Blue is the property of Geoffrey Bates.

Once again, there were long-wheelbase versions of both and there was a Continental chassis designed for high-performance motoring and for bespoke coachwork. The Continental S2 had exactly the same engine and automatic gearbox as the standard chassis, but benefited from a higher axle ratio, so when fitted with genuinely light-weight bodywork – becoming increasingly rare by this stage – it could still out-perform a standard steel saloon.

It was the Rolls-Royce version of the car which sold better this time, perhaps reflecting the greater prosperity of the period. Yet by the early 1960s, the Silver Cloud II and S2 were beginning to look dated. Work was already under way at Crewe on a radically new model which would replace them

Long-wheelbase derivatives had been available since 1957. This is a left-hand-drive 1962 Silver Cloud II (LLCC90) in Sage Green over Velvet Green owned by Alfred Gooding.

H. J. Mulliner remained one of the major coachbuilders throughout this period, although it merged with Park Ward in the early 1960s under Rolls-Royce ownership. This elegant two-door style was offered on the Bentley Continental S2 chassis.

in the middle of the decade, but the V8-engined cars were given a mid-life overhaul and re-emerged as the Silver Cloud III and Bentley S3 in 1962. They still had the same V8 engine, although it now promised better performance from more power and torque. They also still had essentially the same body, although a more steeply raked bonnet and the introduction of twin headlamps (an American fashion of the day) gave them a fresher and more contemporary appearance.

As for the Continental version of the S3, however, it was quite clear that the times were changing. The Continental chassis now offered very little that was special, except for a lower bonnet-line and more comprehensive instrumentation designed to appeal to the sporting driver.

For the Rolls-Royce Silver Cloud III and Bentley S3 models, the V8 engine was uprated and the front end styling was changed to incorporate twin headlamps and a lower grille. This Silver Cloud III (SCX303) (above) with Sand paintwork is a 1963 model owned by Max Brown. Two-tone colour schemes remained popular. This Sable over Sand one (left) is seen on a 1964 Bentley S3 (B56FG) belonging to RREC General Secretary Peter Baines.

During the Silver Cloud III era, the only Bentley chassis available for coachbuilt bodywork was the Continental. However, the Rolls-Royce chassis could be fitted with versions of some bodies originally designed for the Continental. Among them was H. J. Mulliner's Flying Spur four-door sports saloon. This Astral Blue example (CSC43B) is a 1965 model made available by the owner through Martin Sargeant of Goudhurst Service Station.

The bodies designed for it were also made available on the standard chassis, and in 1963 Crewe started to supply coachbuilders with Rolls-Royce chassis which had most of the features once unique to the Continental. As the standard Bentley chassis was no longer available for coachbuilders, choice for the customers was simplified, but the distinction between similarly-bodied Bentley Continental and coachbuilt Rolls-Royce became very blurred indeed.

When the new Silver Shadow saloons were announced in 1965, the Continental chassis and the standard saloons ceased production, leaving coachbuilders with only the Rolls-Royce chassis, which remained available until the new two-door saloon arrived in 1966. While this and the later drophead coupé were quite distinctive visually, they no longer made any pretence at the higher performance which had been so much a part of the Continental chassis that had been their spiritual forebear more than a decade earlier.

The two decades between 1945 and 1965 remain a distinct period in the history of the Rolls-Royce motor car, bounded at one end by the disruption of a world war and at the other by the radical change to monocoque construction. They also saw the manufacture of some remarkable motor cars, many of them graced with hand-built coachwork, which has a character unmatched even by the best of modern cars. At the same time, they demonstrated Rolls-Royce's ability to emulate the best of the coachbuilders' work with its own standardised body designs. The mechanical longevity of the cars covered in this book and the quality of their construction allow large numbers of them still to be enjoyed today, more than 30 years after the last one was built. That is as it should be.

James Young was one of the most distinguished coachbuilders throughout this period but ceased bodybuilding in 1967. The SCV100 four-door body seen here on a 1964 Silver Cloud III (SFU127) was thus one of the company's last designs.

Bentley MkVI, 1946-52

The model name MkVI given to the first post-war Bentley followed on logically from that of the MkV, which had just entered production when the Second World War began at the close of the Thirties. So few of these MkV models were built before the war halted production, however, that the car is often thought to have initiated a new trend in Bentley nomenclature!

The Bentley MkVI was announced in May 1946, a month after the larger and rather grander Rolls-Royce Silver Wraith to which it was closely related. The MkVI was the first car ever to come from Rolls-Royce Ltd with a 'standard steel' body; all earlier models had been supplied in chassis form only for bodying by a coachbuilder of the customer's choice. Around 19 per cent of all MkVI Bentleys were nevertheless fitted with coachbuilt

bodies, but the success of Crewe's standard-body-work strategy was made clear by the fact that the number of coachbuilt cars was tapering off as MkVI production came to an end.

In the mid-1930s, Rolls-Royce had in production three entirely different chassis – the Rolls-Royce 25/30 hp and Phantom III, and the Bentley 4¼-litre – which shared only a few common components. For a small-volume maker, this of course resulted in very high manufacturing costs. So when a strategy for new models was developed after the 1937 split of the company into aero engine and car manufacturing sides, this was one of the problems that had to be addressed.

The basic idea came from W. A. Robotham, who was then deputy to R. W. Harvey-Bailey, the chief chassis engineer. With Harvey-Bailey's

John Gallagher's 1947 MkVI (B181BG) is an example of the very first cars. It still carries its original pass lamp, although this has been supplemented by a pair of later Lucas fog lamps which double as turn indicators.

support, he proposed to streamline the manufacturing operation by introducing what he called a 'rationalised range'. He foresaw a single chassis design, which could be produced in different wheelbase lengths to suit different models; and he believed that should be accompanied by a single engine design, which could be produced with four, six or eight cylinders to give a variety of power outputs. In addition, Robotham believed that Rolls-Royce should offer an 'off-the-peg' standard saloon body, while continuing to make bare chassis available for custom-built coachwork.

Robotham's ideas were approved right at the end of the 1930s, but the 1939-1945 war prevented any of them from going beyond the prototype stage. Nevertheless, discussions with Pressed Steel about the quantity production of a standard saloon body began in January 1944, and several elements of the prototype designs, built in 1939 and used throughout the war, were pulled together to make the first post-war models. The standardised saloon body was drawn up by Ivan Evernden and Bill Allen of Rolls-Royce, and the new car was known at the works as the Ascot. Right from the beginning it was styled in both Rolls-Royce and Bentley forms, the Rolls-Royce being Ascot I and the Bentley Ascot II.

However, the two versions of the car did not appear side by side. There were two main reasons. Firstly, the political climate of the post-war period was not thought to be receptive to the Rolls-Royce image, and secondly the company recognised that the public might take some time to accept the idea of a standardised Rolls-Royce. So the company adopted a careful marketing strategy. The marque image would be maintained by making the first new post-war car a Rolls-Royce in traditional chassis-only form, for coachbuilt bodywork. This was the Silver Wraith, which was actually little more than a long-wheelbase edition of the chassis used for the new Bentley. The standard saloon would follow it and would wear the slightly less prestigious Bentley badges, and only when the public had accepted the idea of a standardised model and the political climate was right would it appear as a Rolls-Royce as well.

So it was that the new standardised saloon was always a Bentley until 1949, when it became available also as a Rolls-Royce Silver Dawn for export only. The catalyst for the appearance of this car had in fact not been political, but was purely pragmatic. The Government of the day was encouraging motor manufacturers to build for export, and Rolls-Royce already had a good market in the US. However, the Bentley name was little-known across the Atlantic, and American customers who were paying Rolls-Royce money for their cars wanted them to wear Rolls-Royce badges.

There were two major variants of the MkVI Bentley. The first 4000 cars, built before the middle of 1951, had a 4¼-litre engine, and the 1200 1951-1952 models had a 4½-litre engine whose increased capacity was the result of enlarged cylinder bores. These later cars are often called the 'big-bore, small-boot' models, to distinguish them from the R-types, which followed them and shared the big-bore engine but had a larger boot. It appears that the new engine was needed less for the Bentley than for the Rolls-Royce Silver Wraith which was mechanically almost identical but which was being fitted with increasingly heavy coachwork.

In 4¼-litre form, the MkVI was of course no slouch, being capable of well over 90mph and 0-60mph in around 17 seconds. The 4½-litre models gave a near-100mph maximum with acceleration to 60mph in just over 15 seconds.

The biggest export market for the right-hand drive MkVI was Australia, and the biggest for left-hand-drive models was the US.

Chassis

Chassis Frame & Fittings

The chassis frame of the MkVI Bentley is constructed conventionally, with deep channel-section side-members and a massive cruciform stiffening member between them. This runs from the front bulkhead area to join the rear side-members at the point where they kick up over the rear axle, and is braced to the side-members near the end of each arm of the cross. There is a box-section pan to support the front suspension components, and a light cross-brace runs between the side-members where they sweep up over the rear axle. Chassis frames were always riveted together on these cars, which all have a wheelbase of exactly 120in.

The body-mounting brackets are on outriggers roughly in the middle of each side-member (below the B/C post on the body), and these double as jacking points for the slide-type jack. Certain chassis, probably always destined for coachbuilt bodywork, had a special bracket fitted to the front chassis members. The shape of the jacking brackets changed after B234CF (standard steel) and B292CF (coachbuilt) when the original Smiths Bevelift jack was replaced by a Dunlop triple screw type. Supplies of the Bevelift jack ran out in 1960, and retailers were advised to supply a Dunlop jack in cases of need; this also entailed swapping the body mounting brackets for the later type. The same modification was recommended for coachbuilt cars, although here the jacking brackets did not double as body mounting brackets.

When a Dunlop jack was supplied to replace a Bevelift type, it was also necessary to change the

jack support bracket and the jack handle bracket in the spare wheel compartment. The number of cars modified to this extent must have been tiny.

The 18-gallon petrol tank is mounted transversely between the chassis side-members, just behind the rear axle. Its breather pipe was extended at chassis number B475CD in 1948. A main fuel strainer is mounted on the chassis crossmember above and in front of the tank, and twin SU type L electric petrol pumps are mounted on the inboard side of the right-hand side-member, slightly behind the central body mounting bracket. All petrol pipes are made of metal. Just ahead of the fuel pumps and also inboard of the chassis side-member is the battery carrier.

Long after production of the MkVI had ended, and with effect from August 1956, a chassis-mounted tow-bar made by Dixon-Bate became available for the standard steel cars. The visible elements could be removed when it was not in use.

Chassis Lubrication System
Automatic one-shot chassis lubrication is provided on the MkVI by a Luvax-Bijur system made by Girling. This lubricates all bearings in the steering and suspension systems, including the main leaf and shackles of each rear spring. A pedal under the dashboard of the car operates the system, and Rolls-Royce recommended depressing the pedal when the car was started for the first time each day and then once every 100 miles.

The system consists of a reservoir tank mounted on the engine side of the bulkhead, an operating pedal inside the car on the toe-board, and a series of small-bore pipes, which duct lubricating oil from the tank to appropriate points on the chassis. The reservoir tank is on the left-hand side of the bulkhead on all cars up to B251EW in 1949 and on some cars between that number and B271EW. On all other cars it is located on the right-hand side. From B165GT, revised pipework was fitted to the rear spring shackles.

Front Suspension & Steering
The MkVI Bentley models all have coil spring independent front suspension with a rubber-bushed lower wishbone, an anti-roll bar and lever-arm hydraulic dampers. The operating arm of the dampers doubles as the upper wishbone. This

The overall styling was unchanged by the time Tony Jenkin's car (B207MB) was built in 1951. However, note the waist-level chrome strip on this car, and the more prominent chrome around the front quarter-light (see text). This car has a non-original central pass lamp and has been fitted with additional fog lamps and a badge bar.

The jacking points underneath the car also act as the central body outriggers. Here, the correct Dunlop screw jack is seen in place on Tony Jenkin's 1951 model.

The MkVI shape had evolved from Park Ward's 1930s styling and no less obviously so than in this rear view. Clearly visible on the rear wing of this 1951 car is the lockable fuel filler flap. The red reflectors were added to meet new regulations during the 1950s, and the amber turn signal lamps are, of course, also a later addition. The twin exhaust pipes show that this is a 4½-litre MkVI.

basic layout remained unaltered, but in 1950 some major changes were made. These were principally designed to provide greater steering accuracy 'by eliminating certain geometrical errors which were present in the original design,' according to Bentley service literature. It was not possible to fit the redesigned front suspension to earlier cars as a service modification.

The rubber bump stops for the front suspension on early cars are located inside the coil

The reservoir for the Luvax-Bijur centralised chassis lubrication system is mounted high up on the front bulkhead. This one is on the 1951 car. Note the voltage regulator and fuse box alongside.

springs, attached to the upper wishbones. However, a change to progressive bump stops was made in 1949, and these central stops were deleted. The progressive bump stops were fitted only to left-hand-drive models at first, starting with B126LEY; the first right-hand-drive car was B466EY, when they became standard.

Other running modifications were made to the early front suspension. The dampers were given screwed inserts at B250AK in mid-1947, and the loading of the dampers was increased with effect from B185BG. Longer upper triangle levers arrived at B134DA, and from B193DZ there were new front springs, which gave a deflection of 8½in.

The fully revised front suspension was introduced at B1GT in 1950. Almost every suspension component was affected, as were the front hubs, but in most cases the changes were to dimensions rather than to design. Brake changes are dealt with below, but the other changes were: Timken taper roller bearings in the hubs instead of ball bearings; a shorter steering drop arm; and an extra steering lever on the front pan (which increased the angularity and effective radius of the track rods by interposing a third section between the two existing swinging track rods). This revised suspension seemed to cure all the ills of the earlier type, and the only subsequent modification came in early 1952 when the front damping was increased at chassis number B210NZ. The earlier type of front wheel fixing studs was also reinstated at chassis B22PV in the early summer of 1952.

The steering on the MkVI models is a Marles cam-and-roller system modified to meet Rolls-Royce requirements. All the first MkVI models had right-hand drive, and there were no left-hand-drive cars before B485LCD in March 1949 (though deliveries to the US began in February 1947). From lock to lock takes 3½ turns of the steering wheel. G-series cars with their revised front suspension have much less understeer and lighter steering than earlier models.

Rolls-Royce steering terminology at this stage needs a little explanation, if only to aid in the use of parts books and workshop manuals! What other makers called the track rod was known at Crewe as the 'cross steering tube', while what is otherwise known as a drag link was called a 'side steering tube'. The layout of the MkVI steering is fairly conventional; with a centre steering lever pivoting on the front cross-member and a drag link running fore and aft attached to this lever. The track rod is in two pieces.

The side steering tube (drag link) socket was modified at chassis number B244FU early in 1950, and the sockets for the cross steering tube (track rod) were modified shortly afterwards at B281FU. The steering geometry was completely revised when the modified suspension was introduced at B1GT in April 1950. There were then no more steering changes until near the end of production in summer 1952, when B89PU became the first car to manage without a packing piece between the cross steering lever and the flange on the stub axle assembly to which the cross axle steering lever is bolted. Rolls-Royce had clearly not rushed their decision that this packing piece was not essential! As details of this change were circulated in a service bulletin, it is probable that the packing-piece was discarded from many cars.

The very last MkVI models built in summer 1952, from B215PU onwards, had steel balls instead of a bronze seat in the front-end socket of the side steering tube. This modification was intended to reduce friction, but in service the balls tended to wear a groove and cause hard steering. So a modification kit, which enabled these later cars to be fitted with a bronze seat, was introduced in September 1953. Late PU-series cars may therefore be fitted with either type of seat.

Rear Axle & Rear Suspension

The live rear axle is a semi-floating type with offset hypoid bevel gears in the final drive, which has a 3.727:1 ratio. Larger rear hub bearings were introduced at chassis B2CF. The axle is suspended on semi-elliptic leaf springs with seven leaves, which have leather gaiters to protect them against dust and road dirt. During E-series chassis production in 1949 (probably at B1EW), larger (⅜in)

rear axle bolts were introduced, with an increased radius between stem and saddle to counter stress. From February 1952 retailers were advised to fit them as service replacements, so the majority of cars probably have them now. A further improvement in this area was the introduction of forged rear spring shackle brackets, at B403EW.

Like the front suspension, the rear axle has Rolls-Royce lever-arm hydraulic dampers, which in this case have an adjustable ride control system. This is operated by the driver from a control mounted on the steering wheel hub. Each damper is linked by pipes to a small gear-type oil pump on the rear of the gearbox. This pump supplies oil under pressure, and a relief valve releases some of that pressure when required. The oil under pressure acts in turn on the damper piston, and the variable pressure available through the system enables the quality of the ride to be varied from soft to firm.

As in the front suspension, the dampers were given screwed inserts at chassis number B250AK in summer 1947. At B200DA, the damper linkage was modified, but the rear spring plate for this linkage then proved unsatisfactory and was changed at B444FV. This second design continued into the GT series as far as B65GT, but also proved unsatisfactory, and so a third design was introduced from B67GT; this time the boss on the plate was wider than before. Retailers were advised to fit this third design to cars retrospectively as they passed through for service, so the majority of cars will probably have been modified.

Brakes

Drum-type brakes are fitted to all four wheels of the MkVI Bentleys. The front brakes have hydraulic operation and the rears are mechanical. The brake pedal operates the rear brakes directly and also engages a friction-disc servo, which is located on the right-hand side of the gearbox casing and driven mechanically from the rear of the gearbox by a cross-shaft at 0.095 times the

The master cylinder for the hydraulic front-wheel brakes is located alongside the battery, under the driver's seat. There is no under-bonnet master cylinder reservoir on these models. This is the 1951 car again.

propshaft speed. The servo operates the front brakes through a balance lever and a hydraulic master cylinder, and at the same time augments the direct application of the rear brakes. Braking is balanced to give about 55 per cent of the total effort on the front wheels, to counteract weight transfer under braking. Both front and rear brake drums have a diameter of 12.25in and are 2.6in wide. The handbrake operates on the rear wheels only, via a cable and mechanical linkage.

The hydraulic components of the front brakes are of Lockheed manufacture, although the drums on cars up to the end of the F series are by Girling. These can be recognised by their external cylinder, which operates the shoes through a wedge mechanism. With the arrival of the G-series cars and their modified front suspension in 1950 came Lockheed 'anti-rumble' front brakes with an internal hydraulic cylinder acting directly on the shoes. The Lockheed drums also have thicker lips than the Girling type.

Three different types of front brake hose were fitted to MkVI Bentleys on production, and a fourth was recommended as a service replacement from November 1954. On cars built up to August 1948, the hoses were smooth-skinned types with a diameter of ⁹⁄₁₆in; on cars built between August 1948 and February 1950 they had a similar appearance but a smaller diameter of 0.43in. Later MkVI cars had hoses with a chevron pattern on their skins, with the same 0.43in diameter but larger end connections. Later examples of these may have carried a green plastic band to indicate that they had been tested to increased pressures.

The replacement hoses recommended from November 1954 were similar to the third production type but carried a yellow plastic band to indicate that they were of three-ply rather than two-ply construction. They also had increased barrelling of the end connections, and later versions had L2 stamped on the hexagon to show they conformed to an agreed SAE specification.

Rear brakes were always made by Girling. At

Beginning with the G-series chassis in 1950, Ace Super Silent wheel discs were fitted. On this 1951 car they were painted to match the body, but some cars have them unpainted and polished.

B493DZ, a revised inter-shoe brake linkage was introduced. The rear axle shaft bearing housing and the brake carrier plate were retained by ⁵⁄₁₆in bolts on cars built before about mid-June 1949, when larger ⅜in bolts were introduced on production at B1EW. At the same time, the rear brake equaliser linkage was reversed and a stiffened linkage fitted. Rolls-Royce requested that all cars should be brought up to the latest standard as soon as possible during service attention to prevent the rear brakes dragging.

The original support for the rear brake equaliser could fracture, and so a modified type was introduced as a service replacement in June 1950 (but was never fitted on production). The modified type was numbered RG5460 and was a U-shaped metal link retained at either end by brackets in Silentbloc bushes. Many cars probably still retain their original supports, although cars in Australia, South Africa and South America should have been fitted with it at their first services after its introduction. A one-piece brake equaliser lever was introduced at B381GT.

The brake pedal on right-hand-drive cars acts directly on the servo, but on left-hand-drive models the pedal is linked to a bellcrank lever which transmits motion across the car to another bellcrank lever behind the servo. This in turn acts on a push rod, which operates the servo. On production, cars were fitted with a plain washer between the brake actuating levers on the servo. If owners complained of brake judder, a corrugated washer was substituted in service.

A number of modifications were made to the servo during the production life of the MkVI. A damper was added very early on, at B70AK. Then several detail changes were made in quick succession during 1948, as Crewe tried to address complaints about fierce or sticking brakes, and about brake balance. The first was a change to 25° servo cams and 13° brake expanders at B17CD in March 1948. A 2.4in balance lever was fitted at B344CF, and then a protection plate for the servo was added at B347CD later in 1948. At B384DA came a chromium-plated servo plate, and then at B241DZ the balance levers were changed to 3in types and servo cams with a shallower 22½° angle were fitted.

The bellcrank lever behind the brake servo on left-hand-drive cars may have a semi-universal bearing where it attaches to the servo operating pushrod. If so, the item is a service replacement component (part number RG2280), introduced to prevent fatigue fractures of the pushrod.

From about January 1950 (some time during the production of F-series cars), the friction surfaces of the brake servo were protected by an undershield which could also be retro-fitted to earlier cars. This covered the triangular gap between the frame side member and the cruciform member forward of the battery container, and included a vertical baffle plate in front of the servo itself. Very late in production, at chassis B284PV in summer 1952, the servo was fitted with solid pins and a shield.

Wheels & Tyres

The MkVI Bentley has pressed steel disc wheels with well-base rims, 5in wide and of 16in diameter. Each wheel is secured by five nuts with handed threads: right-hand threads for the right-hand side of the car and left-hand threads for the left-hand side. The wheels are normally painted to match the predominant colour on the bodywork. They are fitted with balancing weights and chrome-plated covering discs. On early cars, the road wheels were balanced by means of weighting washers. From B2BH in June 1947, the wheel discs had stronger flanges.

New road wheels were introduced with the revised front suspension of the G-series cars in 1950, and these were equipped with Ace Super Silent Discs as standard. These later wheels are easy to recognise as they have 24 holes drilled around the wheel disc, mid-way between the rim and the centre. Four of these are fitted with equal steel weights, at equal distances apart, in order to balance the wheel disc. The later covering discs also have a noticeably larger diameter than the earlier type. Some had their outer rings painted to match the bodywork (or the predominant body colour), while others were simply polished.

The original tyres were India Super Silent rayon in 6.50-16 size, but after these went out of production the recommended tyre was the Dunlop Fort C, in the same size. When these too went out of production in 1960, Rolls-Royce recommended Dunlop Heavy Duty Gold Seal tyres, in either 6.50-16 or 6.70-16 sizes. These could be had with or without whitewalls, and as either tubed or tubeless types. From February 1961, Avon HM Ribbed tyres in either 6.50-16 or 6.70-16 size were also recommended for the MkVI. These could also be had in tubed or tubeless form, but no whitewall option was available. The tyre recommendation changed once again in 1979, when Dunlop Roadspeed RS5 was recommended as the tubeless option and Dunlop RK 3A as the tubed variety. Both could be had in 6.50-16 and 6.70-15 sizes.

Tyre pressures seem to have caused Rolls-Royce a number of headaches over the years. The recommended tyre pressures were originally 23psi at the front and 32psi at the rear, with the tyres cold. The modified front suspension introduced with the G-series cars in 1950 reduced understeer considerably, and owners of earlier cars asked if there was anything they could do to improve their own cars' handling. Rolls-Royce recommended increasing the front tyre pressures to 25psi and reducing the rears to 30psi on standard saloons. For coachbuilt cars of average weight, the company recommended 23psi at the front and 30psi at the rear and suggested inflating the rear tyres by a few extra psi on cars where the bodywork at the rear was noticeably heavy.

Engine

The engine fitted to MkVI Bentleys is an in-line six-cylinder type called the B60, with pushrod-operated overhead inlet valves and side exhaust valves operated directly from the camshaft. All chassis up to and including the L-series have a 4¼-litre (4257cc) version of this engine, which was generally known at Crewe as the '3½in bore' engine. Beginning with the M-series cars in 1951, the bore size was enlarged to give a 4½-litre (4566cc) swept volume, and this engine was known as the '3⅝-inch bore' type. These larger-capacity engines also have an improved full-flow oil filtration system and strengthened crankshaft webs, and when fitted to right-hand-drive cars have a twin exhaust system. All MkVI engines have a 6.4:1 compression ratio.

Rolls-Royce never released power and torque figures for the engines used in the Bentley MkVI. However, the gross power of the 4¼-litre engine has been reliably quoted as 145bhp at 4,000rpm, while that of the 4½-litre engine is now widely accepted to be 153bhp at the same engine speed.

Block, Head, Camshaft & Lubrication System

The cylinder blocks of all MkVI engines are made of cast iron, and are integral with the crankcase. Both 4¼- and 4½-litre engines have a detachable cylinder head made of aluminium alloy, with nickel chrome molybdenum steel inlet valve seats and cast-iron guides. This is attached to the block by means of studs and nuts, and has a 6.4:1 compression ratio. It remained unchanged during the production life of the 4¼-litre and 4½-litre engines. The forged crankshaft in both engines is made of nitrided chrome molybdenum steel, fully machined and balanced with detachable weights. It is hollow and has sludge traps in the crankpins. The crankshaft runs in seven main bearings with Vandervell copper-lead-indium-lined thin steel shells. There is an internal crankshaft vibration damper of the combined spring drive and friction type.

The lubrication system of the 4¼-litre engine incorporates a General by-pass filter. By-pass filters had proved effective on the pre-war 4¼-litre overdrive Bentley, but the copper-lead bearings in the MkVI engine proved less tolerant of dirt than their softer Hall's metal pre-war counterparts, and a number of bearing failures occurred in service.

The long cylindrical air cleaner completely dominates the engine bay on this 1947 4¼-litre car. The SU carburettors are the early H4 type.

By the time this 1951 4½-litre model was built, there was hot air ducting above the air cleaner to feed the demister unit. A Smiths blower at the bulkhead end boosted air flow. These SU carburettors are the later H6 type and the air cleaner is now supported on four feet.

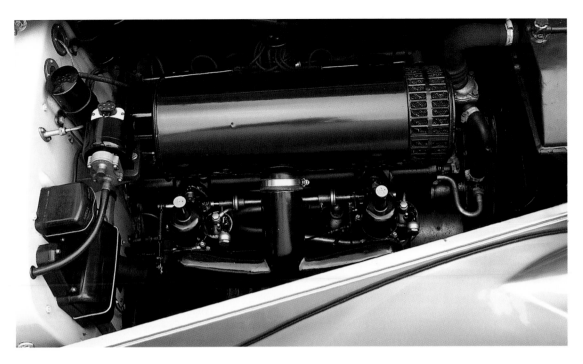

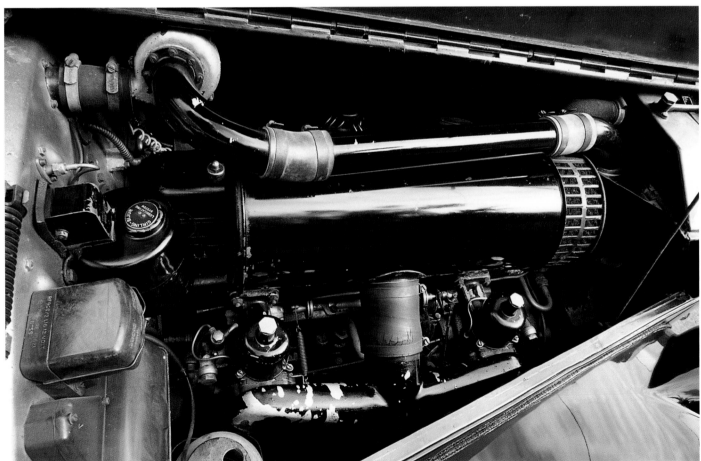

As a result of this, the oil filtration arrangements were improved on the later 4½-litre engines.

The main external finish of all MkVI engines is black, but pipework, bolt heads and the like are left unpainted. The top rocker cover is stove enamelled black and carries a rectangular plate with the Bentley name in raised and unpainted capital letters, positioned within a raised and unpainted border.

The 4¼-litre engine was modified in detail quite regularly throughout its production life. Bottom-end changes began in 1946 at chassis B126AK when a squirt hole was added to the steel connecting rods. The original aluminium alloy core plugs were prone to corrode, and so with the start of the D-series chassis at B2DA in July 1948 came cadmium-plated steel core plugs and aluminium washers. Most cars are likely to be fitted with these by now, as replacement of the originals was recommended as a service modification. Shortly afterwards, at B62DA, the synthetic bungs in number seven crankshaft journal were replaced by metal oil caps.

Mid-1948 also brought an important change to the cylinder block. On the earliest engines, the tops of the cylinder bores were flash-chromed to a thickness of 0.00075in and a depth of 2.25in. However, this sometimes showed unacceptable wear after as few as 40,000 miles, and so from B144DA, the problem was solved by fitting short Bricrome cylinder liner inserts instead, reaching to the same 2.25in depth. These liners could also be fitted as a service modification. The last change made during D-series chassis production was at B95DZ, when ⅜in cylinder studs were fitted.

The light alloy pistons were the main focus of attention during E-series chassis production in 1949-1950, the original solid-skirt type being replaced by a split-skirt design at B2EY, and granodised rings being fitted at B120EY. Graded pistons were introduced not long afterwards, at B111EW. There was then a lull in bottom-end modifications until L-series chassis production in 1951, when steel oil caps were fitted to the crankshaft at B40LJ, and an air bottle was added to the oil feed adaptor at B170LJ.

There were plenty of changes to the top end of the 4¼-litre engine, too. B1AJ in April 1947 brought the first change, when the tappets were Parkerised for longer life, and then shortly afterwards at B31AJ there were hardened pushrods as well. Two modifications were made to the rocker cover during B-series chassis production in 1947-1948, when a breather was added at B198BH and a Nebar rocker cover joint was specified at B303BG. Three more changes came in during C-series production in 1947-1948, these being aluminium tappet doors at B2CF, bronze exhaust guides instead of the original cast-iron type at B26CF, and a copper-asbestos cylinder head gasket at B1CD.

From chassis B2DA in July 1948 there was a new low-lift camshaft (RE6885) in place of the original high-lift type (part number RE5157). The low-lift camshaft was also used as a service replacement on earlier cars, and Rolls-Royce retailers were asked to stamp the letter C into the top left-hand side of the aluminium timing case when fitting one. RE6885 had the camshaft gear retained by four studs. In due course, a modified version (RE19517) was introduced on production, and this had the camshaft gear retained by eight setscrews.

In mid-1949, there was a further modification to the valve gear when B57EW brought closer-fitting tappets. The only subsequent top-end change was then at B2HR in July 1950, when an aluminium cam wheel replaced the Fabroil fabric type. Rolls-Royce recommended that this should be fitted as a routine service modification, when the crankshaft pinion with which it was paired also had to be changed. Retailers were asked to stamp an A on the top left of the timing case when modifying early cars to this later specification.

The camshaft timing was also altered during Mk VI production. Early engines with the high-lift camshaft had different timing from the majority, which had the low-lift camshaft. The later also had different inlet valve springs and was timed to give more torque. Rolls-Royce service data gives the timing for cars from chassis B2DA onwards as Inlet Opens 3½° ATDC, Inlet Closes 43½° ABDC, Exhaust Opens 40½° BTDC, Exhaust Closes 1½° BTDC. There are thus early and late types of flywheel, and as the flywheels for left-hand-drive cars differed from those for right-hand-drive cars throughout, there are no fewer than four different varieties of flywheels.

The position of the timing marks distinguishes flywheels destined for left-hand-drive cars from those destined for right-hand-drive models. The timing marks are at 10 o'clock on the left-hand-drive flywheels and at 2 o'clock on right-hand-drive types. The early flywheels are marked 'IO, IGN, TDC, EC' (Inlet Opens, Ignition, Top Dead Centre, Exhaust Closes), while the later ones are marked 'EARLY, LATE' and in 5° intervals up to 20° either side of TDC.

The 4½-litre engine was introduced in response to demands for more power and more torque, and the first cars fitted with it were delivered in July 1951. Its larger bore of 3⅝in on the same cylinder centres meant that there was not room for cooling passages between all the bores, and so the pairs at each end of the block were siamesed. The big-bore engine was also fitted with a full-flow oil filter, which largely solved the problem of the bearing failures seen on some 4¼-litre engines.

The full-flow oil filter on the 4½-litre engines was made by Vokes. It is fitted on the right-hand side of the crankcase in the oil delivery line between the oil pump and the crankcase oil gallery which feeds the main bearings. Early engines have a Vokes E30 filter distinguished by the six setscrews which attach its lid; later types have a Vokes E62 filter with a single central bolt attaching its lid.

The full-flow lubrication system involved modifications to the crankcase. Its casting was altered to incorporate a new external facing approximately 3in above the oil relief valve unit.

Just visible to the left of the carburettor is the domed top of the oil filter; on this 1947 car it is a service modification to the full-flow type with single-bolt fixing. Originally the car had a by-pass filter.

The vertical oil passage to the gallery was diverted to the lower orifice of this facing, and the upper orifice communicated with the gallery. An adaptor mounted on the facing carried a flow pipe and a return pipe to the oil filter, and a third pipe for the oil pressure gauge.

Earlier engines could be modified to run with a full-flow lubrication system, and Rolls-Royce service literature contains details of two different schemes, one to suit crankcases with the adaptor facing and the other to suit those without.

Even the full-flow system was not faultless, however, and it was possible for oil to pass across the head of a full-flow filter without passing through the filter element if the outer lip of the filter head stood proud of the inner sealing face. In such cases, Rolls-Royce recommended fitting a modified top cap to the filter and putting a spot of green paint on the filter head to show that the modification had been carried out. The original top cap has three grips protruding radially from its top face; the modified type has the grips around its circumference. The modified type was later supplied as a service replacement.

Carburettors & Air Cleaner

There were different carburettor specifications for right-hand-drive and left-hand-drive versions of the Bentley MkVI. The right-hand-drive cars have twin horizontal constant-vacuum SU carburettors. The left-hand-drive cars, however, have the engine in the tune used for the Rolls-Royce Silver Dawn and Silver Wraith models, with a single dual-downdraught Stromberg carburettor. A different inlet manifold is also fitted. Both systems have a small gauze strainer in the fuel line alongside the carburettor or carburettors, to supplement the main strainer near the fuel tank.

The twin SU carburettors are type H4 (with 1¼in choke) up to chassis number B81HP, and type H6 (with 1¾in choke) from B83HP on. The

SU carburettors were initially fitted with SN needles, switched to SC needles at B2BH in June 1947, and then to SP needles at B478NZ in 1952. Rolls-Royce recommended that these should be fitted retrospectively as a service modification to improve engine power and cooling.

Left-hand-drive cars have a Stromberg type AAV26M carburettor. The reason why is not clear: perhaps Rolls-Royce wanted to rationalise spare parts stocks in countries such as the US and Canada, or to simplify the assembly of left-hand-drive Bentley MkVI chassis at Crewe.

The air cleaner is normally a mesh type, in a long black-painted cylinder which lies horizontal to the engine. Early cars have an air cleaner made by Rolls-Royce, but an AC type replaced this at chassis number B2BH. From B111GT, the air cleaner has four mounting feet. Cars that would be operating in dusty conditions were equipped with an oil bath air cleaner, also finished in black.

Cooling System

The pressure-type cooling system has a capacity of four Imperial gallons, and was filled at the factory with a 25 per cent mixture of inhibited ethylene glycol and water. It has a radiator with a corrugated matrix and depends on a centrifugal pump. There is a by-pass thermostat, which allows a minimum running temperature of 78°C. A five-bladed cooling fan is fitted.

The cooling system of the first MkVI Bentleys was pressurised to 4psi, but this was changed during August 1947 (the Service Bulletin announcing it was dated 11 August) to a system operating at atmospheric pressure. Early cars had a ball and spring system inside the steam valve housing, and Rolls-Royce retailers were asked to remove these items during routine service. To indicate that the modification had been carried out, a spot of white paint was to be added to the steam pipe close to the steam valve chamber.

The original radiator was also modified during 1949. Early cars had a shallow matrix with no bottom tank, but with effect from B270DA in 1949, a deeper matrix was fitted. This presented a larger cooling area at the front of the car and the radiator assembly also had a bottom tank with a circular aperture, which allowed the starting-handle to pass through. The later deep radiator could be fitted to earlier cars as a service modification if the mounting yoke at the front of the engine bay was first modified. When the deeper matrix arrived, the radiator was also fitted with an anti-spill valve.

There were also two types of bottom radiator hose. Cars fitted with the deep radiator between 1950 and 1952 had a stiff bottom hose, and the movement of the engine relative to the radiator could cause the fixed pipe on the bottom tank to fracture. During R-type production in October 1952, a more flexible corrugated bottom hose (RE18218) was introduced, and Rolls-Royce recommended that this should be fitted to earlier 'deep radiator' cars as a service modification.

Top hoses were initially in two short lengths joined by a metal pipe in order to give flexibility, which at first the bottom hose was not thought to need. Then from March 1955, a new single-piece replacement hose was introduced with a 2¼in corrugated section at the radiator end to provide a flexible connection. Service literature recommended that the original two-piece installation was discarded so probably few have survived.

Two modifications were made to the water pump, the first being at chassis number B115CD in 1948. The second was the introduction of a modified pump gland ring at B61JN in late 1950. The speed of the cooling fan was also reduced from B213GT in 1950, to reduce fan noise.

Windscreen Washer

In December 1949 a windscreen washer pump was fitted to the engine side of the bulkhead on production at chassis number B1FU. However, its availability was announced in Rolls-Royce service literature some eight months earlier, and between April and December it was probably treated as an optional extra. It is a vacuum-operated device operated by manifold depression, and is made by Trico. The vacuum take-off is at the front of the engine, and replaces a core plug in the inlet manifold. A suction pipe then runs from here to the diaphragm pump on top of the washer fluid reservoir. Early examples have three 1in coils of pipe at the dash end of the suction pipe assembly, but these are not present on later cars, which have a pipe with an increased internal diameter.

There are two types of reservoir for the washer fluid. Most cars have a Trico-Folberth glass bottle on the left-hand side of the bulkhead in the engine compartment. However, cars fitted with an oil-bath air cleaner have a metal storage tank in the shape of a rectangular box. The pump on top of the reservoir takes water to the spray jets, which in all cases are on the scuttle. This pump is operated by a plunger switch, which on right-hand-drive models is located under the right-hand side of the dash, outboard of the wheel.

Exhaust System

All 4¼-litre MkVI models and all 4½-litre cars with left-hand drive have a single exhaust system, which was designed for refinement rather than efficiency, and consumes no less than 28bhp! The right-hand drive 4½-litre cars, however, have a much less restrictive twin exhaust system which consumes just 9bhp.

The single exhaust system consists of four

main parts. These are the front exhaust pipe, two separate silencers, and the tail pipe. The front silencer has an oval section and the rear is circular. The exhaust is flexibly mounted throughout and runs down the left-hand side of the chassis, and the tail pipe is then carried over the rear axle to emerge beneath the rear bumper.

Some customers complained of a hot floor, and so a heat shield was made available for the front exhaust silencer with effect from 3 January 1951. This was an aluminium sheet sandwich, with air in between, and was held in place by four mounting brackets bolted to the left-hand cruciform and frame side-members. It was fitted as standard on production cars from B159PU in 1952.

The twin exhaust system has two oval-section silencers in each branch. The twin pipes run together on the left-hand side of the chassis until they splay just behind the chassis cruciform, at which point the second pair of silencers are positioned. The tailpipes both pass up and over the rear axle to emerge, one on either side, beneath the rear bumper. There are large heat shields for the two exhaust pipes at the rear of the chassis where they pass under the rear seat pan.

The five-blade cooling fan and top hose of a 1947 model; Rolls-Royce recommended fitting this type of hose (a post-1955 replacement) with the corrugated section at the radiator end rather than on the engine, as here. Note the early type of knurled radiator filler cap, just visible at the top of the picture, and the knurled oil filler cap.

Transmission

Gearbox

All MkVI models are equipped with a manually-operated gearbox. This has four forward speeds and a reverse gear, with a positive interlock selector mechanism. There is synchromesh on second, third and fourth gears. The gearbox ratios (with overall ratios in brackets) are: First 2.982:1 (11.113), Second 2.018:1 (7.520), Third 1.342:1 (5.001), Fourth 1.000:1 (3.727) and Reverse 3.157:1 (11.767). A cross-shaft links the gearbox with the change gate and gear lever on the floor on the right-hand side. On left-hand-drive cars the gear lever is on the steering column with an appropriate linkage to the gearbox.

A number of detail modifications were made to the gearbox over the years. On 4¼-litre models, B292BH brought increased synchromesh cam angles in 1947. Square-edged bearings were fitted to the rear of the first and third motion shafts at B150DZ in late 1948, and strengthened third motion shaft splines followed shortly afterwards at B159DZ. The next change was made in the summer of 1950 at chassis number B95HP, when new second- and third-speed bushes brought a closer fit. On 4½-litre models, the only change was to a short-dwell detent on the first gear selector early in 1952; this was introduced on left-hand-drive cars first, at B360LNZ, and reached right-hand-drive models at B500NZ.

Clutch

The clutch on all MkVI Bentleys is a centrifugally-assisted, single dry-plate type. However, three different varieties were used on production. The earliest one is a 10in diameter Borg and Beck type (known as the 'long' clutch), and is fitted up to the end of the G-series cars (B401GT) in 1950. The second type is fitted from chassis B2HR to B298LJ. This has a larger 11in diameter but lightweight construction. The third type, also 11in, was fitted from chassis number B300LJ, and is known as the 'heavy' clutch.

When the cost of providing service parts for the lightweight clutch proved prohibitive, examples returned to the London Service Depot for replacement were automatically exchanged for heavyweight assemblies which, the company reassured its service personnel, 'incorporate several technical improvements over the former lightweight unit'. The heavyweight assemblies consisted of the friction plate, the centre plate and the cover assembly. Some cars earlier than B300LJ will therefore now have 'heavy' 11in clutches.

The original thrust springs for the 10in clutch were rated at 130-140lb and were coloured orange. Replacement springs had a higher rating of 150-155lb and were coloured red. Both the 'light' and 'heavy' 11in clutches are fitted with orange-coloured springs.

A number of detail modifications were also made. The clutch withdrawal bearing was first modified at B164CF in 1948, and then was given a low-rate oil feed when the first 11in clutch was introduced at B2HR in July 1950. At chassis number B83HP came a modified clutch spigot bearing. The next change was not until 1952, when the clutch casing was stiffened with two webs either side of the centre line, at B253NY. Finally, needle rollers were added to the clutch release levers at B185PU, shortly before the end of MkVI production.

Propshaft

The propeller shaft is a divided open type with three needle roller bearing universal joints, one near the centre and one at each end. It is supported in the centre by a flexibly-mounted ball bearing and the centre universal joint is of the sliding type.

Electrical Components

All MkVI Bentleys have a positive-earth 12-volt electrical system, with a dynamo and automatic voltage control. There are two major variations of wiring harness, the first type fitted to chassis up to and including the DA series, and the second type fitted to all later models. In all cases, the wiring harness has an outer casing of black plastic, but there are several different varieties of harness to suit the precise specification of the car. Each harness was hand-made on a peg board so as to cater for extras specified and the differing requirements of export markets.

The fuse box is fitted on the engine side of the bulkhead, ahead of the driver. It has a black cover and contains a main fuse and seven circuit fuses. The fuse wire is 32swg tinned copper wire; three strands are used for the main fuse and a single strand for each of the circuit fuses. A special holder at the bottom left of the fuse box contains spare fuse wire.

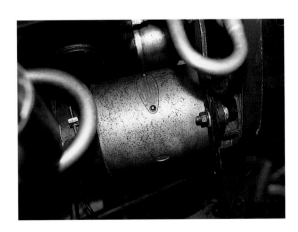

The original 'small' 4½in dynamo is pictured here on a 1947 car.

Battery & Charging System

The battery fitted to MkVI models is a 12-volt, 55amp/hour type, and its positive terminal is earthed to the chassis frame. The original battery was either a P&R Dagenite type 6 HZP9-S or an Exide type 6 MXP9-R. From chassis B252DA, cars were fitted with a battery charging socket on the facia (behind the steering wheel) and a special two-pin plug was provided for attaching the battery charger wires. This socket was also used for the underbonnet inspection lamp.

The electrical system of the MkVI Bentley runs off a dynamo mounted on the right-hand side of the engine and driven by vee-belt from the crankshaft pulley. This belt also drives the water pump and fan. The early type of dynamo, fitted on chassis up to B424CF, is a Lucas C45PV. This is commonly called the 4½in dynamo and has an output of 20-22 amps. Provision was made on the engine for the mounting of the later 5in dynamo as early as summer 1947, at chassis B122BH, but the dynamo itself was not actually introduced until B426CF in 1948. The 5in dynamo is a Lucas RA5, with an output of 25-27 amps. From February 1949, Rolls-Royce retailers were encouraged to fit the more powerful dynamo as a service replacement if customers so wished, and to remember to fit with it the larger securing studs

for the dynamo bracket and the associated voltage control regulator and 0-30-0 ammeter.

The voltage control regulator is fitted to the engine side of the bulkhead, and is a twin-coil Lucas unit with a black case. There are two different types, the first associated with the 4½in dynamo and the second with the later 5in type.

Rolls-Royce was well aware of the problem of silt gathering in the car's cooling system, and attempted to inhibit its formation by electrolytic methods. These involved bonding the dynamo to the radiator and using the current to reverse the natural polarity of the differences existing between radiator and engine. Various methods of bonding were tried as service schemes, and not all of them – as the company admitted in service literature – were successful. A further modification designed to achieve the same end was introduced during 1951, when the dynamo was insulated from the engine, from 4½-litre chassis B313MB.

On cars where the bonding was applied during production, a bolt for the bonding strip was added to the right-hand frame member behind the radiator. A first scheme was used on: B330MD, B334MD to B340MD, B390MD to B400MD, B15MB, B131MB to B137MB, and B233MB onwards.

This scheme had the bonding strip running from dynamo to chassis bolt and then to radiator.

This view of the left-hand side of the 1947 car's engine shows how the plug leads are carried in a metal conduit. The distributor cap is in brown Bakelite; later examples were black. The glass windscreen washer bottle would not have been present when the car was new, but is of the correct type used on later cars and for retro-fits in service.

The early cars were fitted with a Houdaille Berkshire wiper motor, seen here on a 1947 model.

The Lucas headlamps have a 'B' motif behind the glass.

Trafficators were part of the MkVI's original equipment.

It was found to be unsatisfactory, and in May 1954 a service bulletin announced the definitive scheme, with the bonding running from dynamo to radiator to chassis. Rolls-Royce also recommended that the bonding on earlier cars was altered to conform to the new pattern, and many cars in the list above were probably modified.

Starter & Ignition Systems

The starter motor is a Lucas M45G with a Rolls-Royce reduction gear and drive unit. It normally cranks the engine at between 80 and 160rpm.

The distributor is a Delco-Remy type incorporating two sets of contact breaker points, which work alternately to give longer service life. The distributor drive spring ring was modified at chassis B398BH in 1947, and in September 1949, from B2FV, the distributor was given an internal oil feed. The ignition condenser on the distributor was initially a Delco-Remy DRH1386, but from chassis B117KL in 1951, a DRH8859 condenser was fitted. This later type also became the only one available as a service replacement. It is longer than the original and has a distance piece on its mounting bracket. Twin condensers are fitted from 4½-litre chassis B292NZ in 1952.

All the AK-series cars have a single Lucas-type B12 ignition coil, with its terminals marked 'CB' (contact breaker) and 'SW' (switch lead). From B1AJ, all cars have two Lucas B12 coils, the second being intended as a spare. On B5AJ to B121AJ, the second coil is fitted to the dash, but the wires would not reach it and so the two coils had to be swapped over if the first one failed. Longer leads on later cars enable the wires themselves to be switched from one coil to the other.

A Delco-Remy coil was approved as an alternative to the Lucas type from 2 June 1955 in order to guarantee supplies. This coil has its terminals marked '+' and '–'. Then from 22 June 1956, a Lucas UD1984 coil was also recommended. This one is distinguished by a transfer stating 'For use with POSITIVE Earth System only'.

Early cars were supplied without a radio interference suppressor on the coil. However, a suppressor (part number RD4031) was added with effect from 8 August 1947. It was fitted to the input side of the coil and attached by either of the two existing fixing bolts, while its lead was connected to the SW terminal of the coil (or to the '–' terminal on a later Delco-Remy replacement). Retro-fit was straightforward, and the suppressor was probably added to many earlier cars. On cars with two coils, only the left-hand (main) coil was fitted with a suppressor up to and including B25BG. From B27BG, the spare coil was also fitted with a suppressor. At the same time, the coil wires were clipped to the dash by a single clip and fitted with rubber sleeves to prevent chafing.

The sparking plugs on MkVI models all have the same 14mm reach, and in the beginning Champion was the exclusive manufacturer. Later on, three types were recommended: Champion N8, KLG FE60, and Lodge CLN. From 24 May 1954, Champion N8B became the recommended plug. The plug gaps should be 0.025in except on cars where a TV suppressor is incorporated in the high tension lead to the distributor. In these cases, the gaps should be set to 0.030in.

Horns, Windscreen Wipers, & Rear Window Demister

The Lucas twin electric horns are mounted behind the front wings. They can be one of three types: model WT29, WT614 or HF1748. The original horn relay was a Lucas type C585K, but a Lucas type SB40, which became the only available replacement, superseded this in October 1950. The SB40 is a smaller unit, and was fitted with a special mounting bracket, which enabled the existing holes in the valance plate to be used.

An additional radio interference suppressor condenser was incorporated inside the horns from B218CF in late 1947. In this case, the modification to earlier cars was to fit external suppressors in the feed circuit to the horn junction box.

The windscreen wipers on the A-, B and C-series cars are the Berkshire type made by Houdaille. From chassis number B2DA in July 1948, a Lucas single-speed rack system is fitted. With both types, the wiper arms are engaged and disengaged independently of the motor, by means of knobs on the facia capping rail. The knobs also allow the wipers to be parked by hand. The wipers operate in unison with Lucas motors 75186 and 75249 but in counterphase with types 75181 and 75250. (For details of windscreen washer arrangements, see the *Engine* section.)

From chassis B311NY in 1952, a Triplex rear window demister was fitted. This consisted of a laminated glass sandwich with 936 fine wire elements inside it, and was operated by a dashboard-mounted switch. From 15 December 1953, a conversion kit enabled the demister to be fitted to earlier cars. The recommended position for the switch (a push-pull type labelled RW) was in the facia centre above the master switch, where it mated up with an existing hole in the steel instrument panel behind. However, some early cars already had the pass-lamp switch in this position, and in such cases the recommended position for the rear window demister switch was above and to the right of the steering column.

Lighting & Direction Indicators

The lighting system at the front of all MkVI cars consists of a single headlamp partially faired into each front wing, a sidelamp in a faired housing on the crown of the wing, and a pass lamp mounted centrally on the bumper valance ahead of the radiator. The headlamps are twin-filament types and, like the pass lamp, they have a small rectangular 'B' motif behind the glass. The sidelamps are of Lucas manufacture.

The pass lamp deserves a word or two of explanation. It was originally specified as part of the headlamp dipping system. This extinguished the offside headlamp when the lights were dipped, while the nearside lamp switched onto a dipped beam, and the central pass lamp lit up to illuminate the road directly ahead of the car.

A UK regulation introduced in January 1949 stated that pass lamps had to have their centres at least 24in above the ground; the centre of the MkVI's pass lamp was only 22in above the ground, and so the lamp had to be raised by means of a short pedestal between it and the front apron. The pedestal was introduced on production and also became a recommended service modification for cars used in the UK. The original retaining nut for the pass lamp had to be discarded and replaced by a cap nut which held the lamp connector in place in the base of the extension piece or pedestal.

Other changes in lighting regulations around the world brought about the demise of the pass-lamp dipping system altogether, and the familiar

modern double-dip system was introduced on production cars with B193DZ. A service bulletin dated April 1949 gave instructions for retrospective conversion to what Rolls-Royce rather quaintly called the 'Dip and Switch' system. The original MkI Lucas headlamps (RD3970) were replaced at this point by a modified MkI type (RD4544) which had a shallower reflector unit fitted with thicker glass which needed a wider inner rim, and these remained standard until the end of MkVI production. However, supplies of the MkI lamps ran out early in 1955, and Rolls-Royce recommended that damaged lamps should be replaced in pairs because the modified MkI lamps looked very different. Probably relatively few cars survive with their original lamps intact.

The modified MkI Lucas headlamps were used on production until 1952, when B169NY in 1952 brought a change to MkII headlamps. Also made by Lucas, these had a reflector unit secured to the lamp body by three spring-loaded screws, which also adjusted the beam setting. Some of these lamps had a 15-amp fuse fitted to their shells.

After November 1948, MkVI models destined for the US had 7in sealed-beam headlamps to meet new American regulations introduced that year. The American Lucas agents supplied a conversion kit for modifying existing cars. The pass-lamp system was no longer legal in the US from that date, and so cars for that market had two Lucas 7in fog lamps instead, one mounted on each of the bumper irons. This became the standard export specification at the same time.

Two different rear lighting configurations were fitted to the standard MkVI cars. On early cars, the Lucas brake lights are carried in nacelles on the rear wings, and there is a Lucas D-lamp on either side of the number plate housing. These contain the red tail lamp (on the inside, straight, edge of the D), and the bulb for this shines through the side of the lamp to illuminate the number plate as well. The curved section of each D operates as a reversing lamp. On cars built after about the middle of 1947, the wing-mounted nacelles contain double-filament bulbs for the stop and tail lamps, and there are circular Ace Cornercroft reversing lamps in place of the D-lamps alongside the number plate box.

Direction indicators on all MkVI models are the semaphore-arm type, and on standard saloon bodies are fitted in the upper B/C pillars. Early cars have Lucas model SF34N; the later cars have model SF80. A flashing light indicator was fitted to left-hand-drive export cars only. (It is worth noting that when fitting front seat belts – a worthwhile safety modification even though not original – the upper mounting is bolted to the B/C post behind the semaphore indicators. The indicator arms then have to be disabled.)

On early models, the lamps carried in small nacelles on the rear wings had single-filament bulbs for the brake lights only. Before about the middle of 1947, the tail lamps were in Lucas D-shaped lamps alongside the number plate. The clear sections were for the reversing lamps. On later models, the number plate box was flanked by circular Ace Cornercroft reversing lamps and the tail lamps joined the brake lights in the wing nacelles, which now carried twin-filament bulbs.

An oil syringe and two grease guns are clipped to the left-hand inner wing valance, and the starting-handle is just below them.

Body

The differences are hard to spot at first, but early MkVI grilles (below) have ten shutters on each side and later types (below right) have only nine.

The all-steel four-door standard saloon body of the MkVI was stamped out and welded together by Pressed Steel at Cowley before being shipped to Rolls-Royce at Crewe. Painting and trimming were carried out at the Rolls-Royce works before the body was mounted to its chassis. All of the

standard saloon bodies came with a sliding steel sunroof panel.

At the rear, the body is mounted to the chassis by four Silentbloc bushes in the wheelarches. Each bush originally had a two-piece stiffening plate, but a service bulletin in August 1956 recommended that a one-piece stiffener should be used when replacing the originals, to prevent distortion.

A number of modifications designed to meet export requirements were made to the body with effect from chassis number B321BG. This was a special show car completed in November 1947 for US Rolls-Royce retailers J. S. Inskip Inc in New York and described as having a 'Special SSS' (sic) body. It had lowered front wings and several items of special equipment and it is likely that the modified rear lamps (see *Lighting* section opposite) were among the 'export' body modifications.

Front Wings, Bonnet & Grille

The front wings are large, single-piece pressings bolted to the main bodyshell. They contain apertures for the headlamps and chromed horn grilles, and have small extension housings welded to their crowns to incorporate the sidelamps. The headlamps have chromed bezels. On late 1947 and later cars, there is an additional chromed flash running backwards from the top of each headlamp bezel, and a second one on top of each sidelamp housing. During 1950, a longer flash was fitted to the sidelamp housings.

There were no mud flaps on the front wings of the first standard steel saloons, but mud flaps were standardised during B-series chassis production in July 1947 and it was possible to fit them to older cars as well. The mud flaps are attached to the rear underside of the front wings by angle plates and 2BA bolts and nuts.

The side-opening bonnet of the Bentley MkVI has a long piano-type hinge along its centre and opens in two halves. However, only the bonnet top and a small wrap-over actually open, and the side panels of the engine compartment remain fixed. Each bonnet lid can be supported in the open position by a metal strut, which pivots from the side panel. The lids are released and locked shut by a catch operated by a long chromed handle on their side sections. Two bonnet locks of Vaughan manufacture were an optional fitment from October 1948.

Clipped to the inner wing valance under the left-hand side of the bonnet are the starting handle and the oil and grease guns. From chassis number B162EY in 1949, there is also an inspection lamp in two clips at the top of the bulkhead under the right-hand bonnet lid. This is plugged into a socket on the facia when in use.

The radiator grille has fixed vertical shutters, and carries the winged-B mascot at its crown. On the earliest cars, the mascot leans backwards, and on later cars it leans forwards. There are three different varieties of grille, too. The first type has ten shutters on each side and is fitted to cars up to and including chassis number B318CF. To cure overheating problems encountered in some markets, the opening angle of these shutters was widened at B320CF to create the second type of grille. Then from B163DZ in late 1948, the overheating problem was tackled in a different way by fitting a third type of grille with only nine shutters on each side.

The grille projects rearwards to form a forward support for the bonnet lids. This rearward projection is unplated and carries a braided cloth strip, woven in and out of slots in the metal, which acts as a buffer.

Bulkhead, Scuttle & Windscreen

The engine side of the bulkhead is unpainted, and the scuttle panel top and sides are attached to it and painted to match the bodywork. At the top left of the scuttle, on the painted section normally covered by the bonnet lid, is a small plate. This is stamped with the body number of the car, and is painted the same colour as the surrounding metal. The body number has seven digits; an example is B004639, which is the body number of 4½-litre chassis B207MB.

The 4¼-litre models have an air vent positioned centrally in the scuttle panel, ahead of the windscreen. This vent contains two metal grilles; its drain was given a larger diameter at B492DA in early summer 1949. Enlarged air apertures were used from November 1949, and it was possible to increase airflow even further by removing the two grilles and substituting a nickel-plated wire mesh screen. The central vent proved prone to leaks and was therefore deleted shortly after the 4½-litre models were introduced in 1951. From B29MB, it was replaced by a hinged ventilator on each side panel, just ahead of the door.

The upper scuttle sides also carry a chromed finisher for the side trim strip on cars built from late 1947 onwards. When a windscreen washer is fitted (as it is to most of these cars by now), the twin washer jets are fitted in the top of the scuttle, just ahead of the windscreen. The jets themselves are chromium-plated, and each consists of a slotted screw fitted with a hexagon nut, which provides jet adjustment.

The MkVI has a single-pane laminated-glass windscreen made (like all of the body glass) by Triplex. It is mounted to the body in a rubber seal, which in turn carries a bright finisher. When supplies of the original type of windscreen seal dried up, an improved type was introduced as a replacement in March 1951.

The windscreen wipers are fitted to the lower

section of the windscreen surround panel, and when parked should lie on this panel and point towards the outsides of the car (ie in opposite directions). All MkVI models had a radio as standard, and the chromed telescopic aerial for this is fitted centrally above the windscreen. It stands erect when in use, but can be turned through 90° by means of a knob inside the car, to lie parallel to the top of the windscreen and give more clearance for entering low garages and the like.

Doors

Both front and rear doors are hinged on the central body pillar or B/C post. The window frames are incorporated within the main door panel, and each front door has an opening quarter-light in a separate frame. On early cars, the drop-glass has no front guide above the door panel, and carries a chromed finisher on its leading edge. However, this arrangement proved unsatisfactory. After an unsuccessful modification to the window channels at B131DZ, Rolls-Royce settled on a full-length fixed guide for each drop-glass at B237DZ towards the end of 1948. As a result, the chromed finisher was removed from the drop-glass. The quarter-lights were then further modified at B311NY during 4½-litre production in 1952, so that they could open to 120°. Modified catches seem to have been introduced at the same time, or possibly later.

On early cars, the chromed trim strip on the bonnet sides divides into two on the scuttle panel and the doors thus carry a strip both above and below their chromed handles. From late 1947, a simpler single chromed moulding is fitted, which runs directly behind the handles.

The door hinges are fully concealed when the doors are closed, and operate on ingenious slides, which allow the door to move away from the

On early cars, there is no fixed guide for the front door drop-glass, which carries a chrome finisher that descends with the glass on its leading edge. On later types, there is a fixed guide for the drop-glass. Quarter-light windows have a limited opening and a quadrant-type lever.

The door hinges operate on slides, which move the opening door away from the body. Above is the courtesy light switch.

bodywork as it opens. Stronger hinges were fitted during 1949, at chassis number B420DA, and in August 1950, two holes were added in the slide piece to allow use of a grease gun. The original door lock striker plates had a spring-loaded safety catch, but a solid safety catch was introduced at B206CF in 1948. As Rolls-Royce instructed their retailers to fit the improved type when servicing cars, it is unlikely that many of the original spring-loaded safety catches have survived.

Both window and door seals gave some trouble, and there were a number of modifications in these areas. Softer door seals came in with B347CD in 1948. These had a roughly triangular section, and were made of very soft white sponge rubber. The same seal was also used sideways (at an angle) for the boot lid. The bottom sealing rubber on the outer edge of the sill tended to spread with age and prevent water drainage. So from January 1950, this was cut back to leave a quarter-inch gap. A retrospective modification was recommended at the same time, and so most earlier cars were probably modified. As for the windows, the U-shaped sealing strips at the front of their frames tended to distort over time and allow the windows to rattle. So in April 1950, a service modification was introduced, consisting of a one-inch long rubber buffer strip which could be added at the top corner of the window frame.

Rear Wings

The rear wings are incorporated in the rear quarter-panel pressings and are welded to the main bodyshell. Their shape is carried forwards into the rear doors. Early MkVI cars have open wheelarches, but cutaway spats – 'fairings' in Rolls-Royce language – were available in late 1947. Each spat is secured by two tongue-and-slot fittings inside the wing flange, and there should be Rexine piping between spat and wing.

The first cars had no stone guards on their rear wings. However, moulded rubber stone guards were introduced on production from June 1947. These were cemented in place and covered the front of the rear wings and the rear of the sills. Retro-fitting appears to have been possible.

The left-hand rear wing is home to the fuel filler, concealed under a hinged flap. This flap is sprung, and pops up when a button just below it is pressed. It could be fitted with a Yale lock to special order with effect from April 1949, and the lock could also be fitted retrospectively.

Boot, Spare Wheel & Number Plate

The MkVI boot lid hinges downwards in pre-war fashion to provide a flat area for carrying oversize loads. Fabric straps can be fastened through metal loops in the coachwork to secure the load in place when the boot lid is open. There are also two hinged and chromed arms on the inside of the boot lid, which can be erected as suitcase supports. These are spring-loaded and when not in use close flat on rubber buttons. There is a chromed thumb-wheel on either side to lock the lid in the desired position. A weather-proof roller shutter, made of black-painted wood, could be fitted to protect the contents of the boot.

The boot lid is opened by a long, vertical, chromed handle with its own keylock. Early cars have a plain boot lid, but in late 1947 a vertical chromed embellisher was added to the panel directly behind the opening handle. Opening the boot lid operates the internal boot illumination. The boot floor inside the car is flat, although the boot area does not extend very far back. The floor and sides of the boot are carpeted in Wilton, and there is a soft felt covering on the rear bulkhead. A water trap was fitted to the boot at chassis number B264EY in 1949.

Underneath the boot floor is the spare wheel compartment, which is reached separately from outside by opening the cover panel which contains the rear number plate. The cover panel is released by a catch located behind it on the left-hand side; this can only be reached when the boot lid is partly open. The panel hinges back and outwards on two arms, which then lie across the rear bumper. It closes against a spring stud on each side. The spare wheel compartment also contains the jack, jack handle, wheel brace, wheel disc spanner, tyre pump and tyre levers. The spare tyre's pressure can be checked through a flap in the boot floor. This obviates the need to open the spare wheel compartment – as long as the valve has been correctly positioned, of course!

The number plate is fitted behind a glass panel, and its compartment is illuminated internally when the side lights are on. The number-plate box was modified at B165GT in mid-1950. Cars that

Displayed in the boot of Tony Jenkin's 1951 MkVI are the Dunlop screw jack and large tools normally carried under the floor with the spare wheel. The longest handle is for the jack, the wheelbrace is made up of two sections, there is a special spanner for removing the hubcaps and a set of tyre levers. The tyre pump is in the background. The two chromed 'spears' on the inside of the boot lid could be erected to provide anchor points for luggage carried on the open lid.

went to the US from May 1949 have a modified support bracket for the rear number plate. This bracket tilts the number plate so that the existing lamps provide the direct illumination required under newly-introduced lighting regulations. Some export cars have the number plate mounted externally on the hinged spare wheel door, with a black-finished lamp unit fitted below it.

A set of six suitcases could be ordered as an optional extra to make the most of the rather limited luggage space. These were designed to fit neatly into the boot of the MkVI, but it was important to load them in the right order!

Bumpers

The large chromed bumpers carry separate over-riders, which are mounted alongside the number-plate at the front and further outboard at the rear of the car. There are two types of bumper, the standard type made by Wilmot Breeden and the larger and heavier 'export' type made by Pyrene, which became available during 1949. Overall length of the MkVI is 15ft 11½in with Wilmot Breeden bumpers. The Pyrene bumpers have a more rounded section than the standard type and come with bigger overriders. They increase the overall length to 16ft 4½in. Rear bumpers of all types have a winged-B emblem in the centre.

Both front and rear bumper support brackets are Y-shaped and bolt directly to the chassis side members. At the front, the brackets are covered by a neat curved valance on each side. Some coachbuilt cars have different rear bumper support brackets, with the bumper-support stiffening web bolted additionally to the side of the chassis member. This arrangement was used in

cases where there were more than 8in between the rear face of the bracket (where it bolted to the bumper) and the rearmost fixing bolt holding it to the chassis frame. All chassis for coachbuilt cars were drilled to accept this additional fixing with effect from B190CF in December 1947.

Interior

Facia & Instruments

The MkVI instrument panel is a neat, rather formal and rather old-fashioned construction made of wood with a figured walnut veneer. It consists of three main sections, with a capping rail above. On 4¼-litre models, the rear view mirror is on a pedestal screwed to this capping rail, but on the 4½-litre cars it is fixed above the windscreen and hangs downwards.

In the centre of the capping rail is a Bakelite switch for the direction indicators. The original clockwork switch was made by Trico, but a Scintilla type was recommended as a replacement when supplies of the original dried up in 1957. On either side of the capping rail is a knob, which allows the windscreen wipers to be engaged or parked, and there is a large chromed grab handle on the passenger-side of the rail, above the glove box. Later cars have hinged chromed metal strips (familiarly known as 'eyebrows') covering the demister vents in the capping rail, and these can be closed when the demister is not in use.

In the middle of the main facia panel is the traditional Rolls-Royce switchbox for ignition and lighting, flanked on the driver's side by a speedometer and on the passenger's side by a dial containing four instruments. The speedometer

The dashboard of the MkVI was plain but elegant. Originally this 1951 example would have had an HMV Radiomobile set with black knobs and push-buttons.

By the time of this 1951 car, the flap concealing the tool tray was fitted with a Yale lock. The glove compartment had always been lockable. This is one of the later Smiths electric clocks.

has its zero mark at one o'clock rather than the more familiar seven o'clock. From B31HP in mid-1950, a main beam warning light was added to its face. The four instruments in the combined dial are (clockwise from 12 o'clock) an ammeter, a water temperature gauge, a fuel gauge and an oil pressure gauge. The ammeter reads 0-25-0 on early cars, but a 0-30-0 gauge is fitted to those with the 5in dynamo (for details, see page 30). The ammeter was further modified at B64KM in 1951.

Major switchgear is arranged vertically on the outer edges of the central panel, and there are additional switches at top and bottom. The precise layout depends on the age of the car, but it is always symmetrical. A typical right-hand-drive layout for a car from chassis B311NY has the windscreen wiper control at the top left, the instrument lighting switch below it and a Smiths cigar lighter at the bottom. At top right is the switch for the demister booster fan, below that is the rear window demister control and at the bottom is the heater switch. During 4½-litre production in 1952, at B311NY, the heater and demister switches were changed from two-position to three-position types.

Underneath the central panel is a pull-out ashtray, and the standard radio is mounted below this, in a neat wooden housing. An HMV Radiomobile Model 4200 was usually fitted to early cars, and later cars had a Radiomobile 100. Both types offer Medium and Long Wave reception, with push-button tuning.

There is an open glovebox on the driver's side. Alongside it, and just above the steering column, a two-pin socket for the inspection lamp is fitted from chassis number B162EY in 1949. This socket also serves for connecting a battery charger, using the special plug supplied. Some cars were fitted

optionally with a three-way switch for the fuel pumps, just above the steering column on the wooden facia. This is finished in black and carries the letters A and B. It allows separate operation of each pump and a double pump check. This was an option introduced to meet demand from customers who had appreciated the similar three-way switch on pre-war Bentleys; the standard MkVI system has both pumps running together.

On the passenger side is a glovebox with a lockable wooden lid which contains a clock. The clock was a hand-wound type up to the end of the G-series chassis, but an electric clock was fitted from B2HR. When supplies of hand-wound clocks dried up during 1958, a scheme was introduced which enabled the later electric clock to be fitted as a replacement. Below the glove compartment, all models have a hinged wooden flap, which conceals the tool tray. From late 1947, this flap was fitted with a Yale lock, located just inboard of the clock. The tool tray pulls out to reveal spare lamp bulbs and hand tools for roadside repair and small maintenance tasks, each one individually fitted into the moulded rubber lining of the tray. Under the tray is a holder for the car handbook.

Steering Wheel, Gear Lever & Handbrake

The steering wheel is a large three-spoke type made of black plastic over a steel armature. Its hub contains the horn push, and around its circumference are three operating levers. In the top left segment is the hand throttle lever, and the hub is stamped with the words 'OPEN, CLOSED' and, between and below them, 'THROTTLE'. All letters are painted white. In the top right segment is the mixture control lever, and here the hub is stamped 'START, RUN' and (below and between them) 'MIXTURE'. The bottom segment contains the ride control lever which regulates the rear damper settings. The words here are 'NORMAL, HARD' and 'RIDING'.

From chassis B185AJ, the horn push-button assembly was strengthened where the contact pillar screws into the horn push itself, and was sweated into place rather than locked by a taper pin. Earlier cars so modified should have a P stamped on the nearside lug of the steering box.

The gear lever on right-hand-drive cars is mounted alongside the driver's seat and outboard of it. It has a chromed stem with a black plastic grip, and operates in the traditional Rolls-Royce gate. Reverse is selected by depressing the lever to release a catch, allowing the lever to move left and forwards into the reverse slot. All left-hand-drive cars have the gear lever mounted on the steering column, and the lever itself was lengthened in late 1949, at chassis number B138LFV. On cars prior to B281LGT in 1950, the gearchange has two cross-tube assemblies and a gearchange pull-rod

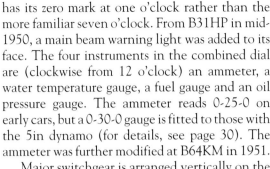

The steering wheel hub carries three sliding controls, with the functions of each one clearly labelled.

Small tools carried in the moulded tool tray of a 1951 model.

assembly. Later cars have keyhole-type sockets in the gearchange, and the modified assemblies were also supplied as service replacements.

Handbrakes also differ between models with right-hand and left-hand drive. Both are mounted under the dashboard, outboard of the driver, but on right-hand-drive cars there is a release button in the pistol-grip handle, while left-hand-drive cars have a T-handle which is released by twisting.

Pedals

Accelerator pedals differ between right-hand-drive and left-hand-drive cars. The right-hand-drive type is a small rectangular pedal with a ribbed black rubber pad. The left-hand-drive type is a much larger treadle-type pedal with a plain metal finish. Out of sight below the floor, the accelerator was fitted with a countershaft guard at B1CD in March 1948.

The brake and clutch pedals are mounted on shanks, which protrude through the toe-board, and each one has a rubber pad embossed with a 'B' symbol. On the early cars, the shank of the clutch pedal was fitted with a pressed cup and rubber washer beneath the pedal pad, which acted as a stop. However, these tended to work loose and rattle, and so Rolls-Royce suggested removing the cup and letting the carpet act as a stop.

There is also a dipswitch with a bare metal cover, mounted on the toe-board to the driver's left on both right- and left-hand-drive models. On early cars, the Bijur chassis lubrication pedal is on the toe-board inboard of the steering column. On later ones, the pedal is outboard of the column.

Seats & Carpets

The early MkVI Bentleys have rather austere interiors which matched the spirit of their times admirably, but were nonetheless luxurious by the standard of other cars. Cars built before the end of 1947 have plain rather than pleated leather seat upholstery, and there are no picnic tables in the rear of the front seats. From late 1947, the seats have pleated wearing faces and plain panels over the bolstered sections, which give thigh support and sideways location. All seats are upholstered in top-quality Connolly Vaumol hide (which is now available again as Connolly Classic). The edges of the seats are piped, and this piping is sometimes finished in a contrasting colour.

Two types of stitching exist on the early front seats with plain leather upholstery. The leather covering on the first examples suffered from splitting at the rear corners where the top leather of the cushion was stitched to the side panel. So in July 1947, modified stitching was introduced to withstand the strain better. Retailers were advised to modify the older seats to the new pattern in cases of need.

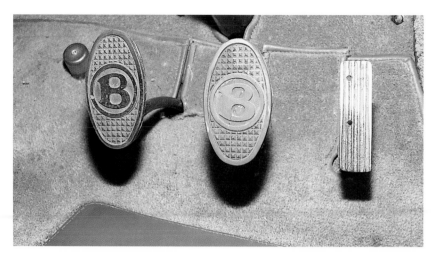

These are the pedals of a 1947 right-hand-drive car. On the left is the bare metal dipswitch. The pedals come up through the floor to provide the optimum operating arc.

From the beginning, these cars were normally fitted with separate front seats rather than the bench seats that were favoured by many other makers at the time. A bench seat was available to order, though, and with it came a folding centre armrest. After late 1947, cars with individual front seats have a pull-down wooden picnic table in the rear of each front seat, and there are chromed grab handles for the rear seat passengers mounted above them. Cars with a bench front seat built after this date normally have a single, larger, picnic table in the seatback. The rear seat is always a bench, flanked by fixed outboard armrests and carrying a pull-down central armrest.

Several interior changes accompanied the change to the 4½-litre engine in 1951, at chassis number B2MD. These were most noticeable at the rear, where tall, padded side bolsters were added to the outboard edges of the seats and provided headrests for dozing passengers. Their curved tops made it necessary to alter the shape of the vanity mirrors. The rear armrests took on a curved section, and the piping now ran around their forward faces instead of around the sides as on the earlier square-section armrests. In addition, the configuration of the central armrest altered; its box-like top section became shallower and the curved lower section became correspondingly deeper, presumably to improve the backrest padding when the armrest was folded away and a third rear seat passenger was being carried.

There is a pull-out ashtray in the front face of each rear armrest. These ashtrays have bright metal bodies and housings, with a Bakelite front cover made to look like wood. The rear picnic trays are of walnut-veneered plywood on a wooden frame, and are matched to the rest of the interior woodwork.

Top-quality Wilton carpet covers the front floor of the passenger compartment. This is in no fewer than seven sections. One runs right across the footwell and toe-board area. Under each front seat are two further pieces, which meet around the

Pleated leather upholstery and picnic tables give this 1951 model a great deal of its charm. Note the footrests at the bottom of the front seat backs. The seat belts are a modern addition.

battery box cover on the right-hand side and around the heater on the left-hand side. There is a separate piece of carpet on the battery box cover, and a further small piece over the forward-facing heater duct. All carpet edges are stitch-bound in leather, as are the cut-outs for the pedals and dip-switch. There is a black rubber heelmat for the driver, which is bound to the carpet with stitching. The carpet for the rear compartment is a single piece running right across the car, and is leather-bound at its edges. There are footrests for the rear seat passengers at the base of the front seats, and these are also covered in carpet material to match the main carpet.

Door Trims & Headlining

The interior door panels are covered in leather, neatly tooled into panels. Each one has a carpeted kick-panel at its base, and at the top there is a deep wooden fillet, which extends all the way around the window. Its figured walnut veneer matches that on the instrument panel and other wooden parts of the interior. The front doors also carry raked armrests which are fixed on early cars and adjustable in the vertical plane on later cars. The driver's door trim on right-hand-drive cars has a special cut-out for the hand on the gear lever.

Each door carries a chromed release handle

and a chromed window winder, while cars up to B115DZ in late 1948 have an extra-long handle for the window on both front doors. This is a quick-lift handle, which raises an open window with a single action. (On some early examples, these handles were found to work loose, and so a tapered plug was introduced at an unspecified point during production to hold the securing screw in place.) At B117DZ, the quick-release handle on the passenger side only was replaced by an ordinary winding handle. Modified interior door locks had been introduced in 1947 at chassis number B228BH.

The headlining is made of beige West of England woollen broadcloth, and the sun visors above the windscreen are covered in leather. There is a large knob above the centre of the windscreen which is connected to the radio aerial and turns it through 90° so that it can be positioned parallel to the windscreen top rail or vertically for improved reception. The rear-view mirror hangs down from the windscreen capping rail on a chromed stalk. There is also a circular courtesy lamp above the rear passenger area, and the sunroof aperture has veneered wooden edges.

The rear quarter-panels contain vanity mirrors. These are sometimes called 'companions', and can be illuminated by bulbs concealed behind a shallow pelmet made of frosted glass. The companions are edged with figured walnut veneer to match the other interior woodwork. On the 4¼-litre models, the mirrors are rectangular, but on the 4½-litre models (B2MD onwards), their shape was altered to accommodate the large head-rests introduced on these cars. The left-hand companion also contains a cigar lighter.

The rear window can be obscured by means of a translucent silk roller blind, operated by a cord, which runs above the windows and behind the headlining on the driver's side of the car. It is attached to a chromed sliding control above the driver's door; there is a fixing clip there to hold the cord (and thus the blind) in position. When not in use, the blind retracts out of sight onto a roller between the rear window and the false lining of the rear compartment.

Heater & Demister

The interior heater and windscreen demister are not part of the same piece of apparatus on the MkVI Bentley. The passenger compartment heater is located under the front passenger seat, and is supplied with hot water from the engine cooling system. Heat is distributed by an electric blower motor through a forward- and rear-facing vent between the seats. A tap at the front or rear of the engine block (just above the exhaust manifold) allowed the heater to be turned off when not required. On cars up to and including B235DZ, the heater has a shallow matrix; from B237DZ, a deeper matrix is fitted. Early cars have a heater return tap, but this was deleted during 1947 at B70BH, when a drain tap was added. At B273DZ, the return tap was then reinstated.

From February 1950, it was possible to buy a supplementary heater, which was fitted into the

hot water circuit in series with the existing heater. This was a circular type with a trapdoor in its front cover to allow hot air into the footwells or to shut off the footwell flow so that all the hot air could be used for demisting. It was attached to the centre of the dash behind the facia panel.

To make room for this supplementary heater, the powerpack fitted behind the radio had to be relocated on a bracket behind the tool tray. The radio mounting tray also had to be modified to clear the demister adapter at the top of the heater cover. Part of the hot air output of this supplementary heater was directed into the two existing demisting ducts, and so the electrically-heated demister element fitted in the right-hand duct on early cars became redundant. With this option came a rheostat switch, replacing the existing

The driver's door trim of this 1947 model (above left) shows the pull-out ashtray, the cutaway to clear the outboard gear lever, and the long quick-release window handle. The front passenger door of a 1951 car (above) shows the ordinary window winder and the adjustable armrest.

PAINT & INTERIOR TRIM

It is not easy to establish for certain what were the standard colour schemes at any one time for the Bentley MkVI. What follows should not therefore be viewed as definitive. Coachbuilt bodies were trimmed and painted to the customer's choice, of course.

1946 to July 1949 (approx)
There were seven standard exterior paint finishes, of which one was two-tone. Each was available with a pre-defined choice from five interior colours. The exterior colour schemes (with upholstery colour in brackets) were: Black (Beige, Blue, Brown or Grey), Dark Blue (Blue or Brown), Fish Silver metallic (Grey), Maroon (Beige or Maroon), Mistletoe Green metallic (Beige), Pearl metallic (Blue), and Two-tone Grey (Blue).

August 1949 to March 1950 (approx)
Six standard paint finishes were on offer, again including a single two-tone. There were now six interior colours but there was a rather more limited choice of combinations. The exterior colour schemes (with upholstery colour in brackets) were: Black (Brown), Dark Blue (Dark Blue),

Maroon (Maroon or Tan), Metallic Grey (Grey), Pearl metallic (Light Blue), and Two-tone Grey (Light Blue).

April 1950 to March 1951 (approx)
There were once again six standard finishes, including a single two-tone. This time, there was an even more restricted choice of four interior colours. The exterior colour schemes (with upholstery colour in brackets) were: Black (Brown), Dark Blue (Beige), Metallic Grey (Grey), Moss Green (Beige), Pearl metallic (Light Blue) and Two-tone Grey (Light Blue).

April 1951
The final 4¼-litre models came with a choice of six exterior finishes yet again, of which one was a two-tone. Two of the new colours, which would be available on the 4½-litre cars, now made an appearance. The interior colour choice was still restricted, with just four colours on offer. The exterior colour schemes (with upholstery colour in brackets) were: Black (Brown), Dark Blue (Beige), Moss Green (Beige), Pearl metallic (Light Blue), Shell Grey (Light Blue), Tudor Grey (Grey), and Two-tone Grey (Light Blue).

May to December 1951 (approx)
These colour schemes were announced shortly before the introduction of the 4½-litre models, and may have been available on the final 4¼-litre cars as well. Once again, there were six exterior paint options, including one two-tone. Metallic paints were no longer available. There were just four different upholstery colours. The exterior colour schemes (with upholstery colour in brackets) were: Black (Brown), Dark Blue (Beige), Shell Grey with (Light Blue), Tudor Grey (Grey), Two-tone Grey (Light Blue), and Velvet Green (Grey).

January to August 1952
There were again six exterior finish options for the final MkVI models, one of them a two-tone. A choice of six upholstery colours was offered also, and customers could in theory match these to exterior colours to suit their own preferences.

The exterior finishes were: Black, Midnight Blue, Shell Grey, Tudor Grey, Two-tone Grey, and Velvet Green.

The upholstery options were: Beige, Brown, Grey, Light Blue, Maroon, and Tan.

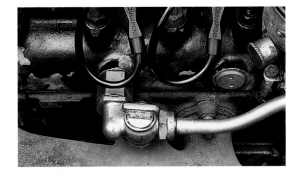

This underbonnet heater isolation tap is the only way to turn off the underseat interior heater for the summer.

The chassis plate of a Bentley MkVI is much plainer than its Rolls-Royce equivalent. Note the delightful invitation to have the car serviced by the supplying dealer!

push-pull demister switch on the facia. According to the Rolls-Royce Chassis Numbers Booklet, a three-position switch was offered as an alternative to the rheostat type from B311NY.

This additional heater was not the same as the optional additional heater fitted to R-types, and was not the same as the standard under-dash heater on the R-type Continentals.

There were three types of windscreen demister over the years. The demister on the earliest cars consisted of an electric heating element under the scuttle on the driver's side to warm incoming air. A blower motor then directed the heated air through vents in the capping rail onto

the windscreen. Starting with B193DZ in 1948-1949, this electric demister was replaced by a demister heated by warm air brought from the radiator by ducting running above the engine.

The third type was introduced as an intermediate scheme from chassis number B149HP late in 1950, and also used hot air collected from behind the radiator but allowed cold air to be admitted through the vents as well. Cold air was drawn in from the intake below the right-hand headlamp, and hot air came through the radiator matrix. Both were ducted to the windscreen via the blower unit mounted on the scuttle, and there was a changeover valve on the front left-hand side of the engine which allowed the hot side of the system to be switched into or out of circuit. The final triple by-pass demister scheme was introduced at B2KM in early 1951, and the definitive hot-and-cold demister system arrived in 1952 at B53PU in the final MkVI chassis series.

Division

A division was available for the standard saloon bodies from October 1949, and was accompanied by the bench front seat with 4in of sliding movement. Locking catches were fitted in the rear compartment on either side of the seat to prevent adjustment while the division was raised. It had a single pane of glass, which could be wound down into the lower section by hand from the rear compartment. A separate lock was required for one of the rear doors to guard against slam-locking the rear doors with the partition glass raised. The division could be fitted retrospectively if the separate front seats and some of the trim were replaced.

IDENTIFICATION, DATING & PRODUCTION FIGURES

The chassis number of a Bentley MkVI is found on the car's identification plate, which is fixed to the engine side of the front bulkhead. It is also stamped on the left-hand chassis frame member just ahead of the bulkhead.

There were 5,200 production MkVI chassis, of which 4,000 had the 4¼-litre engine and 1,200 the 4½-litre. To these figures may be added two prototype cars (one with each engine) which were sold off by the factory and renumbered within the production chassis sequences.

CHASSIS NUMBERS

The chassis number sequences for the MkVI models are set out below, together with delivery dates. All chassis numbers have a B prefix followed by up to three digits and two letters. The penultimate suffix letter denotes the chassis series. Cars with left-hand drive have an L before the suffix letters, eg B281LGT. Sequences beginning with 1 use odd numbers only and always except 13; sequences beginning with 2 use even numbers only.

4¼-litre models, 1946-1951

B2AK to B254AK[1]	November 1946 to July 1947	
B1AJ to B247AJ	April to October 1947	
B2BH to B400BH	June 1947 to January 1948	
B1BG to B401BG	September 1947 to March 1948	
B2CF to B500CF	December 1947 to August 1948	

B1CD to B501CD	March to December 1948
B2DA to B500DA	July 1948 to May 1949
B1DZ to B501DZ	October 1948 to May 1949
B2EY to B500EY	February to November 1949
B1EW to B501EW	June 1949 to February 1950
B2FV to B500FV	September 1949 to March 1950
B1FU to B601FU	December 1949 to March 1950
B1GT to B401GT	April to September 1950
B2HR to B250HR	July 1950 to January 1951
B1HP to B251HP	July 1950 to March 1951
B2JO to B250JO	September 1950 to February 1951
B1JN to B251JN	November 1950 to May 1951
B2KM to B200KM	January to July 1951
B1KL to B201KL	February to August 1951
B2LJ to B400LJ	March to September 1951
B1LH to B401LH	May to December 1951

[1] To this sequence must be added B256AK, renumbered from experimental car 1BVI.

4½-litre models, 1951-1952

B2MD to B400MD	July 1951 to January 1952
B1MB to B401MB[2]	September 1951 to February 1952
B2NZ to B500NZ	November 1951 to May 1952
B1NY to B501NY	February to September 1952
B2PV to B300PV	April to July 1952
B1PU to B301PU	June to August 1952

[2] To this sequence must be added B403MB, renumbered from experimental car 4BVI.

ENGINE NUMBERS

The engine number is stamped either on the front left-hand crankcase lifting lug, or on a boss on the crankcase immediately above. Engines are numbered consecutively. The numbering sequences are:

4¼-litre engines

B1A to B250A	A-series chassis
B1B to B400B	B-series chassis
B1C to B500C	C-series chassis
B1D to B500D	D-series chassis
B1E to B500E	E-series chassis
B1F to B500F	F-series chassis
B1G to B200G	G-series chassis
B1H to B250H	H-series chassis
B1J to B250J	J-series chassis
B1K to B200K	K-series chassis
B1L to B400L	L-series chassis

4½-litre engines

B1M to B400M	MD- and MB-series chassis
B1N to B500N	NZ- and NY-series chassis
B1P to B300P	PV- and PU-series chassis

Bentley R-type, 1952-55

The Bentley MkVI had not been on sale long when Rolls-Royce began to receive criticisms of its boot capacity. So the tail end of the car was restyled by John Blatchley, formerly of the coachbuilder Gurney Nutting and by then Chief Styling Engineer for Rolls-Royce and Bentley cars. He extended the boot, incorporated a lift-up (instead of drop-down) lid and relocated the spare wheel. The results were a useful increase in boot capacity from 6cu ft to 10.5cu ft, and a much better balance to the overall styling.

While the revised car was under development, it was referred to as a Bentley MkVII. Indeed the chassis cards for these cars describe them all as 'Bentley 7' up to and including B205SP on 4 December 1952. The first card to call the chassis a 'Bentley R' is for B207LSP, destined for Switzerland, on 19 December 1952. However, it is unlikely that Rolls-Royce ever planned to release

the car to the public as the MkVII. By the time work started on the new car in 1951, Jaguar had already announced their MkVII saloon – leapfrogging the MkVI designation already used by the Bentley even though the previous Jaguar was called a MkV. Rolls-Royce would certainly not have wanted their new model to carry the same name as the Jaguar, which was to some extent a cheaper competitor for the Bentley. So when the new body and longer chassis were introduced in September 1952, the car was simply known as a Bentley Sports Saloon. The R-type name which is now usually applied to this model stems from the chassis series (RT) at which the styling change took place.

The R-type Bentley is a development of the MkVI. It is therefore generally similar to the 4½-litre MkVI in all respects, except for those highlighted in this section.

The styling balance was not upset by lengthening the MkVI's rear wings and boot; indeed, to some eyes, the R-type was the better-balanced shape.

The lengthened tail of the R-type is readily apparent in this picture of Graham Pearce's 1953 model (B435SP). This Midnight Blue and Cream car has the MkVI style of colour split.

The R-type's usual two-tone colour scheme is shown on David Clarke's 1954 model (B40ZY) in Velvet Green over Donegal Green.

Chassis

Chassis Frame & Fuel Tank

To support the longer boot of the R-type, the MkVI chassis frame was extended rearwards by six inches. The rear suspension was modified to cope with the potentially greater weight over the rear wheels, and the fuel tank was modified to fit around the spare wheel and allow it to be accommodated further forwards.

Like the MkVI chassis before them, the early R-type chassis frames are riveted together. However, Rolls-Royce moved to all-welded frames in 1953, and these were standardised at B349LTO. A few earlier cars had been built with all-welded frames, these being B161SP, B23TO, B57TO, B199TO and B123TO. In addition, two cars were built with riveted chassis frames after, theoretically, the welded type had been standardised! These were B387TO and B401LTO.

The fuel tank on the R-type is made of aluminium and has a distinctive shape at its forward end which cradles the spare wheel. It has the same 18 Imperial gallon capacity as the MkVI type. As on the earlier models, the twin fuel pumps are fitted inside the right-hand chassis rail and there is a strainer in the line between pump and tank.

Steering

All 1952 cars and a number of those built in 1953 (ending with B388TN) had steel balls in the front end socket of the side steering tube. These had been introduced on the last MkVI cars and were intended to reduce friction in the steering. However, the balls tended to wear a groove and cause hard steering, and so a bronze seat replaced the steel balls on production, beginning with B390TN. A modification kit, which allowed the bronze seat to be fitted to earlier cars, was introduced on 23 September 1953.

Other changes were a revised slow leak rate of 3½ seconds for the dampers at chassis number B61SP, and the deletion of the non-opposed springs in the side steering tube at B313TO.

Rear Axle & Rear Suspension

The rear road springs of the R-type Bentley are longer and wider than those of the MkVI. The rear shackle bracket by which they are mounted to the chassis side-member is located differently from its

MkVI equivalent, to bring the shackle eye above the frame instead of below it. In tandem with a lowered front spring shackle, this change was made to counteract roll oversteer. The rear dampers are also differently calibrated.

From chassis number B433SP in 1953, an axle ratio of 3.417:1 (12/41) was introduced as an optional alternative to the standard 3.727:1 (11/41) ratio on export chassis. This taller overall gearing became standard in 1954 at B1YA, and is found on all Y-series and Z-series cars.

All axles with the 3.417:1 gearing, and the 3.727:1 axles from B380SR, have a pinion thrust bearing which consists of a pair of Timken taper roller bearings. On earlier 3.727:1 axles, a double thrust bearing is fitted.

Brakes

By the time of the R-type Bentleys, the specification of the braking system had settled down and there were relatively few modifications. However, the jaws on the front brake operating links were strengthened at chassis number B60XF in summer 1954, and the chromium-plated servo pressure plate was no longer fitted with effect from B123YD in the autumn of that year.

When new R-type Bentleys were fitted with two different types of brake hoses. Cars built up to November 1953 had front brake hoses with a chevron pattern on their skins and a diameter of 0.430in, exactly like those on the final MkVI models. Later examples of these hoses carried a green plastic band to indicate that they had been tested to increased pressures.

From November 1953, the specification of the hoses was changed from two-ply to three-ply. They had the same chevron pattern on their skins but carried a yellow plastic band to indicate this tougher construction, and they had increased barrelling of the end connections. Later versions had L2 stamped on the hexagon to show they conformed to an agreed SAE (Society of Automotive Engineers) specification. These hoses were recommended as service replacements for the earlier type from November 1954.

Just as on the MkVI models, there may be a semi-universal bearing on the bellcrank lever behind the brake servo on left-hand-drive cars where the lever attaches to the servo operating pushrod. If so, the item is a service replacement component (RG2280), introduced to prevent fatigue fractures of the pushrod.

From approximately B311YA on in 1954, a spring clip was fitted to the upper brake actuating lever on the servo to eliminate clonks. However, this was removed if it fouled the corrugated washer, which was sometimes added in service to prevent judder. (The corrugated washer replaced a plain washer between the brake actuating levers.)

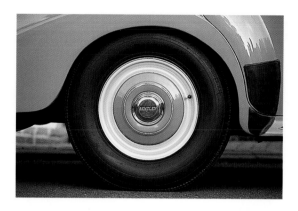

Wheels & Tyres

Bentley R-types have the same disc wheels as the last of the MkVI cars, with four steel balancing weights spaced equally around the 24 holes drilled in the disc itself. Like the MkVIs, these cars were originally equipped with India Super Silent rayon 6.50-16 tyres. When these went out of production, the same alternatives were recommended as had been recommended for the MkVI cars.

Tyre pressures do not seem to have given so much trouble as on the MkVI models. The recommendations for R-types remained consistent at 24psi for the front tyres and 33psi for the rears.

The wheel cover discs are the same as on the final MkVI models, with outer rings painted to match the bodywork (or the lower colour).

Engine

The engine in all the R-type Bentleys is the 4½-litre 'big-bore' type introduced during 1951 on the MkVI. However, all the R-type engines have the same twin-SU carburettor installation, and there are none with the Stromberg or Zenith carburettors used on contemporary Rolls-Royce Silver Dawn models. Unlike the 4½-litre MkVI, all R-type engines have an automatic choke.

Cylinder Head, Cylinder Block & Bellhousing

The specification of the 4½-litre engine remained fairly constant during the production life of the R-type Bentley, the main change being to the cylinder head when a higher compression ratio type was introduced during 1953. By this time, the poor-quality petrol which was universal in the early post-war years had largely disappeared, and as octane ratings began to stabilise, so Rolls-Royce saw its way clear to raise the compression ratio and thus increase power and torque.

The cylinder head on the first R-types is the same component (RE10429) as on the MkVI engines, and gives a 6.4:1 compression ratio. The head itself remained unchanged until replaced by the high-compression type. However, during 1953, Parco lubrized tappets were fitted from

All R-types have the 4½-litre 'big bore' engine carried over from the later MkVIs. Seen from the left-hand or exhaust side (above), this is the engine of the 1954 car. Note the single coil, now at the front. This 1953 car (right) has the combined hot-and-cold demisting system. Note the horizontal hot air pipe above the engine and the cold air ducting (in foreground) joining it. Compare it with the earlier and simpler hot-air demisting type on the 1951 MkVI (page 25).

chassis number B425SP, and a hard clay gasket was used from B372TN.

The high-compression cylinder head (RE19451) gives a 6.75:1 compression ratio. It is fitted as standard from B93TO, but was also on a few earlier cars: B11TO, B15TO, B17TO, B19TO, and B49TO to B87TO inclusive. The two types of head are easily distinguished because their castings bear part numbers on the top left-hand side. The later cylinder head uses the same copper and asbestos gasket (RE14764) as is found on Continental chassis prior to the change.

The crankcase was fitted with cadmium-plated core plugs in place of the earlier aluminium alloy plugs with effect from B257SP in 1953. As on the 4½-litre MkVI engines, the early type of core plug tended to corrode, and most will have been replaced by the cadmium-plated steel core plugs and aluminium washers that were recommended as a service modification. The cadmium-plated plugs were also fitted on production to the engines in some chassis before the full changeover. These were B171SP to B185SP, B203SP and B205SP.

The crankshaft vibration damper was modified very late in production at chassis B212ZY, when Ferodo washers and drain slots were added.

The bellhousing is normally made of aluminium but the early cars with automatic transmission had a cast iron bellhousing. An alloy housing was used again from early 1953, the first car with it being B35UL. All cars with automatic transmission were fitted with a flywheel inertia ring from chassis number B236WH in early 1954.

Carburettors & Fuel System

The R-type engines have twin SU type H6 carburettors, with a 1¾in choke. An automatic cold starting device of Rolls-Royce design is fitted. This consists of a butterfly strangler between the air intake silencer and the carburettors, operated by a temperature-sensitive bi-metallic strip in the water-heated inlet manifold, and a fast idle cam to raise the idling speed on a cold engine.

The automatic choke was modified three times during R-type production. From B1SP in January 1953, trip levers were added to the choke flap to counter flooding problems under some conditions. In the late summer of 1954, at B158YD, an oil-pressure-operated switch was incorporated into the solenoid circuit of the automatic choke to improve cold-start performance. Then from B1ZX in October 1954, a heat-sensitive switch was added to take account of underbonnet temperatures; this was fitted to the engine side of the bulkhead, just below the fuse box.

Cooling System

There were just two modifications to the cooling system during R-type production. From chassis

B68RT in 1952, a corrugated bottom hose was fitted to the radiator to allow for the movement of the engine, and from B160YD in mid-1954, the water pump was fitted with a Flexibox seal.

Transmission

The first R-type Bentleys all have the same four-speed synchromesh gearbox as the final MkVI models, and the accompanying clutch and propshaft are also the same. A four-speed automatic alternative became optional for export models only right from the start of R-type production, and the first chassis with the new option (B16RT and B26RT) were both delivered to their coachbuilders on 11 June 1952, although the completed cars were not shipped until January 1953.

The automatic gearbox became an option on home-market cars as well a year later. The first home market R-type automatic was B88TN, a company car built for W. A. Robotham. However, B134TN, which was the 1953 Earls Court Show car, was the next to be built and traditionally has been considered as the first of its kind. The automatic transmission quickly proved popular, and was standardised on left-hand-drive chassis from B1TO in 1953 and then on right-hand-drive chassis as well from B2WH. Nevertheless, a few customers still specified the synchromesh gearbox, which remained an option to the end.

The automatic transmission installation was envisaged from the beginning of R-type production, and the transverse mounting bracket for the

On synchromesh models with right-hand drive, the gear lever remained outboard of the driver, on the floor.

The selector for the automatic transmission is mounted on the steering column. A push-button at the end of the lever has to be depressed to move from Neutral to 4 (drive) or into Reverse from 2.

Two-pedal control on an automatic R-type: note the umbrella-type handbrake lever. The cable-operated heater controls are on the left of the modern chrome switch panel.

rear end of the gearbox tie-rod was designed to suit both the existing synchromesh gearbox and the eventual automatic. It therefore differs from the type used on MkVI models. However, this new bracket proved to be weak in service and was replaced in about April 1953 (from B212UM) by the MkVI type of bracket. Rolls-Royce recommended that a service modification was carried out to earlier cars; those with riveted chassis frames were to have the tie rod bracket stiffened, while those with welded frames were to have the MkVI type of bracket added. Probably few of the original brackets survived unmodified.

Synchromesh Gearbox

Just one modification was carried out to the four-speed synchromesh gearbox during R-type production. This was the fitting of a thicker thrust washer for the third speed motion shaft in 1954, at chassis number B89WG. Rolls-Royce recommended that earlier gearboxes should be so modified if they needed service attention. A service replacement washer was available, and gearboxes so modified should have been stamped 'W1'. When the production type of washer was fitted, the gearbox should have been stamped 'W2'.

From chassis B433SP, a 3.417:1 (12:41) rear axle ratio became optional and was standardised at B1YA, so although the internal gearbox ratios of cars so fitted remained unchanged the overall ratios now became: First 10.187:1, Second 6.893:1, Third 4.584:1, Fourth 3.417:1 and Reverse 10.786:1.

Automatic Gearbox

The automatic transmission fitted to the R-type Bentley is an American General Motors Hydra-Matic. It gives four forward speeds and has a fluid

flywheel, but it was considerably modified to suit its Bentley and Rolls-Royce applications and therefore differs from gearboxes of the same type installed in contemporary American cars. In particular, the Rolls-Royce gear selector allows manual override options denied on the American original, and makes it possible to change gear by using the column-mounted selector lever rather than the kick-down switch.

Perhaps most useful is the second-speed hold which permits engine braking for steep descents. Third speed has a safety override, which allows the transmission to change up to top gear if the road speed exceeds about 60mph; this prevents the driver from over-speeding the engine. In addition, the upshift characteristics are slightly different from those of the American original. If the driver selects Reverse before switching off the engine, the transmission is locked to assist when parking on steep inclines. Starting the engine is possible only in Neutral.

The rear extension casing of the transmission is also to a Rolls-Royce design, and incorporates the friction-disc brake servo, the speedometer drive gear, the gearbox output drive shaft and the ride control pump.

The gear ratios (with the overall ratios in brackets) of the automatic transmission model are: First 3.819:1:1 (14.236), Second 2.634:1 (9.818), Third 1.450:1 (5.404), Fourth 1.000:1 (3.727) and Reverse 4.306:1 (16.050). Cars fitted with the 3.417:1 (12:41) rear axle ratio, which was optional from B433SP and standard from B1YA, retained the same internal automatic gearbox ratios but the overall ratios became: First 13.049:1, Second 8.999:1, Third 4.954:1, Fourth 3.417:1 and Reverse 14.712:1.

The first Hydra-Matic gearboxes used in Rolls-Royce cars were actually manufactured in Detroit to meet Rolls-Royce requirements. An initial batch of 300 to the 1952 specification was followed by a further 300 to the 1953 specification, which had eight sets of clutch plates instead of seven. Not all of these were fitted to R-type Bentleys; some were used in Rolls-Royce Silver Dawn and Silver Wraith chassis. They carry a plate on their right-hand sides which reads 'GM Detroit Transmission Division. Built for Rolls-Royce Ltd'. Their serial numbers are preceded by an X, and the first two digits are 52 or 53, to indicate the year of manufacture. Thus, X52 123 would be the 123rd gearbox made in 1952. The factory started to fit the later gearboxes with the X53 prefix before all the earlier X52 versions had been used up and gearboxes were allocated to chassis in no particular order.

Subsequent gearboxes were manufactured under licence by Rolls-Royce at Crewe, and these carry a plate listing patent numbers under the heading 'Licensed under General Motors Corporation's British Patents Nos'. Their serial numbers are prefixed by 'C' (for Crewe) and these gearboxes began to be fitted before all the X53 versions had been used up. Recent research makes clear that Rolls-Royce encountered a number of difficulties when it first began to manufacture these gearboxes. Nevertheless, those released to customers maintained the proper Rolls-Royce tradition, and just two modifications were made after full production had started. These were at chassis number B183WG in summer 1954, when a compensator pipe was added between the front and rear servo, and at B73ZX later that year, when the automatic transmission was arranged to give a smoother start in second gear unless overridden by the kick-down switch.

Fluid Coupling

The fluid coupling occupies the position of a normal clutch between engine and gearbox. However, its effect is as if it were fitted between the two epicyclic gear trains, so that when first or third gear is selected, the coupling rotates at only 70 per cent of engine speed, to eliminate 'creep' at tickover. The fluid coupling slips freely at low engine revs but locks up at higher engine speeds due to the inertia of the fluid rotating between its steel guide vanes.

Ride Control Pump

A flexible pipe runs from the ride control pump to a four-way union mounted on the frame cruciform member just behind the gearbox. On left-hand-drive automatics, this pipe could burn if it fouled against the exhaust pipe. So, beginning in 1953, Crewe fitted a shorter pipe to B20UM and then to B26UM and all subsequent cars. This shorter pipe was supplied as the only service replacement after November 1954, and was recommended as a service modification if the foul could not be cured by repositioning the flexible pipe on earlier cars to run vertically.

Electrical Components

Fuses & Fuse Box

There are two fuses boxes attached to the engine side of the bulkhead. The larger of the two contains the eight circuit fuses, which are made of 32swg tinned copper wire, as on the MkVI. The smaller fuse box alongside it contains only the main fuse, which consists of three strands of the same copper wire.

Dynamo

The R-type is fitted with the fully-insulated Lucas RA5 dynamo used on the final MkVI cars. The dynamo was originally earthed to the chassis by

This two-pin socket, just inboard of the steering column, is for the under-bonnet inspection lamp and also for battery charging using the special plug supplied.

Like the later MkVIs, all R-types had an inspection lamp clipped to their bulkheads, with a lead that could be plugged into a socket on the facia.

Early R-types have twin Lucas B12 ignition coils on the bulkhead, as do MkVI models.

means of a strip running from dynamo to chassis bolt and then to radiator. However, this scheme was found to be unsatisfactory in inhibiting the build-up of silt within the cooling system, and from mid-1953 the earth bonding was altered to run from dynamo to radiator to chassis. The change was at B210TN, and the last coachbuilt car with the old system was B130TN. Rolls-Royce also recommended that the bonding on earlier cars was altered to conform to the new pattern, and no doubt many cars now do so.

Lighting & Direction Indicators

The R-types inherited their double-dipping MkII headlamps from the last of the MkVIs.

The standard direction indicators on the R-type were always Lucas semaphore-arm trafficators in the upper B/C pillar. However, some export models were fitted with flashing direction indicator lights. These operate through a second filament in the bulbs of the front fog lamps, and through the stop lamps in the rear lights, when they interrupt the stop lamp circuit if the two are in use at the same time.

The flasher unit is mounted on the valance plate. The original Scintilla flasher units were 36-watt types, which operated 18-watt bulbs. However, an international agreement reached during 1954 settled on 21-watt bulbs and an operating speed of between 90 and 120 flashes per minute. From the end of November that year, Rolls-Royce retailers were advised to fit a new

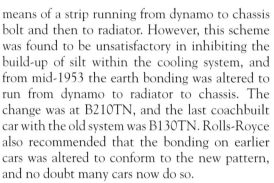

The rear lamp nacelles were modified during 1954 to take the red reflectors now demanded by law.

Late R-types from chassis B210TN have a revised radiator grille with nine shutters on each side of a central bar.

flasher unit labelled 36/42w when changing to 21-watt bulbs, because the original unit gave too slow a flash rate if used with these higher rated bulbs.

The 1953 Road Transport Lighting Act in Britain also had an effect on all R-types sold on the home market. Among the Act's requirements was one for cars to carry two red reflectors at the

rear, the rationale behind this being that the headlights of a following car would pick these up even if a tail lamp bulb had failed. So to meet the requirements of the Act, which became effective on 1 October 1954, Rolls-Royce added small circular reflectors below the tail lamps in a modified nacelle on the final R-types.

Starter Motor

The starter motor mounting strap was changed in 1954 at chassis number B270WH to the type used for the dynamo. Then from B138YD later that year there was a long-stroke starter pinion, which was designed to prevent accelerated wear of the flywheel ring gear teeth. This was also fitted to a few earlier YD-series cars with right-hand drive, namely B2YD, B4YD, B6YD, B18YD, B24YD, B62YD, B74YD, B80YD, B88YD, B90YD, B92YD and B94YD. The new starter assembly was also recommended as a service modification, and is therefore likely to be found on many cars not in this list.

Ignition Coils

Most R-types have Lucas B12 coils, but from 2 June 1955 a Delco-Remy type was approved as an alternative to ensure supplies. The terminals of the Lucas coil are marked 'CB' and 'SW', whereas on the Delco-Remy type the markings are '+' and '−' respectively.

Windscreen Wipers

Two-speed windscreen wipers were introduced from the start of R-type production. They have a Lucas motor with a thermostatically controlled cut-out, which operates if the wiper is overloaded. The motor is mounted to the engine side of the bulkhead on the left-hand side.

Body

The front section of the R-type body is the same as its MkVI equivalent as far back as a point just behind the B/C post. Between there and the tail of the car, however, there are major differences. The swage line on the body sides follows the shape of the new and longer wings rather than returning forwards along the wing's leading face, as on the MkVI. The boot is very noticeably longer than the MkVI type at the top as well as at the bottom and the lid is deeper.

Radiator Grille

The radiator grille and shutters are the same as on the late MkVI models. However, some cars may have had the angle of the shutters modified to improve cooling. The recommendation was made in a February 1952 Service Bulletin, and concerned cars which had been found to overheat

The boot lid of all R-types carries twin reversing lamps, as seen here. The number plate pivots, to remain vertical when luggage prevents the boot from being closed The rear wing lamp nacelles are different from the MkVI type to allow for the altered rear wing shape.

The R-type boot opens to reveal the spare wheel and wheel-changing kit beneath a shaped metal platform. The flap, seen open here, gives access to the tyre valve without the need to remove the spare wheel first. Note the oil syringe and starting handle, now located in the boot.

elongated to suit the shallower slope of the wing line. On the final cars the lamp nacelles are modified to accommodate a circular reflector below each lamp. This must have been to meet new UK lighting regulations, which came into force on 1 October 1954. A keylock for the fuel filler flap in the left-hand wing is fitted just below the swage line and has a chromed metal keyhole cover which swings aside on a pivot.

Boot Lid & Interior

The boot lid of the R-type is completely different from that of the MkVI. It is hinged at the top rather than at the bottom, and its hinges have torsion bar springs which support the lid in the open position without the aid of a prop. The panel is made of Birmabright aluminium alloy (Birmal sheet BB3) for lightness, and is the only panel on the car that is not made of steel. However, there is a steel frame to the boot lid, which also carries an interior light operated by a mercury switch.

The spare wheel compartment does not have the separate cover of the MkVI. Instead, the boot lid reaches right down to bumper level, and the spare wheel compartment is exposed when the boot is opened. The number plate is carried on a hinged bracket with a coarse ratchet which allows it to be tilted to a more visible position if the boot is over-filled and the lid cannot be shut properly. For such an eventuality, a leather strap in the tool kit can be used to hold the lid down. The number plate is illuminated from below by lamps in a large chromed nacelle, which also carries the twin reversing lamps.

The boot capacity of 10.5cu ft is considerably more practical than that of the MkVI. The boot floor has a flat centre section, but falls away on either side of the spare wheel, thus providing some

during Alpine climbing in hot weather. Changing the angle from the standard 43° to 37° improved airflow, and was effected by removing a rivet from each end of every shutter, and by soldering the shutters in the new position. In late 1953, from chassis B210TN, a centre bar was added to the grille so that these later types have 19 bars in total.

Rear Wings

The R-type's rear wings have a long, flowing rearward extension which is absent from the more rounded MkVI panels. They have their own swage line, which runs back from the curved closing line at the trailing edge of the rear door and follows the line of the wing crown. No spats are fitted. The rear lamps are fitted in pedestals attached to the wings, as on the MkVI, but the pedestals are

The dashboard of the R-type is essentially similar to that of the MkVI, but note that the tool tray is no longer under the glove box of this 1954 car. Note that the capping rail on the R-type did not have the windscreen wiper controls of the MkVI.

On this 1954 car a picnic tray is concealed within the dashboard and, when pulled out, brings the HMV radio with it. There is also an ashtray in the front of the sliding section. On late R-types the lockable fitted tool tray (far right) was repositioned under the driver's seat.

The hub of the steering wheel has only a single sliding control, for the ride control. The sunroof aperture (far right) was veneered to match the rest of the interior. Note the cloth headlining. Interior of the 1954 model (below) with automatic transmission.

The right-hand rear companion included a cigar lighter and its own illumination. Note the large shoulder bolster on the seat and the braided dowager strap, the latter an extra.

The pendant rear view mirror and radio aerial knob are shown on a 1954 model. The arrow on the knob indicates the position of the roof aerial.

additional storage space for small items. The boot floor and sides are carpeted. A seven-piece fitted luggage set was available as an optional extra. The spare wheel compartment contains the wheel-changing tools, as on the MkVI.

Bumpers

R-types for the home market have the same Wilmot Breeden bumpers as the MkVI models but an overall length of 16ft 7½in. As before, export models are fitted with heavier bumpers made by Pyrene. According to Rolls-Royce service literature, these increase the car's overall length by 4in, rather than the 5in difference they made to the MkVI! Some left-hand-drive models have a third, still heavier type of bumper, which was also made by Wilmot Breeden, and this increases the car's overall length by no less than 10½in to 17ft 6in.

Interior

Facia & Instruments

The basic layout of the R-type facia is the same as that of the later MkVI. Detail differences include a pop-out cigar lighter, and the absence from the capping rail of knobs for the windscreen wipers. There is a button for the windscreen washer on the capping rail outboard of the steering column. The Trico clockwork direction indicator switch is again mounted centrally on the capping rail; Scintilla replacements were recommended when supplies of the original switch ran out in 1957. From chassis number B2TN in summer 1953, the facia was actually made of metal behind the wooden panels, and the radio was built into the underside of the pull-out picnic tray so that it moves with the tray. There is a radio speaker behind a slotted veneered grille immediately above the recessed instrument panel.

The first R-types have a tray containing hand tools underneath the passenger side glove box, exactly as on the final MkVIs. However, at chassis number B66UM in late 1953, the tool tray was moved to a new position under the driver's seat and the glove box was enlarged.

Steering wheel, Controls & Handbrake

The steering-wheel hub differs from the MkVI type because it contains only one sliding control instead of three. The remaining lever is the ride

The front quarter-lights opened to 120°, as on the final MkVIs. The extra piece of glass in the vee prevented water from dripping into the car if the quarterlight was opened in wet weather.

PAINT & INTERIOR TRIM

In October 1952, the paint and trim options were exactly the same as those for the final MkVI models. Any combination of the six standard paint colours could be ordered to make a two-tone car, and as the flowing lines of the R-type lent themselves to two-toning rather better than the MkVI, it is probable that a greater proportion of R-types were ordered with this option.

On two-tone cars with the standard bodywork, the boundary between the two colours differs from that on MkVI models. The colour boundary on the R-type follows the swage line along the top of the rear wing to terminate at the back of the car.

The rear wing and the valance panel below the bumper are therefore the same colour as the lower body panels, and not (as in the MkVI short-boot body) the same as the roof and upper panels.

In 1954 there were nine standard paint colours. These could be combined to achieve two-tone schemes in addition to the 'standard' two-tone offering. It was usual on Bentley models (as distinct from the contemporary Silver Dawn) for the bonnet top to be finished in the lower body colour.

The nine colours were: Black, Donegal Green, Lugano Blue, Maroon, Midnight Blue, Shell Grey, Tudor Grey, Two-tone Grey and Velvet Green.

Upholstery colours were then: Beige, Brown, Grey, Light Blue, Red and Tan.

control for the rear damper settings, and is still at the bottom of the hub. The Mixture and Hand Throttle controls were made redundant of course by the standardisation of the automatic choke on the R-type.

Cars fitted with automatic transmission have the gear range selector in a quadrant on the right of the steering column. This quadrant is not illuminated when the main lighting is on. There is a stepped gate with five positions, these being N, 4, 3, 2 and R. The step is between 3 and 2 and was intended to prevent accidental downshifts. N and R can only be selected after first depressing a button in the end of the gear knob to operate a detent. The R position serves as a parking lock when the engine is switched off.

Pedals

There were revised throttle controls for cars fitted with the synchromesh gearbox, introduced at chassis B436TN.

Heater & Demister

The standard heater is fitted under the front seat, as on the earlier MkVI models. Cable controls are fitted from chassis B2TN. Some cars are also fitted with an optional additional heater, located under the dash. This differs from the standard under-dash heater fitted to R-type Continentals and also from the optional under-dash heater in the MkVI.

Earlier R-types have a hot/cold changeover valve for the demister underneath the bonnet. From B2TN, however, there is a flap valve at the junction of the hot and cold air ducts. This is operated by a control on the steering column worked by a Bowden cable. From chassis number B246YD in 1954, the Bentley Continental demister arrangement is fitted.

Seats

From B66UM, the driver's seat base carries a sliding tray, which contains the small tools. This tray pulls out from the front of the seat base.

The rear compartment of the R-type was similar to the MkVI. Picnic tables and footrests were included in the specification. The rear window blind was still operated by a cord (right) from above the driver's door.

IDENTIFICATION, DATING & PRODUCTION FIGURES

The chassis number of an R-type Bentley is located in the same place as on MkVI models.

There were 2,320 production R-type chassis. To these figures must be added two prototypes which were given production chassis numbers and then sold off by the factory.

Chassis Numbers

The chassis number sequences for these cars are set out here, together with build dates. All chassis numbers have the prefix B followed by up to three digits and then two suffix letters, the first of which denotes the chassis series. Cars with left-hand drive had an L in front of the two suffix letters, eg B35LUL. Sequences beginning with 1 used odd numbers only and always excepted 13; sequences beginning with 2 used even numbers only.

Chassis	Date
B2RT to B120RT[1]	June 1952 to April 1953
B1RS to B121RS	September 1952 to April 1953
B2SR to B500SR	September 1952 to May 1953
B1SP to B501SP	January to December 1953
B1TO to B401TO	April to September 1953
B2TN to B600TN	June to December 1953
B1UL to B251UL	October to December 1953
B2UM to B250UM	November 1953 to May 1954
B2WH to B300WH	January to May 1954
B1WG to B301WG	March to June 1954
B2XF to B140XF	May to July 1954
B1YA to B331YA	June to October 1954
B2YD to B330YD	August to November 1954
B1ZX to B251ZX	October 1954 to January 1955
B2ZY to B250ZY	December 1954 to February 1955

[1] To this sequence must be added B122XRT, renumbered from experimental car 14BVII, and B124XRT, renumbered from 12BVII.

Engine Numbers

Engine numbers are found in the same place as on MkVI models. The numbering sequences are:

Engine	Chassis series
B1R to B120R	R-series chassis
B1S to B500S	S-series chassis
B1T to B500T	T-series chassis
B1U to B250U	T-series chassis
B1W to B300W	W-series chassis
B1X to B70X	X-series chassis
B1-Y to B330-Y	Y-series chassis
B1Z to B250Z	Z-series chassis

Rolls-Royce Silver Dawn, 1949-55

Over the three years after the introduction of the Bentley MkVI, demand for an owner-driver Rolls-Royce along similar lines gradually built up, and the mothballed Ascot I design which had been drawn up in 1945 was prepared for production. The Rolls-Royce edition of the MkVI was given the name of Silver Dawn and was seen in public for the first time at the 1949 International World's Fair in Toronto. This choice of exhibition was an appropriate one, because the Silver Dawn was made available exclusively for export markets.

Not until the Earls Court Show of October 1953 (effectively from the start of SNF-series chassis) was the car offered to the British public.

The first Silver Dawns (A- and B-series cars) had the 4¼-litre engine, and the model switched to the big-bore 4½-litre type with the C-series cars during 1951, at the same time as the MkVI Bentley. The Rolls-Royce version took on the enlarged boot and became available with automatic transmission in 1952 at the same time as its Bentley equivalent, from chassis number SKE2

The early Silver Dawn was the Rolls-Royce equivalent of the A- to D-series Bentley MkVI. This 1951 example (SDB134) in Tudor Grey over Shell Grey belongs to Dermott Kydd.

With the exception of the Rolls-Royce radiator and badging, this Silver Dawn appears identical to the contemporary Bentley MkVI (see page 21). All 'small-boot' Dawns were exported originally; this car went to Kenya.

The upright Rolls-Royce grille made the car appear more square-rigged from the front than its Bentley equivalent. This 1951 car has retained its original Kenyan registration number.

(E-series). However, whereas the Bentley was renamed the Sports Saloon for public consumption, the Rolls-Royce remained a Silver Dawn. For ease of reference, its is possible to divide the cars into A- to D-series models, which equate to the MkVI Bentley, and E- to J-series models, which equate to the R-type Bentley.

By far the majority of the 761 Silver Dawns were delivered with the standard Pressed Steel saloon body.

The Silver Dawn was similar in every respect to the contemporary MkVI and R-type, except as noted in this section. Important changeover points for detail differences are also noted here. Nevertheless, it is important not to see the Silver Dawn as simply a MkVI or R-type wearing Rolls-Royce badges. Its character is quite different from that of the Bentleys, and its single-carburettor engine gives more refinement (and slightly less performance) than the twin-carburettor Bentleys.

Chassis

Chassis Frame & Suspension
The lengthened chassis frame and modified rear suspension were introduced with the E-series chassis in 1952. All chassis frames up to and including the E series were riveted together; welded chassis began with the F-series cars, at SNF1. Forged brackets for the rear spring shackles were introduced at chassis SBA16 in early summer 1949.

Chassis Lubrication System
The chassis lubrication system was the same as for contemporary MkVI or R-type Bentley models. From SBA140, the pipes running to the rear spring shackles were modified.

Front Suspension & Steering
The most important alteration to the front

Brian Palmer's 1954 Silver Dawn (SOG90) in Black over Shell Grey shows off the longer tail and the later style of two-tone colour scheme associated with the R-type Bentleys.

Jack Henley's Shell Grey 1955 model (SVJ75), finished in a single colour and with polished rather than painted wheel covers, shows the final rear lamp arrangement and twin exhausts. Note the Silver Dawn's different bonnet profile.

suspension was made at chassis SCA1, when the whole geometry of the system was revised. This change was the same as the one made on the first G-series Bentley MkVI chassis. The new wheel fixing studs introduced at this stage were changed for the earlier type at LSHD56. Stiffer damping was provided from SFC92 in early 1952, and the dampers' slow leak characteristics were modified at SLE31 about a year later.

Steering changes began with a modification to the drag link sockets at SBA16, but this modification did not reach left-hand-drive cars until LSBA106. From SKE2 in July 1952, friction within the steering connections was reduced, but the modifications associated with this were deleted at SNF27 in summer 1953. SKE2 also brought castor angle wedges. Then the non-opposed springs in the drag link tube were deleted at SMF70 in autumn 1953.

Rear Axle

The standard final drive ratio of the Silver Dawn was 3.727:1 until the end of the G-series cars in 1954. From 1953, a 3.417:1 ratio was optional,

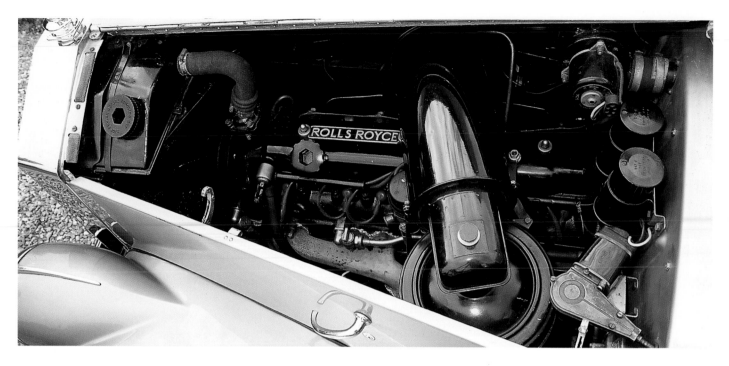

and this ratio then became standard at chassis number SRH2. The double thrust bearings on the rear axle pinion were changed to taper roller bearings on 3.727:1 axles from chassis number SLE11. The 3.417:1 axles retained the early type of bearings until SMF42, when they also took on the taper roller bearings.

From SBA16, ⅜in rear axle bolts were fitted. The multiple damper modifications began with new rear damper plates at LSBA46 in 1949, and this change was followed by a further modification of these components at LSBA138 in June 1950. There were longer bosses on the rear damper plates from LSCA51, and then thicker plates shortly afterwards at LSDB2 in November 1950. From SCA29 in late 1950, the lower bush was deleted from each rear damper linkage.

Brakes

The anti-rumble brakes and Lockheed drums were introduced at the same time as the revised front suspension in 1950, at SCA1. From LSCA17 there was a one-piece rear brake equaliser lever, and from LSCA23 (and SCA27 on right-hand-drive chassis) there were three bushes on the rear brake equaliser support. Stronger jaws were fitted to the front brake operating links at SRH4, and the brake servo lost its chromium-plated pressure plate at chassis SRH50.

Tyres

Silver Dawns were equipped when new with Dunlop tyres rather than the India tyres fitted to Bentleys. This helped to differentiate the Rolls-Royce model from the Bentley: the India tyre also absorbed less horsepower, and so was more appropriate for the Bentley performance image.

Engine

The engine fitted to the Silver Dawn is essentially the Silver Wraith version of the six-cylinder B60. It has a single Stromberg, or on later models Zenith, carburettor instead of the Bentley's twin SUs, and all except the final 4½-litre models also have a milder camshaft to improve smoothness and low speed refinement. The top rocker cover casting is finished with the same stoved black enamel as the Bentley equivalent, but bears the Rolls-Royce name. The air cleaner sits diagonally across the engine rather than parallel to it as on the twin-carburettor Bentley. An oil-bath air cleaner was fitted to many export cars, especially those destined for dusty territories.

The changeover to the 4½-litre engine was made in summer 1951, and the first car to be fitted with the big-bore engine (and attendant full-flow oil filter) was LSFC2. In 1953 the high-compression cylinder head, giving a 6.75:1 compression ratio in place of the earlier 6.4:1, was fitted from chassis number SMF62. From SMF66 in 1953, the Bentley MkVI type of camshaft was fitted to left-hand-drive cars only.

Internal engine modifications were the change to steel oil caps in the crankshaft at LSDB58 in 1950, the specification of Parco lubrized tappets at chassis SMF50, and the addition at SVJ101 of Ferodo washers and drain slots in the crankshaft vibration damper.

There were several other minor modifications. At the top end of the engine, the fabric camshaft gear wheel was replaced by an aluminium one at chassis LSCA23 during 1950. The head gasket switched to a copper and asbestos type at SBA16 in mid-1949, and then during 4½-litre production

An oil-bath air filter was fitted to export models, and is seen here on a 1951 car. Note the earlier type of wiper motor and the knurled oil filler cap.

The Silver Dawn's air cleaner is positioned diagonally across the engine. Note the Lucas two-speed wiper motor on the bulkhead, the Rolls-Royce name on the rocker box cover and the dual exhaust system on this 1955 car.

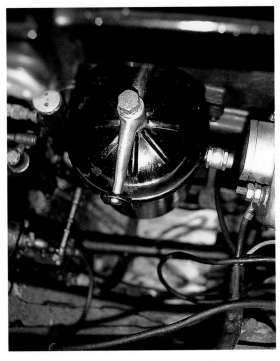

By-pass oil filter fitted to the 1951 car.

The Silver Dawn engine always had a single carburettor instead of the twin SUs of the Bentley. This 1955 example has the later Zenith.

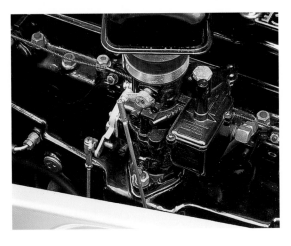

a hard clay gasket was fitted from chassis SNF15 in mid-1953.

On the crankcase, the oil gauge connection was relocated from LSHD6 in March 1952. An aluminium flywheel housing was introduced at SRH72 in mid-1954 and the flywheel was fitted with an inertia ring on engines destined for cars with automatic transmission from SOG86 in the summer that year.

Inlet Manifold & Carburettor

The inlet manifold of the Silver Dawn engine differs from that on the Bentley engine in that it is designed to take a single carburettor rather than two. On cars up to SFC100 in 1952, the carburettor is a dual-downdraught Stromberg, type AAV26M, exactly as fitted to left-hand-drive export Bentleys of the time. On cars from LSFC102 onwards, the carburettor is a single downdraught Zenith, type DBVC42. It appears that the single carburettor was thought to maintain traditional Rolls-Royce standards of refinement better than the twin-SU installation used on the Bentley. Rolls-Royce customers were also expected to drive rather more gently than Bentley owners, and Crewe imagined that they would not miss the better top-end performance available with the twin carburettors!

There are just three recorded modifications to the carburettor. The first was a change to the throttle return spring at chassis number LSBA28. An unspecified change was made at SBA128 in early summer 1950, and there was a revision to the throttle control on cars which were fitted with the synchromesh gearbox. This last alteration probably occurred late in the SNF series, at the end of 1953 or early in 1954.

Cooling System

The fan speed was reduced at LSCA9 in mid-1950, and a modified pump gland ring was fitted at SDB12 a few months later. A Flexibox seal for the water pump was introduced, probably on STH-series chassis in autumn 1954. The radiator bottom outlet was corrugated from chassis SKE10 in summer 1952.

Exhaust System

The first cars have a single exhaust system, mainly to improve refinement. A twin exhaust like that of the Bentley is fitted from SRH2 in 1954.

Transmission

The Bentley MkVI type of gearbox tie-rod is fitted to all chassis from SNF113 in late 1953.

Synchromesh Gearbox

The synchromesh gearbox fitted to the Silver Dawn is exactly the same as on the contemporary Bentley, with the traditional right-hand gearchange except on left-hand-drive cars which had a column gearchange. Even after the optional, and then standard, automatic was introduced a number of customers continued to specify the manual gearbox. Later synchromesh gearbox cars are: SLE3, SNF53, SNF63, SNF73, SNF103, SOG14, SOG40, SOG64, SOG92, SOG94, SOG96, SPG1, SPG3, SPG23, SPG27, SPG43, SPG45, SPG51, SPG53, LSRH82, LSTH41 (special centre change), STH61, STH73, STH75, STH77, STH89, STH99, SUJ44, SUJ46 and SVJ113. It is believed manual gearboxes were also fitted to SMF38, SMF44, LSMF58, SMF60, SMF62 and SMF72.

From LSCA51, there are closer-fitting bushes for the second and third speeds. The short-dwell detent on the first gear selector came in at chassis number SFC122 in early 1952.

Clutch

The early cars are fitted with the same 'long' 10in clutch as contemporary Bentley models. At SCA27, the 'lightweight' 11in clutch was introduced on right-hand-drive cars, and this was fitted also to left-hand-drive models from LSCA41. The final 'heavy' 11in clutch arrived at SDB76.

Other modifications also followed the Bentley pattern. A low-rate oil feed for the clutch thrust bearing was introduced at SCA29, and the spigot bearing was modified shortly afterwards at SCA45. The clutch casing was stiffened at SHD18, and the clutch release levers had needle rollers from SKE2 in July 1952.

Automatic Gearbox

The first left-hand-drive chassis fitted with the

A Triplex heated rear window was standard from 1952 and contained fine wires in a laminated glass sandwich. This one is on Brian Palmer's 1954 car.

All Silver Dawns had the 5in dynamo, seen here on a 1954 car; compare this with the 4½in type pictured on page 29. Note the full-flow oil filter behind the dynamo.

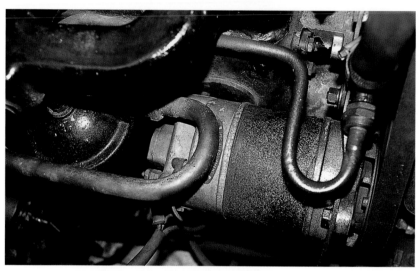

The 'RR' symbol behind the headlamp lens is seen here on a 1951 car.

The kneeling version of the Rolls-Royce Flying Lady mascot was used on the Silver Dawn.

Early cars had a single central ventilator on the scuttle, as seen here. However, this 1951 car exported to Kenya has both the central ventilator and the later side ventilators!

Note how the spare wheel cover panel (above) on the A- to D-series cars hinges down on cantilevered arms which rest on the bumper. This is exactly the same arrangement as on the contemporary Bentley. The 'small-boot' Rolls-Royce and Bentley models sometimes had a wooden roller shutter (below) to protect the contents of the enclosed area when luggage was being carried on the open boot lid. The chromed luggage stays are seen here erected (see Bentley MkVI, page 35).

automatic gearbox was LSKE10 in summer 1952. It became optional on right-hand-drive chassis at SLE5 slightly later in the year, and was standardised on the F-series cars (at SMF2) in 1953.

Production modifications again followed the Bentley pattern. A compensator pipe was fitted between the front and rear servos at SPG37 in summer 1954, and a second-gear start was standardised at SUJ50 at the end of that year.

Electrical Components

Fuses
The main fuse was housed separately from the circuit fuses with effect from chassis SKE2.

Lighting
Silver Dawns were built exclusively for export before 1953, and so all of them had the twin 7in foglamps standardised on export models of the Bentley MkVI in November 1948. By the time cars became available for the home market, the old pass-lamp system had been replaced by the double-dipping headlamp system on the R-type Bentley, and so the Silver Dawn followed suit. As a result, all Silver Dawns have double-dipping headlamps, and none was ever fitted with the central pass lamp.

The change to Lucas MkII headlamps was made at chassis number LHSD56 in 1952.

Starter Motor & Dynamo
There was a modified solenoid starter switch at SCA27 in mid-1950. The starter motor was fitted with a dynamo-type mounting strap at SPG11 on right-hand-drive chassis and at LSRH72 on left-hand-drive chassis. The long-stroke starter pinion was introduced at STH57 in autumn 1954.

The dynamo was insulated from chassis number SFC64 in 1951.

Distributor
A new type of condenser was fitted from SDB40, and twin condensers from SFC94.

Windscreen Wiper Motor

The two-speed Lucas wiper motor was fitted from the first of the 'big-boot' models, SKE2.

Rear Window Demister

The rear window demister was standardised at chassis number SFC94.

Body

Standard-bodied cars switched to the 'big boot' body of the R-type Bentley at chassis number SKE2 in July 1952.

Bonnet, Grille & Scuttle

The bonnet panel on the Silver Dawn is not the same as that on the MkVI and R-type Bentley models. It has a different profile at the front, to suit the less rounded shape of the Rolls-Royce grille. The rear profile is the same, however, because the scuttle and bulkhead are the same on Rolls-Royce and Bentley versions.

The Silver Dawn was the first Rolls-Royce motor car to be made with fixed grille shutters. Even the contemporary Silver Wraith had the thermostatically-controlled shutters for so long associated with the marque. The Silver Dawn grille has 22 shutters, and its proportions are different from those of all other Rolls-Royce models. The shutter opening is 25.65in tall by 19.9in wide and the radiator shell is 4.35in deep from front to rear. To suit these proportions, the Spirit of Ecstasy mascot is kneeling rather than standing.

The original central air vent in the scuttle was changed for side ventilators from chassis number SDB44 in early 1951.

Doors

From SFC94, the front quarter-lights opened to 120°, and their catches were modified to suit.

Rear Wings

As on the final R-type models, the lamp nacelles were modified to incorporate red reflectors.

Note the minor differences of the dashboard layout between the 1951 car (with well-worn switchbox!) and the 1954 model (right). The later car has cable-operated heater/demister controls and the special battery-charging plug is in its socket.

The positions of the smaller dials varied; this is a 1954 right-hand-drive car for the home market (top). Export models, like this 1951 car (centre), all had the smaller dials arranged differently. The final cars, like this 1955 example (above), had the Bentley dashboard layout with a four-in-one instrument and a central switchbox.

On early Silver Dawns the tool tray lived under the glovebox.

On the later cars, the tool tray pulled out from beneath the driver's seat.

The tool tray, seen here on the passenger seat, could be removed completely and contained a variety of small tools.

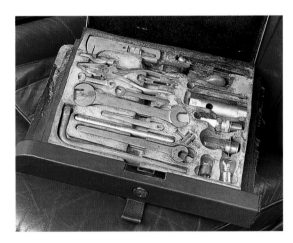

This silk rope-pull was an extra ordered by the original owner of this 1955 car. Note that a cigar lighter was fitted only to the rear companion on the driver's side of this RHD car.

Boot

The improved number plate box on the 'small-boot' cars was introduced at SCA1 in June 1950.

Bumpers

The Pyrene heavy-duty bumpers, as fitted to export-model Bentley cars, are standard on the Silver Dawn. The E-series cars (1952 and later) could be fitted optionally with extra-heavy-duty Wilmot Breeden bumpers. All rear bumpers carry a small central Rolls-Royce emblem.

Interior

Facia and Instruments

The central panel of the Silver Dawn dashboard differs from that of the contemporary Bentley with four separate small gauges. In 1954, probably from chassis LSRH2, it changed to the layout used on Bentley models from B2TN onwards with a four-in-one instrument and was mounted on the same kind of metal armature.

The earlier Silver Dawn central instrument panel has the same layout as that of the contemporary Silver Wraith, with the instruments and switches grouped around a central speedometer. The switches are arranged in vertical rows at each end of the central panel, as on the Bentley. Their layout is also similar. On right-hand-drive cars, the switches further from the driver are (reading from the top) for the wipers, the instrument panel lighting and the cigar lighter. Nearer the driver, the topmost switch is for the fog lamps, the middle one for the demister booster fan, and the bottom one for the heater rheostat. There are additional controls on the facia capping rail: a centrally-placed trafficator switch, a knurled wiper arm engagement knob on each side, and a windscreen washer button just outboard of the driver. There are four smaller dials, two on either side of the central speedometer. Their positions differ between home market and export cars. On home market cars, the fuel gauge is at top left and the clock below it, while the ammeter is at top right above the combined oil pressure and water temperature gauge. On export models, with right- or left-hand drive, the ammeter is at top left with the fuel gauge below it, and the clock is at top right above the combined gauge. In all cases, the switchbox is outboard of the steering column.

Modifications were made during production in the usual way. The speedometer and its drive differ slightly on chassis starting with SBA130 in summer 1950. From LSFC102 in 1952, three-position switches are used for the heater and demister. From SKE2 there is a pop-out cigar lighter, and the tool tray moved from the dashboard to under the right-hand front seat at SNF109 in late 1953.

PAINT & INTERIOR TRIM

The standard paint finishes on the Silver Dawn were broadly the same as those on contemporary Bentley models, but with detail differences in areas such as trim options. Where two-tone exterior colour schemes are used, the bonnet top is usually painted in the upper colour.

Mid-1951

There seem to have been six paint finishes for the final 4¼-litre and early 4½-litre models, of which one was a two-tone. There were five different interior colours. The exterior colour schemes (with upholstery colours in brackets) were: Black

(Beige, Brown or Tan), Dark Blue (Beige), Metallic Grey (Grey), Moss Green (Beige), Pearl metallic (Light Blue), and Two-tone Grey (Light Blue).

Autumn 1952

With the introduction of the 'big-boot' models came a new choice of 10 paint colours and six interior colours. There was just one two-tone paint finish. In theory, any combination of paint and interior colour was available.

The exterior finishes were: Black, Donegal Green, Lugano Blue, Maroon, Midnight Blue, Shell Grey, Silver, Two-tone

Grey, Tudor Grey, and Velvet Green. The upholstery options were: Beige, Brown, Grey, Light Blue, Red, and Tan.

1953

There were seven exterior finishes, one of them a two-tone. Seven upholstery colours were offered, and customers could in theory match these to exterior colours as they wished.

The paint colours were: Black, Midnight Blue, Shell Grey, Silver, Tudor Grey, Two-tone Grey, and Velvet Green.

The upholstery options were: Beige, Brown, Grey, Light Blue, Maroon, Red, and Tan.

Steering Wheel & Gear Lever

The steering wheel is the same as on contemporary Bentley models except for the RR symbol at the top of its hub. A- to D-series cars have three hand controls on the hub, but from the beginning of the E-series there is only one control, which is for the rear damper settings.

All the left-hand-drive Silver Dawn models have a gear lever on the steering column, whether for the synchromesh transmission or the automatic. As on the Bentley MkVI, the synchromesh gear lever was lengthened during 1949 at SBA26, (although LSBA28 had the earlier short type). Right-hand-drive manual Silver Dawns have the traditional right-hand floor gearchange.

Two further changes were made early in Silver Dawn production. A felt bush was added to the

gearchange at LSBA44, and then the linkage was modified and an extra rubber grommet was added at chassis LSBA76. From LSCA11 in summer 1950, there are keyhole sockets fitted on the gear control mechanism.

Windscreen Demister

The intermediate scheme triple-pass demister was introduced at chassis number LSCA53 in 1950, and the final version of this scheme shortly afterwards at LSDB6. The hot-and-cold demister system is fitted to cars beginning with SKE2 in July 1952, and the tap-operated hot/cold air blender is replaced by a flap-operated type with cable control from chassis number SNF1 in 1953. From SUJ14 in late 1954, the Bentley Continental type of demister is fitted.

Apart from the different facia arrangement, the Silver Dawn's driving compartment was similar to the Bentley R-type. Most UK market cars, like this 1955 example, had automatic transmission.

The rear compartment was also similar to the Bentley R-type. All upholstery was in Connolly Vaumol leather. The rear side armrests contain pull-out ashtrays (right), seen here on a 1951 Silver Dawn.

The Silver Dawn's traditional Rolls-Royce chassis-number plate was much grander than its equivalent on the Bentley.

IDENTIFICATION, DATING & PRODUCTION FIGURES

The chassis number of a Rolls-Royce Silver Dawn is located in the same two places as on the Bentley MkVI and R-type models.

There were 761 Silver Dawn chassis, of which 170 had the 4¼-litre engine and 591 the 4½-litre. All 4¼-litre cars had the 'small boot' body. Of the 4½-litre chassis, there were 110 'small-boot' and 481 'big-boot' types.

CHASSIS NUMBERS

The chassis number sequences for these cars are set out here, together with delivery dates. Chassis numbers consist of three letters (always beginning with S) followed by up to three digits. The final letter denotes the chassis series. Cars with left-hand drive had an L prefix, eg LSBA108. Sequences beginning with 1 used odd numbers only and always excepted 13; sequences beginning with 2 used even numbers only.

4¼-litre Small Boot models, 1949-1951

SBA2 to SBA138	April 1949 to June 1950
SCA1 to SCA63	June 1950 to March 1951
SDB2 to SDB140	November 1950 to August 1951

4½-litre Small Boot models, 1951-1952

SFC2 to SFC160	July 1951 to July 1952
SHD2 to SHD60	March to September 1952

4½-litre Big Boot models, 1952-1955

SKE2 to SKE50	July 1952 to January 1953
SLE1 to SLE51	November 1952 to May 1953
SMF2 to SMF76	December 1952 to September 1953
SNF1 to SNF125	July 1953 to February 1954
SOG2 to SOG100	February to August 1954
SPG1 to SPG101	March to September 1954
SRH2 to SRH100	May to August 1954
STH1 to STH101	August to October 1954
SUJ2 to SUJ130	October 1954 to January 1955
SVJ1 to SVJ133	November 1954 to April 1955

ENGINE NUMBERS

Engine numbers are located in the same place as on contemporary Bentley models. The numbering sequences are:

S1A to S100A	A-series chassis	4¼-litre engines
S1B to S70B	B-series chassis	
S1C to S80C	C-series chassis	4½-litre engines
S1D to S30D	D-series chassis	
S1E to S50E	E-series chassis	
S1F to S100F	F-series chassis	
S1G to S100G	G-series chassis	
S1H to S100H	H-series chassis	
S1J to S131J	J-series chassis	

Bentley Continental, 1952-55

Work began on a new Bentley chassis during 1937, and towards the end of 1938 a specification was issued for a lightweight version of this. The car was thought of as a Continental model, after the short-chassis high-performance Phantom II Continental of the early Thirties, but the 1939 prototype was actually called a Bentley Corniche. An accident during testing in France, and the outbreak of war, prevented the project from going any further, but the idea of a high-performance lightweight sports saloon remained alive with the postwar car design team.

In the late 1940s, there was pressure from some of the major coachbuilders on the European continent to produce a chassis with a lower bonnet line and a less upright steering column than were fitted to the standard MkVI chassis. The main reason was that the coachwork taste in Europe favoured lower lines than were common from the established British coachbuilders. Beginning in 1948, a number of special MkVI chassis were produced to 'Cresta' specification at Crewe, with a lowered bonnet line and more steeply raked steering column. All of these were bodied either by Farina in Italy or by Facel-Métallon in France.

These chassis pointed the way forward, although they did not have a direct influence on what happened next. Ivan Evernden – creator of the original Phantom II Continental – picked up the threads of the pre-war Corniche experiments in 1950. He wanted a car capable of 120mph, which calculations showed could be achieved with the existing chassis and drivetrain if the weight was limited to 33cwt and the frontal area was restricted to 22sq ft.

So Evernden drew up plans for what he called a Corniche II, based on a modified Bentley MkVI chassis and featuring a special streamlined light-

weight body with a reduced frontal area and striking fastback styling. This was designed by Ivan Evernden and the Rolls-Royce styling team, but H. J. Mulliner had already made some lightweight bodies with some of the characteristics needed for the new car, and so the company was asked to build a prototype. In doing so Stanley Watts, H. J. Mulliner's chief designer, altered some details from the Rolls-Royce drawing, such as the rear of the roof, sloping back, rear wings, boot lid shape and rear quarterlight shape.

This prototype was completed in August 1951. The car was registered as OLG490 and has been affectionately known as 'Olga' ever since. Olga proved that the design targets could be met, and series production began in the spring of 1952. Olga was sold into private ownership in 1960, but before then she lost her original experimental chassis number (9BVI) and was renumbered by Rolls-Royce as an extra A-series car (BC26A).

Production cars were known as Bentley Continental models when they were new, but when they were replaced by the S-series Continental in 1955 they were generally referred to retrospectively as R-type Continentals. Although the vast majority of Continentals (192 out of 208, including Olga) had the standard H. J. Mulliner two-door sports saloon body, the 4.9-litre Continental chassis was made available separately in 1954 and 16 were given special bodies. These are listed at the end of this chapter.

The Continental was an outstanding success, and today it remains one of the most desirable of all Classic cars. When new, it was the fastest genuine four-seater in the world, with a near-120mph maximum (and Olga had reached 124mph on test in France). Acceleration to 60mph was much the same as that of a standard Bentley saloon, as the taller gearing offset the light weight of the body. Above that speed, however, the Continental could show a clean pair of heels to almost any other car on the road in the early Fifties.

The Continental was produced initially for export, and the whole of A series was sold overseas; Olga was the sole exception. Home market sales began at the end of 1952, and the majority of Continentals (107 out of 207) found first buyers in Britain. Only 28 Continentals were sold new in the USA, although many more have since found their way across the Atlantic.

The Continentals are essentially coachbuilt variants of the contemporary Bentley saloons and therefore share a number of components with these cars. However, they also have a number of special features, and these are set out below.

Chassis

Chassis Frame & Fittings

The chassis frame of the Continental is essentially the same as that of the contemporary Bentley

For its day the two-door sports saloon body by H. J. Mulliner for the Continental chassis had remarkable lines, which mixed flowing wings with the traditional upright Bentley grille and a streamlined fastback. This was effectively the 'standard' body for these cars, although several were fitted with other types from March 1954. This is a late 1954 D-series car (BC45D).

saloon in most respects. The frames of the first Continentals are riveted together like those of the contemporary standard models, but a switch to all-welded frames was made in September 1953. The first all-welded frame was for BC21LC, the Paris Show car. Five cars had specially-strengthened frames: BC36C, BC73C, BC8D, BC25D and BC28D. The latter four had Park Ward bodies.

One of the interesting questions about the Continental is when its chassis switched from a MkVI-based type to an R-type. The prototype, Olga, was quite clearly numbered as a MkVI experimental car (9BVI) and the prototypes of the R-type were quite clearly numbered as MkVII models (e.g. 12BVII). The first production Continental chassis was completed in February 1952, and the first production R-type in September that year. The final Continental in the A-series was completed in November 1952, so it is tempting to suggest that the A-series were strictly MkVI-based while the B-series and later cars were based on the R-type. However, there appear to be no chassis differences to confirm this, and the most likely explanation is that the Continental pioneered features which later filtered down to the R-type.

The Continental chassis also has a special fuel tank, shaped to allow the boot floor to be as low as possible with the low-height bodywork. Its capacity is the same 18 Imperial gallons as the standard tank.

Front Suspension & Steering

The Continental chassis has the same front suspension as was fitted to MkVI chassis from the start of the G series in 1950 and to the contemporary R-type chassis. Colonial-type front suspension with stiffer springs was fitted to chassis BC37LC, BC39LC, BC48D and BC73D.

From chassis number BC38LC, in February 1954, the front wheel castor angle was increased from 1° to 1½° positive by incorporating wider-angled taper packing (part number RF8070) instead of taper packing (part RF8069) in pairs on either side of the lower radius arms.

From the beginning of production, the front-end socket of the side steering tube (drag link) was normally fitted with the same bronze seat found on the standard chassis of the time. The so-called reduced-friction modification of steel balls replaced this bronze seat on BC11A, BC12A and BC15A to BC29C inclusive. However, the steel balls tended to wear a groove and cause hard steering, and so from BC30C the bronze seat was reinstated on production. A modification kit was also introduced in September 1953, so that the bronze seat could be fitted to cars with the reduced-friction steering, and probably many of these cars have been so modified.

Cars up to BC17C have non-opposed springs in the side steering tube, but on BC18C and later chassis these springs are not present.

The steering column of the Continental is mounted at a lower angle than on the standard saloons. This matches the lower scuttle height, which in turn was designed to allow the lower grille to reduce the frontal area of the car and so improve its aerodynamics.

Rear Axle & Rear Suspension

The Continental rear axle carries higher gearing than that of the standard car, with a 3.077:1 (13/40) ratio.

Brakes

From BC5D, there are strengthened jaws on the front brake operating links, and from BC12D, there is no chromium-plated servo pressure plate.

As on MkVI and standard R-type chassis, the bellcrank lever behind the brake servo on left-hand-drive cars may have a semi-universal bearing where it attaches to the servo operating pushrod. If so, the lever is a service replacement component (part RG2280), introduced to prevent fatigue fractures of the pushrod.

Wheels & Tyres

Tyre wear was always a problem on Continentals which were used enthusiastically. In fact, one reason why the car's weight had to be limited was because the best tyres available when it was being designed in 1950 could not cope with weights of over 34cwt if the car were to be driven at sustained speeds of more than 115mph.

The original tyres specified for the Continental were India Speed Special six-ply 6.50-16 with about half a normal tyre's tread depth. India Super Silent Rayon tyres of the same size could also be fitted, but were not suitable for over 100mph.

At a later date, Dunlop Roadspeed RS3 tyres, again 6.50-16, were recommended. These went out of production in 1960, and the replacement RS4 type, in 6.50-16 or 6.70-16 sizes, was suggested. By 1979, Rolls-Royce recommended the same tyres for the Continental as for the MkVI, standard R-type and Silver Dawn. These were 6.50-16 or 6.70-16 Dunlop Roadspeed RS5s as a tubeless tyre and the same sizes of Dunlop RK3A as a tubed type.

Engine

Two different engines are found in Continentals, and both are versions of the Rolls-Royce B60 six-cylinder. Cars in the A, B and C chassis series have a 4½-litre engine which is essentially the same as that in the contemporary MkVI and R-type cars. The first Continentals delivered 137bhp at the wheels thanks to a special exhaust system. The

Underbonnet appearance is almost the same as the saloon with the engine hidden under the massive cylindrical air cleaner. The carburettor dashpots are correctly finished in black. Note that the inspection lamp is now clipped to the inner wing, which is braced by a diagonal tubular strut. The large diagonal pipe feeds air to the windscreen demister blower. The windscreen washer jets are fed from the glass bottle just behind the inspection lamp.

later D and E-series cars have an enlarged 4.9-litre engine, which was unique to the Continental at the time and has a 3¾in bore to give 4887cc. A small number of the A- to C-series cars has been fitted with later 4.9-litre engines since leaving the factory. The prototype car, Olga, was fitted with a 4.9-litre engine in July 1954 and BC49C was built with the larger engine in July 1954, prior to being bodied by Pininfarina for Rolls-Royce.

Cylinder Block & Cylinder Head
Cylinder head RE16876 is fitted to 4½-litre Continental engines up to chassis number BC3C, and is not the same as the cylinder head on the contemporary standard R-type. On chassis up to BC18A, it gives a compression ratio of 7.27:1; from BC19A, reduced-height pistons lower the compression ratio to 7.10:1 but the head itself remains unchanged. A copper-asbestos gasket is used with this cylinder head.

From January 1954 and chassis number BC4C, Continentals have the same cylinder head as the standard R-types. This is part number RE19451, the so-called high-compression head introduced on the R-type during 1953. However, on the Continental it is fitted with a different cylinder head gasket, made of steel, which raises the compression ratio to 7.20:1.

With the introduction of the 4.9-litre engine on the D-series cars in July 1954, the compression ratio was raised to 7.25:1. These engines have high-phosphorous iron cylinder liners, and their aluminium alloy pistons have a chrome-plated top compression ring.

The crankcase core plugs were made of aluminium alloy on Continental engines up to and including BC14B, except for BC17A. Just as on contemporary R-type engines, these core plugs tended to corrode, and most will have been replaced with the cadmium-plated steel type and aluminium washer recommended by Rolls-Royce as a service modification.

From chassis number BC70C, a flywheel inertia ring was fitted to all engines destined to drive through an automatic transmission.

Carburettors & Fuel System
To ensure positive cold starting, an oil-pressure-operated switch was incorporated into the solenoid circuit of the automatic choke from car number BC37D. There was a further improvement to the automatic choke in October 1954, when a heat-sensitive switch was added to take account of under-bonnet temperatures at BC43D.

Cooling System
The water pump seal was changed to a Flexibox type at BC35D.

Exhaust System
The exhaust system of the Continental has a larger bore than the standard Bentley type and

special low-loss silencers. The two combined to make an extra 25bhp available at the wheels.

Transmission

As a high-performance sports saloon, the Continental was always intended to have a synchromesh gearbox, and all the A- and B-series cars did so. This is a special close-ratio gearbox made only for the Continental and gearbox ratios (with overall ratios in brackets) are: First 2.672:1 (8.222), Second 1.544:1 (4.750), Third 1.216:1 (3.741), Fourth 1.000:1 (3.077), and Reverse 2.860:1 (8.802). One chassis, BC77C, was supplied to special order with the standard Bentley saloon gearbox. Most manual cars had the usual right-hand gearchange, but 29 cars were specified with the optional central floor change and 11 left-hand-drive cars had a column gearchange.

However, customer pressure eventually persuaded Rolls-Royce to fit automatic transmission to a small number of cars, of which the first was BC42LC exported to the USA in April 1954. Five more of the C-series cars were supplied to special order with the Hydra-Matic gearbox, and then from the start of the D-series cars with their 4.9-litre engines in July 1954, automatic transmission was made available as an option. Automatic gearbox ratios (with overall ratios in brackets) are: First 3.819 (11.752), Second 2.634 (8.105), Third 1.450 (4.462), Fourth 1.000 (3.077) and Reverse 4.306 (13.249).

In total, the manual gearbox was fitted to 166 Continentals, and the remaining 42 had the automatic. Details of which gearboxes and gearchanges were fitted originally to which chassis are given at the end of this chapter.

From the start of the B-series cars in April 1953, a modified transverse mounting bracket for the rear end of the gearbox tie-rod was fitted to all Continentals. However, the new bracket proved weak, and Rolls-Royce recommended that it should be stiffened on cars with riveted chassis frames (BC1LB to BC20C) or replaced by the MkVI type of bracket on cars with welded frames (BC21LC to BC49LC). All the cars affected had manual transmission, except for BC42LC. It is unlikely that any of the original brackets survive in unmodified condition, and the MkVI tie-rod was fitted as standard on production from BC50C.

Manual Gearbox

From chassis number BC78C, manual gearboxes have a thicker third motion shaft washer.

The letters W1 and W2 stamped on the gearbox casing have the same meaning as on regular R-type gearboxes (see under *Synchromesh Gearbox* in the *Transmission* section of the R-type chapter on page 47).

Clutch

All Continentals have the 'heavy' 11in diameter clutch, which was already being fitted to the standard chassis before Continental production began.

Automatic Gearbox

From BC1D, a compensator pipe is fitted between the front and rear servos. From BC47D, the automatic transmission starts in second gear unless overridden manually.

Electrical Components

Lighting

Continentals have the same Lucas headlamps as the contemporary standard saloons, and there is a Lucas sidelamp with a white lens in the nose of each wing. All of the first series of chassis were destined for export, and so were fitted with export specification lighting, which meant double-dipping headlamps, twin 7in Lucas fog lamps and flashing direction indicators. The front indicators work through the fog lamps. Home market cars were to be fitted with semaphore-arm indicators according to the 1952 sales brochure, but it is unlikely that any cars actually had them.

On each rear wing there are two circular red Lucas lamps, mounted as a vertical pair. One of these is for the tail lamp, and the other doubles as a brake light and direction indicator. A pair of vertically-mounted lamps with chrome bodies illuminate the number plate from each side and also double as reversing lamps.

Starter Motor & Dynamo

Just as on the standard R-type saloon, cars with automatic transmission were fitted with a new long-stroke starter drive assembly from January 1955. The first Continental so equipped was BC37D, but many others will have been fitted with the revised starter drive because it became a recommended service modification.

By the time the Continentals entered production, a production scheme already existed for inhibiting silt formation in the cooling system by bonding the dynamo to the radiator and using the current to reverse the natural polarity of the differences existing between radiator and engine. As on contemporary standard cars, the dynamo was insulated from the engine and a bonding strip ran from dynamo to a bolt on the right-hand chassis member and thence to the radiator. This scheme was applied to Continentals up to BC23C.

As on the standard cars, the bonding was altered when it proved unsatisfactory. Later Continentals had the bonding strip running from dynamo to radiator and then to chassis frame, and there was a service recommendation to modify the bonding on early cars to conform to the new

The prototype and a few cars had no radiator mascot in deference to aerodynamics. This car has the correct 'winged B' mascot, which was fitted to most Continentals.

pattern. Many early cars were no doubt modified as a result.

Distributor & Sparking plugs

The rev counter's drive is taken by flexible cable from the distributor housing.

The Continentals were initially fitted with Champion N8 sparking plugs, but from 5 June 1953, type NA8 plugs with a greater heat range were recommended. These plugs were not recommended for MkVI or standard R-type engines, where they had been found likely to cause misfiring. From 12 August 1954, Lodge CLNP plugs were added to the list of recommended types. They lasted longer and resisted misfires, although they were more expensive than Champions.

Horns, Windscreen Wipers & Rear Window Demister

The twin horns are mounted behind the front number plate, and the windscreen wipers have the same two-speed Lucas motor as is fitted to the standard chassis of the time.

An electrical blower, fitted under the parcels shelf, demists the sloping rear window.

Body

The Continental body is totally different from the standard saloon type, and there are no common panels. The majority of cars have the two-door sports saloon body built by H. J. Mulliner, and all comments here refer to this type of body. It was fitted to all the A- and B-series chassis, and it was not until the spring of 1954 (with chassis BC49C to Farina) that any Continental chassis was supplied to another coachbuilder.

The main features of this body, which was evolved by Ivan Evernden of Rolls-Royce and Stanley Watts of H. J. Mulliner, are its aerodynamic fastback shape and its light weight. The low-drag shape was achieved partly by a lower build than on the standard saloons, and this in turn was made possible by a lower radiator grille and scuttle. The shape was wind-tunnel tested in quarter-scale form at the Rolls-Royce aeronautical establishment in Hucknall before a full-size car was built. The roofline of the production cars was also lowered by an inch compared with the prototype, Olga. The light weight was achieved by making the bodywork out of aluminium panels over a light alloy framework of Reynolds metal and the body weighed about 750lb at the outset. However, before long extras demanded by customers had increased this to around 900lb, with the heaviest bodies topping 1000lb.

Even though 192 of the Continental chassis carried the Mulliner two-door sports saloon body, it is important to remember that the car was seen as a coachbuilt model and that minor variations on the design were made to suit individual customer tastes. A revised version of H. J. Mulliner's drawing 7277 dated July 1954 shows differences in interior seating and dimensions. The front seats are wider apart and narrower without a cutaway for the gear lever but the cushion length has increased from the original 19in to 20½in. The interior body width is 1½in greater; 51½in at the front and 44½in at the rear between the armrests. The rear seat cushion is 1½in longer at 20in and the squab has a less upright angle, reducing the boot length by 3in to 34in. The bigger seats mean that rear kneeroom is down from 11in to 8in, while headroom is reduced by ½in to 37in at the front and by 1in to 34in at the rear.

Front Wings

The front wings are hand-beaten aluminium panels, with apertures for the headlamps, sidelamps and chromed air intakes in the front faces. A single swage line leads back into the doors. The wings are fixed to the engine valance panel and are part of the structure, so cannot be unbolted and removed in the normal way. There is a wing support bracket in each wheelarch. Early cars suffered from flexing and cracking of the front wings so diagonal braces were fitted between scuttle and wings to stiffen the structure.

Bonnet

The bonnet has a central piano hinge, as on R-type saloons, and each side opens individually.

Scuttle

The scuttle is lower than on the standard car and carries chromed windscreen washer jets with screwed, adjustable nozzles.

Doors

The doors carry swivelling quarter-vent windows in addition to the main drop-glass. The window frames are made of light alloy.

Rear Quarterlights

The rear quarterlights are hinged at their forward ends, and at the rear they are attached to a hinged chromed arm which acts as a stop to prevent them from opening too wide.

Rear Wings

The aluminium rear wings are integral with the rear quarter-panel. Each one carries a small oval mounting plinth for the rear lamps. The left-hand wing carries the fuel filler flap, which can be locked by the master key. Detachable rear wheel spats were fitted to the early cars to improve the steamlining but were omitted on many cars at the request of customers.

Boot Lid & Interior

There is a long, chromed vertical release handle at the lower edge of the Continental boot lid, and above it is a winged Bentley emblem. The lid is hinged at its top edge, and opens onto a boot that is more capacious than it at first appears. Small tools are arranged in the underside of the lid, and others are carried in a box built into the floor.

The boot has a stepped floor, which rises over the rear axle. The spare wheel lies flat on the left-hand side towards the front, and has a circular wooden cover plate with carpeted top and sides. The floor and sides of the boot are carpeted in Wilton, with leather-bound edges.

Bumpers

The bumpers on the Continental are totally unlike their equivalents on the standard saloons, and the Mulliner two-door sports saloon body comes with one of three different types. The very earliest cars have bumpers made of heavy-duty polished aluminium alloy (to save weight), but these gave way quite early to similar bumpers made of chrome-plated steel. Many of the later export cars have the third type of bumper, which is heavier still. In all cases, the front number plate is mounted in the centre of the bumper.

The rear bumper consists of two separate sections, which curve elegantly backwards at each end before wrapping around the rear wings. The number plate is mounted on the body between the bumper sections.

The overriders are once again unique to the Continental. They are much taller and more ornate than those used on the standard saloons. At the front, they stand on either side of the number-plate; at the rear, they are fitted just inboard of the sides of the boot opening.

Grille & External Trim

The Continental's radiator grille is 1½in lower than its equivalent on the standard saloons. On most cars, it carries a dummy radiator cap, which bears the winged-B mascot. However, some cars (BC1A, BC4A, BC9C, BC30C, BC65C, BC69C, BC14D, BC33D and BC70D) have a plain top to the grille, with neither dummy cap nor mascot. The prototype, Olga, originally had this plain grille but was modified to the later standard before being sold. BC39D had a winged B mascot fitted direct to the radiator shell and no dummy cap.

The front wings carry circular, chromed slatted grilles on the air intakes. Usually the sides of the car are completely devoid of ornamentation, with only the long and elegant chromed door handles to break up the compound curves of the wing lines. Some customers specified a chrome strip on the door sills and one car had a chrome strip along the bottom of the spats and rear wings.

Windscreen

The windscreen has a heavy curvature because tests at Hucknall showed that a slip angle as close as possible to 45° was needed to achieve low aerodynamic drag. This was difficult to make in safety glass at the time, and the prototype had a two-piece windscreen. All the production cars have a one-piece screen, however, in a light alloy frame.

Interior

Facia, Instruments & Steering Wheel

The Bentley Continental's facia is completely different from the standard steel saloons, with some additional instrumentation. As the model was coachbuilt, not all facias were exactly the same. The Continental's facia consists of a single, flat piece of polished wood with lighter cross-banding running right across the car. Immediately in front of the driver are the speedometer (on the left) and rev counter, both deeply recessed, with a small oil temperature gauge between them. On the prototype, 'Olga', these three dials were located in a raised oval binnacle. Outboard of the rev counter is a dual instrument for oil pressure and water temperature. The switchbox is located in the centre of the main panel. There are then three further small dials in a line on the passenger's side of the switchbox, the clock being flanked by fuel gauge (nearest driver) and ammeter. The position of these five smaller gauges was sometimes interchanged to suit a customer's wishes. A pull-out veneered ashtray was fitted beneath the switchbox and a cigar lighter below the fuel gauge. Knobs and switches are arranged in a line along the lower edge of the facia, below the three smaller dials, and towards the top on the passenger side is a long chromed grab-handle.

On some cars, below the main facia is a shaped

The wraparound of the windscreen, resulting from Rolls-Royce's aerodynamic tests, is clearly seen here and was necessary to achieve speeds approaching 120mph. The front fog lamps on this car are smaller replacements for the original 7in lamps.

central section, again cross-banded, and slightly recessed on the passenger's side is a third flat section, which incorporates a lidded glove-box. The facia's central section could be fitted with a wireless but Rolls-Royce argued that it added unnecessary weight, and so although it was included in the chassis price an HMV Radiomobile set was fitted only when specifically requested! When installed, the radio speaker was positioned behind a slatted veneered grille immediately below the chrome grab-handle.

Right-hand-drive cars normally have the outboard gear lever found on the contemporary saloons, and left-hand-drive cars have the gear selector on the steering column. However, 29 cars of both types were fitted with a central floor-change lever (see page 75), the first being BC16LA in January 1953. In these cases, the gearchange gate remains in its traditional position on the right-hand side of the chassis.

Handbrake & Pedals
The handbrake is the same as on the standard saloons of the period, with a pistol-grip type on right-hand-drive cars and a twist-grip type on left-hand-drive types. Pedals are also the same as contemporary standard chassis, with the same differences between right-hand- and left-hand-drive types. On chassis BC15C there was a central handbrake. A pedal provides an additional method of operating the twin horns.

Seats
The Continental was originally fitted with lightweight seats, but customer demand for larger, heavier, and ostensibly more comfortable types on later examples nullified some of the painstaking weight-saving which had been engineered into

the car. The front seats are individual bucket types, on a sliding base-frame, and on the earliest cars their squabs wrap around to give lateral support to the body. These early seats also have light alloy frames. The leather upholstery is arranged to provide plain cushions and pleated squabs with a plain inverted horseshoe panel around the edge. A bench-type front seat was fitted to chassis BC18D. Cars known to have been equipped with heavier front seats are: BC26C, BC30C, BC35LC, BC37LC, BC38LC, BC50LC, BC56LC, BC67C, BC68C, BC69C, and BC70C.

The rear bench seat is made of Dunlopillo cushion supported on a lightweight wire frame. It has a folding central armrest and a fixed armrest at each side. These fixed armrests carry pull-out ash-trays in their forward faces. The upholstery of the cushions and armrests is in plain leather, while the squabs are pleated.

Trim & Headlining
The door trims have sculpted panels with a carpeted kick-panel at their bottom edges. There is a thin strip of veneered wood running all round the windows, with a dark centre section and light cross-banding. A separate wood fillet, veneered to match the lighter of the two wood colours, is screwed to the B/C post by chrome-plated screws in chromed countersinks. The headlining is made of West of England cloth.

Heater & Demister
The Continental's recirculatory heater is under the dash rather than under the left-hand seat as on the standard saloons. The demister blower, fed with ambient air ducted from a circular grille in the front wing, is fitted under the bonnet. There are pedal-operated fresh air scuttle vents.

The facia of the Continental was completely different from that of the contemporary saloon, although it did use the standard instrument dials and switches. This customer specified a radio, which was supposed to be standard, so the otherwise plain veneered panel to the left of the instruments was slotted to accommodate the speaker. Note the foot-operated scuttle vents and the right-hand gear lever for the manual gearbox.

This 1953 H. J. Mulliner-bodied car (BC8C) has the original weight-saving interior with lightweight wrap-around seats, ruched leather door pockets and manual window winders. The facia is to the standard RHD design with the oil temperature gauge on the extreme right and speedometer and rev counter separated by the combined oil pressure and water temperature gauge. To the left of the central switchbox, which controls ignition and lighting, is the fuel gauge. To its left the ammeter and clock have been interchanged from the standard positions, with the clock here in front of the passenger. The steering wheel on this early car has both throttle and ride controls. The indicator switch on the steering column, fire extinguisher and manual choke knob are later additions.

The heater return pipe on early Continentals was prone to fracture through strain at the point where it joined the underwing demister unit. So from BC29C, a new pipe with a strong saddled junction was fitted. At the same time, a short length of rubber hose and two clips replaced the screwed union on the return pipe from the demister unit. These two modifications were recommended as a service retro-fit.

Special Bodies

There were 16 special-bodied Continental chassis. The most popular coachbuilder was Park Ward, who built six bodies. Franay built five, Graber three, Farina one, and H. J. Mulliner built one special coupé.

Park Ward & Co Ltd
The two Park Ward designs were numbers 647 (drophead coupé) and 648 (two-door saloon). Both were styled by John Blatchley at Rolls-Royce, who had taken over the exterior styling of Park Ward coachwork in 1952 to introduce a

Continentals have individual front seats, with plain leather on the cushions but a pleated pattern on the backrests. These are the later heavier seats and this car (BC45D) also has electric windows, both features that added weight.

degree of family resemblance between the coach-built and standard saloons. Of the six bodies, two were fixed-head coupés, on chassis BC24D and BC29D. The others were drophead coupés, on BC73C, BC8D, BC25D and BC28D.

Carrosserie Franay
Full details of the five Franay-bodied cars are not known. BC51C certainly had a saloon body and BC21D was a two-door saloon, but the body type fitted to chassis BC20D, BC66LD and BC9LE remains unidentified.

IDENTIFICATION, DATING & PRODUCTION FIGURES

Bentley Continentals carry their chassis numbers in the same two places as their saloon counterparts.

CHASSIS NUMBERS

The chassis number sequences for these cars are set out below, together with delivery dates. All chassis numbers have the prefix BC followed by one or two digits and then a suffix letter, which denotes the chassis series. Cars with left-hand drive have an L in front of the suffix letter, eg BC8LA. Both odd and even numbers were used in all sequences, but 13 was always omitted.

There were 207 production Continentals, of which 124 had the 4½-litre engine and 83 the 4.9-litre type. To these must be added the prototype, sold off by the factory.

4½-litre models (1952-1954)

BC1A to BC25A[1]	June 1952 to April 1953
BC1B to BC25B	April 1953 to September 1953
BC1C to BC78C	August 1953 to July 1954

[1] The prototype Continental (Olga) was renumbered as BC26A, having originally carried the experimental chassis number 9BVI. It was built in 1951.

4.9-litre models (1954-1955)

BC1D to BC74D	July 1954 to March 1955
BC1E to BC9E	April to May 1955

ENGINE NUMBERS

Continental engines have their serial number stamped in the same place as contemporary R-type saloon engines. The numbering sequences are as follows:

BCA1 to BCA24	A-series chassis 4½-litre[1]
BCB1 to BCB24	B-series chassis 4½-litre
BCC1 to BCC77	C-series chassis 4½-litre[2]
BCD1 to BCD73	D-series chassis 4.9-litre
BCE1 to BCE9	E-series chassis 4.9-litre

[1] The prototype, BC26A, later had a 4.9-litre engine, BH11. [2] BC49C was built with a 4.9-litre engine, BCC48.

GEARBOXES

The 137 chassis originally equipped with manual gearboxes with a right-hand gearchange were: BC1A to BC7A, BC9A to BC12A, BC15A, BC17A, BC19A to BC26A, BC3B to BC7B, BC9B, BC12B to BC16B, BC18B, BC19B, BC21B to BC25B, BC1C, BC3C to BC14C, BC16C to BC20C, BC22C to BC 32C, BC34C, BC36C, BC43C, BC52C, BC53C, BC55C, BC59C to BC61C, BC64C, BC65C, BC67C to BC69C, BC71C, BC72C, BC74C to BC78C, BC3D, BC4D, BC12D, BC18D to BC21D, BC23D to BC27D, BC34D to BC36D, BC40D, BC41D, BC45D, BC48D, BC49D, BC52D, BC53D, BC56D to BC61D, BC63D to BC65D, BC68D, BC69D, BC72D, BC1E, BC2E and BC4E.

The 29 cars that originally had a central floor gearchange were: BC16LA, BC8LB, BC11LB, BC17LB, BC20B, BC15C, BC21LC, BC33LC, BC35LC, BC38LC, BC39LC, BC40LC, BC45C, BC46LC, BC47LC, BC49C, BC50LC, BC51LC, BC54C, BC56LC, BC57C, BC63LC, BC2LD, BC5LD, BC7LD, BC10LD, BC16LD, BC17LD and BC22LD.

The 11 left-hand-drive chassis originally fitted with a steering column gearchange were: BC8LA, BC14LA, BC18LA, BC1LB, BC2LB, BC10LB, BC2LC, BC37LC, BC41LC, BC44LC and BC48LC.

The 42 cars originally fitted with automatic transmission were: BC42LC, BC58C, BC62LC, BC66LC, BC70C, BC73C, BC1LD, BC6D, BC9D, BC14D, BC28D to BC32D, BC37D to BC39D, BC42D to BC44D, BC46D, BC47D, BC50D, BC51D, BC54D, BC55D, BC62D, BC66LD, BC67LD, BC70D, BC71D, BC73D, BC74LD, BC3E and BC5E to BC9E.

Carrosserie Graber

The three Graber-bodied Continentals all had open coachwork. There were drophead coupé bodies on BC55C and BC68D, while BC77C was a two-seater cabriolet.

Carrozzeria Farina

The single Farina body was a two-seater coupé on chassis BC49C.

H. J. Mulliner & Co Ltd

The special body built by H. J. Mulliner was a 2+2 coupé on BC50D with a standard (taller) Bentley radiator. The specially-shortened body, designed by owner R. G. McLeod, reduced the car's overall length to 15ft 2in.

PAINT & INTERIOR TRIM

As the Continental was always seen as a coachbuilt car, which was built to individual order, there were no standard paint finishes or trim colours. Customers could – and did – choose from the range offered on the standard saloons, but also cars were painted or trimmed in other colours to the individual customer's choice.

The plain, almost austere, upholstery style H. J. Mulliner used on the Continental is well illustrated here. The rear seat's thin Dunlopillo cushion is supported on a wire frame and the thin squabs also helped to reduce weight. There was sufficient room for two adults to sit in the back comfortably. Note the opening rear quarterlights for ventilation at speed.

Rolls-Royce Silver Cloud & Bentley S-series, 1955-59

The Rolls-Royce Silver Cloud was introduced as a replacement for the Silver Dawn models in April 1955. At the same time, its twin, the Bentley S-series, replaced the R-type models. Styling work had started in 1951, and the first prototype car was on the road in October 1952. During the pre-production period the design was known as Siam or Bentley IX. The cars were designed with an eye to sales in the lucrative US market, and for that reason offered more space, lighter steering and softer suspension than the models they replaced.

The £4669 Bentley proved more popular than the more expensive £4796 10s (£4796.50) Rolls-Royce, and 3072 Bentley chassis were built as against 2238 Silver Clouds. This was probably a hangover from earlier times, when the Bentley MkVI and R-type were more numerous than their Rolls-Royce Silver Dawn equivalents.

The Silver Cloud and S-series models are physically larger than the Silver Dawns and R-types, with a wheelbase 3in longer and a greater overall length at 17ft 7¾in. The exact difference in length depends on which bumpers are fitted to the R-type used for comparison, but is typically about 15in. The 1955-59 standard-wheelbase cars, which are covered in this chapter, all have versions of the 4.9-litre six-cylinder engine first seen in the later Bentley R-type Continental models. Automatic transmission was standard, although a few early examples of the standard steel saloons and the Bentley Continental S-series were fitted with manual gearboxes to special order.

The Silver Cloud/S-series body was styled by John Blatchley at Rolls-Royce, and was the first from the company to be developed with the aid of quarter-scale wax models. It was a beautifully well-balanced design, which has stood the test of time extraordinarily well, and it proved so popular that

The rounded grille of the Bentley somehow toned down the car's appearance compared with the Rolls-Royce version.

the number of coachbuilt bodies declined yet again. This seriously affected the specialist coachbuilders: Freestone & Webb ceased coachbuilding in 1958, and in 1959 H. J. Mulliner was bought out by Rolls-Royce and Hooper built its last bodies.

The Bentley version was correctly known as an S-series, although it is often called an S-type. When the Silver Cloud II and Bentley S2 models arrived in 1959, the six-cylinder cars became known as the Silver Cloud I and S1 respectively.

The original versions of both cars had a maximum speed of around 100mph. After the engine compression ratio was raised in 1957, the maximum speed increased to about 105mph.

The cars are identical in all respects except where indicated in the following text. All nuts and bolts on these chassis have UNF threads.

Chassis numbers for Rolls-Royce Silver Clouds have a sequence of three letters and up to three numbers (eg SWA206). Bentley S-series chassis numbers start with the letter B followed by one, two or three digits and two letters (eg B270AN); Bentley Continentals have the prefix BC instead of B. Left-hand-drive chassis are identified by an L in front of the chassis letters.

Chassis

Chassis Frame

The chassis frame was built by John Thompson Motor Pressings, and has welded box-section side-members of 16-gauge steel with a massive cruciform centre brace. The wheelbase is 123in – 3in longer than that of the R-type. At the front is a substantial cross-member, and there are two further, lighter, cross-members behind the rear axle. This construction gives the frame a torsional rigidity which is 50 per cent greater than that of a MkVI or R-type channel-section chassis, with a weight penalty of a mere 14lb. There are 12 body mountings on the chassis, those on the outriggers being adjustable and set to a predetermined load on assembly.

At chassis numbers SZB113/B218CK, welded stiffeners were added to each side of the jacking bracket at the centre of each side rail. From chassis numbers SZB139 and B27CM in August 1956, the frame was revised with a splayed front end. Bumper brackets are bolted to the front and rear of the chassis rails; the front ones differ between the two types of chassis.

Chassis Lubrication System

Like its predecessors, the Silver Cloud/S-series chassis has a Luvax-Bijur centralised lubrication system operated by a pedal under the dashboard. However, on these cars it lubricates only the front suspension, and not the rear springs. Flexible hoses deliver the lubricating oil to the kingpins and, on early cars only, the steering ball-joints. From chassis number SHF1 in July 1958, the Bijur lubrication was deleted from the idler lever, the

The Rolls-Royce Silver Cloud seen here is John McGlynn's Mason's Black 1959 model (SNH116), which has been re-registered with a 1963 A-suffix number.

track rod ends and the centre steering lever. Grease lubrication was substituted. This change took place more gradually on the Bentley chassis, the idler lever being the first to change at chassis number B136FA, the track rod ends next at B556FA, and the centre steering lever being deleted from the Bijur system at B644FA.

The combined oil reservoir and foot-operated pump for this lubrication system are located on the engine side of the front bulkhead, next to the main fuse box on right-hand-drive cars. The reservoir/pump unit is finished in black with bare metal on top of the filler cap, which has a black-finished, knurled rim.

Front Suspension & Steering
The coil-spring front suspension was designed to give longer wheel travel than the MkVI and R-type suspension. It has unequal-length semi-trailing wishbones, the lower being longer than the upper. The upper pairs are pivoted on the shafts of the horizontal piston-type dampers, and the lowers on the front frame cross-member. The wishbones are channel-section pressings, and all bearing and attachment brackets are bolted to them. There is also an anti-roll torsion bar, which is mounted to each lower wishbone by a rubber bush and to the chassis frame on each side by a further rubber bush.

A number of running changes was made to the various components of this suspension. Some distortion of the lugs on the front pan was encountered on early cars, and so at SWA14/B296AN, a thick washer was added under the fulcrum bracket lock plate to compensate. This was also fitted to several earlier chassis. Stabiliser bracket attachments were welded to the coil spring support plates at B430AN (SWA-series Rolls-Royce) during 1955, and these plates were strengthened

at SWA70/B87AP later in the year. Then at SXA187/B109BC, the fulcrum bracket for the lower wishbone was strengthened.

The dampers (made by Rolls-Royce) were modified twice, first by introducing a sleeve in their mounting bolt bores and by strengthening their bodies at SDD98 and B170EG, and then with stronger damper casings at SDD350 and B316EG. The dampers had larger end cover studs from B555EK and mid-way through the SFE series. A seal was added between the front damper and the bearing housing body at B35GD in early 1959, and early on in the SKG series.

Stub axles and hubs also changed. Modified yoke seals were fitted in late 1957 at SFE23/B377EK, and in May 1958 at SGE66/B214FA, the radius of the stub axles behind the inner hub bearing was changed. This was recommended as a service modification: solid stub axles were to be stamped MS and hollow ones with an M to show that the modification had been carried out. In late 1958, the stub axles were strengthened at SJF122/B458FA. Stronger front hubs arrived with SHF1/B65FD in July 1958.

The steering is a Marles cam-and-roller type. Power-assistance became optional in 1956. The steering box is connected by a transverse link to a three-piece track rod. The transversely-mounted drag link is connected to an extension on one of the two slave levers pivoted between the chassis and the centre member of the track linkage. The unassisted steering on all right-hand-drive cars has a ratio of 20.6:1 and gives 4½ turns of the wheel from lock to lock. When power-assisted steering became available, it was higher geared with an 18.7:1 ratio, giving 4¼ turns of the steering wheel from lock to lock and this ratio was then fitted to left-hand-drive cars with unassisted steering.

Power-assisted steering was theoretically

This side view of Professor Edward Thornton's Tudor Grey 1955 S-series Bentley (B84AN) shows off the car's beautifully balanced profile.

The jacking points on the chassis are just ahead of the rear wheels, as shown here, and just behind the front wheels. The jack is a Smiths Bevelift.

introduced at LSCC69 and B46LDB in October 1956 and was initially available only on export models as an option. However, a number of customers whose cars were being built at the time demanded that the new option should be fitted before they took delivery – and so it was, at considerable expense and inconvenience to Crewe. Thus the records show that the first Bentley export chassis with power-assisted steering was actually B171BC in March 1956, while the first home-market chassis to have it was B296DB in October that year. The last Bentley chassis fitted with unassisted steering was B630EG in June 1957. The first Rolls-Royce chassis to be built with power-assisted steering was LSXA101, which was for the US, but for the UK there were no cars with power-assisted steering until SCC123 in June 1957. Meanwhile, SYB24 was converted to power-assisted steering, and SYB194 was built with right-hand drive and power-assisted steering for a Californian customer, but otherwise the first right-hand drive car with power-assisted steering was SYB244 for Australia. The last Silver Cloud built with unassisted steering was chassis SED307, in July 1957.

Power assistance is provided by a Hobourn Eaton pump driven by a single rubber vee-belt from the fan pulley and mounted on a bracket on the left-hand side of the engine. A separate fluid reservoir is mounted above this, with a knurled screw-type filler cap. Reinforced rubber pipes take oil under pressure to an hydraulic ram, which is mounted at the front of the chassis and protrudes below the radiator. This in turn is linked to one of the centre track rod idling levers. An hydraulic control valve is incorporated in the system and is actuated by movement of the steering wheel.

The steering components also underwent a number of production modifications, beginning in late 1955 at SWA56 and B340AN, when new

On cars with power-assisted steering, the pump and reservoir are mounted at the front of the engine, on the left-hand side when looking forwards.

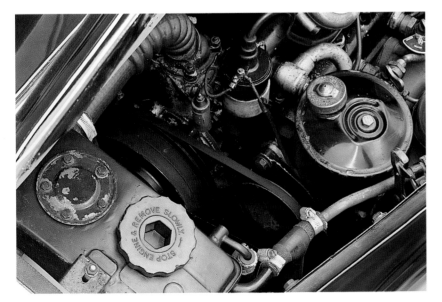

ball joint castle nuts with a larger bearing surface were fitted. Shortly afterwards, at SWA168 and B383AP, the drag links were strengthened to resist kinking under compression; they were strengthened once again at SFE109 and B379EK in late 1957. Then taper roller bearings replaced bushes on the steering lever at SXA151 and B51BC, and there was a stronger adjusting sleeve for the steering cam at B635EK and towards the end of SFE-series production.

There were modifications to the power-assisted steering, too. There was a modified sealing ring for the centre steering operating lever at SYB2/B178CK, and from SZB183/B262CM, the power cylinder mounting bolt was reversed. All the first cars had an expansible hose of Chrysler manufacture, but from early in the Rolls-Royce SFE series and from B375EK, a Dunlop hose was an alternative.

Rear Axle & Rear Suspension

The rear axle of the Silver Cloud has a hypoid bevel final drive with a four-star differential and semi-floating half-shafts. The final drive ratio is 3.417:1 (12/41). The live axle is sprung by semi-elliptic leaf springs mounted inside the frame. A Z-shaped control rod is pivoted on the top of the right-hand-side chassis member, with the other end mounted on top of the rear axle. The Z-bar absorbs vertical movement under acceleration and braking and also acts as an anti-roll bar.

The springs have nine leaves each, those on the right-hand side of the car being slightly thicker than those on the left, to compensate for greater weight and also to give a degree of torque resistance under acceleration. All leaves are Park-erised to improve lubricant retention, and the top four leaves on each side are interleaved with rubber. The whole spring is packed with grease (originally Ragosine 204G with 20 per cent molybdenum disulphide) and enclosed in Wefco leather gaiters to exclude road dirt.

The spring eyes and shackles are rubber bushed. The front eye of the right-hand spring is bigger and stronger to cope with the extra loading from the Z-shaped control rod. Extensions on the outer ends of the shackle bolts engage with shackle stops fitted on the top of the chassis frame, to prevent the rear spring shackles from going over-centre.

Early production changes strengthened various components. The bosses on the rear axle side tubes were modified to give additional strength at SWA62/B476AN, and the clamps for the Z-shaped control rod were strengthened at SWA146/B341AP in late 1955. During 1956 it was the turn of the axle shaft splines at B404CK and during SZB series production, but this was clearly not enough, because larger-diameter splines were specified at SHF1/B590FA in July 1958. There were improved axle shaft flanges during 1957 at B243EK and early in the SFE series. Then the number of fixing holes in the rear axle tube was increased at SXA67/B198FA, and a similar change was made to the rear axle centre casing at SBC112/B122DB.

The Silver Cloud and S-series cars have an electrically-operated ride control system on the rear axle, replacing the gearbox-driven oil pump and associated pipework used on earlier models. The rear dampers, made by Rolls-Royce, are fitted with solenoids which alter their 'slow leak' characteristics. A switch on the side of the steering column selects Normal or Hard damping, the latter being twice as hard. There were three production modifications: an oil deflector plate was added to the dampers at SCC119/B249DE; the dampers gained larger end cover studs at B555EK and mid-way through the Rolls-Royce SFE series, and stronger Silentbloc bushes for the damper links were fitted at chassis SFE367/B54FA.

Brakes

The Silver Cloud and S-Series have an all-drum, combined hydraulic and mechanical braking system, which is assisted by a friction disc servo driven by the gearbox and located on its right-hand side. The braking effort is biased towards the front wheels, on a ratio of 1.23:1. A direct mechanical linkage from the brake pedal supplies 40 per cent of rear braking, acting as a fail-safe and giving the pedal 'feel'. From SYB50 and B245BC in April 1956, the front hydraulic circuit is duplicated, with one circuit operating one trailing shoe in each brake drum and the proportion of mechanical rear braking reduced to 24 per cent.

Cars with the dual-circuit system have a second master cylinder and fluid reservoir. The two master cylinders are different sizes; the larger one is for the circuit covering the rear brakes and one half of the front brakes, while the smaller one covers the remaining half of the front brakes only. The fluid reservoir on single-circuit systems is mounted to the top of the inner wing valance on the driver's side, and the two reservoirs are mounted side by side there on dual-circuit cars.

The brakes are Girling Autostatic types, with twin trailing shoes on the front wheels and leading-and-trailing shoes at the rear. The drums are 3in wide and have a diameter of 11.25in. The front brakes of the later cars with dual hydraulic circuits have an extra set of expanders for the shoes. The shoes themselves are also different and are not interchangeable with those for the single-circuit brakes; the dual-circuit type of shoes are identifiable by the additional strengthening pieces at their operating ends.

The friction-disc servo is geared to revolve at

Cars fitted with the dual-circuit braking system have twin reservoirs mounted on the inner wing valance. This is a 1959 right-hand-drive model.

0.179 times propshaft speed – a higher speed than on earlier cars, which had been criticised for servo lag. The pedal operates directly on this servo through a pull rod on right-hand-drive chassis. On left-hand-drive cars, it acts on the pull rod through a cross-shaft. Part of the pedal linkage to the rear wheels is also operated by the handbrake. The sealing arrangements for the servo were changed twice during production of the six-cylinder Clouds and S1s. The first change was at SWA62/B41AP, and was intended to keep out water and oil mist. The second change was at SDD316/ B278EG but retrospective modification was recommended only if the servo had to be disturbed.

Early cars suffered from brakes which tended to stick on, so at SWA56/B492AN, the brake shake-back stops were given more friction, and the servo return spring load was increased. The shake-back stop collars on both front and rear brakes were modified at SXA187/B115BC, and then a third modification in 1959 brought enlarged shake-back stop slots on the brake shoe webs at B43FD. These were introduced on Rolls-Royce chassis at the end of SGE or the beginning of SHF series.

The rear brake expander wedges were also improved at SHF1/B454FA in 1958. There were modified linkages for the front shoes in 1959 at B4GC and very early in the SMH series, and the handbrake cable was also re-routed at B45FD, a change which was probably introduced late in

SGE series Rolls-Royce chassis. Then B129FD brought plain washers at each end of the braking pivot distance piece direct and intermediate linkages; on Rolls-Royce chassis, the change was probably made early in the SHF series.

The original master and wheel cylinders were cast iron, but aluminium types replaced both in late 1955. The wheel cylinder was changed first, at SWA136/B273AP, and then the master cylinder at SWA162/B20BA. The external finish of both master cylinder types is similar; the cast iron one has six spanner flats on its end cap but the aluminium type has just two. Meanwhile a gauze filter had been added to the fluid reservoir at SWA152/B287AP, to prevent foreign matter from entering the braking system.

Problems with air being drawn into the system on chassis with the dual-circuit brakes also led to modifications. From SZB69/B376CK, larger-diameter pipes were fitted between the twin master cylinders and the fluid reservoir. Also the pipes were re-routed so that they ran uphill from the master cylinders. Some earlier cars were fitted with an intermediate scheme which consisted of a larger-diameter recuperation pipe for the lower master cylinder, clipped to the underside of the floor panel instead of to the right-hand frame member. The final modification in this area came at SKG1/B513FD in January 1959, when the check valve was deleted from the brake fluid supply pipes.

Fuel Tank & Pumps

The 18-gallon fuel tank is made of light alloy and is mounted at the rear of the chassis, transversely across the frame and behind the rear axle, where it is attached by two metal securing straps. It has a large curved cut-out in its rear face, to accommodate the spare wheel. On early chassis, the fuel pipes are made of aluminium, but they were prone to corrosion by road salt, and were replaced by copper pipes at chassis SZB29/B326CK.

There is a filter in the line between tank and pumps, held to the chassis rail by a bracket. Its lower body is finished in black, and the rest of the filter is unpainted. The twin SU fuel pumps are mounted back-to-back on a bracket outside the right-hand chassis rail, towards the rear of the cruciform brace. Both pumps work all the time. From SZB27/B312CK in April 1957, an improved stoneguard was fitted to protect the pumps, and could be fitted retrospectively. Better waterproofing arrived in December 1958, with a new joint seal between body and end cover of each pump.

Wheels & Tyres

The 15in diameter wheels are five-stud disc types with 6in well-base rims (type 6Lx15). Recommended tyre pressures are 22psi (front) and 27psi (rear). Wheel nuts on the left-hand side of the car have left-hand threads, those on the right-hand side have right-hand threads – to prevent the wheel nuts undoing if not fully tightened.

Engine

The 4887cc six-cylinder engine in these cars is the final derivative of the B60, with a 95.25mm bore and 114.3mm stroke. Its power output, never revealed officially by Rolls-Royce, was 178bhp by the time production ended.

The engine is generally similar to the unit used in the final R-type Continentals, but has a number of improvements. Most important of these is a different cylinder head with six inlet and six exhaust ports (instead of the four inlet and three exhaust ports of the earlier engine) and a two-piece inlet manifold. The forged crankshaft has integral balance weights (rather than the earlier detachable type) on either side of the centre main bearing, on the outsides of the numbers 2 and 6 webs, and on the insides of numbers 1 and 7. The crankshaft damper is a metallic mass attached to a thin flange on the shaft by spring-loaded friction linings. There is an oil thrower as well as an oil return scroll behind

Silver Cloud wheel discs carry the 'RR' motif in their centres. Just visible below the front bumper of this 1959 Rolls-Royce is the ram for the optional power-assisted steering.

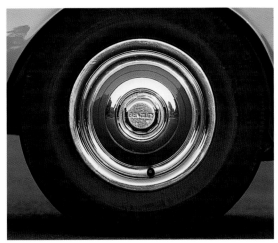

S-series wheel discs have the full Bentley name in their centres.

the rear main bearing. The pistons have four rings instead of three, the top one being a chromium-plated compression ring, and the block has full-length cylinder liners made of 30 per cent chrome iron. The 1.85in diameter exhaust valves (made by Rolls-Royce) have heads coated in nickel-chrome, the large inlet valves are of 1.625in diameter and there are screwed-in steel valve seat inserts in the aluminium alloy cylinder head.

The rear engine mounting was modified twice, first at LSWA34/B43AN (except B172AN) for standard saloons and at SWA60/B17AP for coachbuilt chassis. This change brought a modified bracket and larger-diameter mounting bolt to prevent fatigue fractures of the bolt. Earlier chassis were modified as necessary in service, by machining a counterbore in the underside of the rear extension bracket and, in some cases, by fitting washers and a longer distance tube. A spot of yellow paint on the mounting bracket indicated the alteration. The second modification came at SWA206/B411AP, when the rear engine mounting itself was revised.

Block, Head, Manifold & Bellhousing
The cast iron cylinder block should be finished in black externally, against which the bare metal finish of the bolt heads, pipework and timing cover makes an elegant but business-like contrast.

The bellhousing should be unpainted.

Internally, set screws replaced studs on the main bearing caps early on at SWA24/B39AP. Hepolite pistons with four rings were introduced during 1956 at B54CK (and probably during SYB series Rolls-Royce production) and the cam wheel was strengthened during 1957 at chassis B41EK and during SED-series production. A combined inertia and starter ring was fitted from chassis numbers SED131/B530EG (to go with a new starter, qv), and the bellhousing was strengthened at the same time.

The cylinder head is attached to the block by 37 set bolts of ⅜in diameter, rather than by the studs used in earlier engines. Its visible elements should be finished in black to match the engine block. The cylinder head gained new valve seats and guides to improve cooling at B324EG in summer 1957, and strengthened valve seat inserts shortly afterwards at B474EG. On Rolls-Royce chassis, these changes probably occurred towards the end of the SDD series.

Early engines have a compression ratio of 6.6:1. Beginning with LSDD136 in 1957, Rolls-Royce chassis originally destined for the USA have a revised cylinder head with larger 2in inlet valves. These larger valves are accompanied by a raised compression ratio of 8:1, and by bigger carburettors (see below). From SFE9, the big-valve,

The exhaust side of a 1959 Rolls-Royce six-cylinder engine. The ignition coil is incorrectly installed here; it should be mounted upside down. The windscreen wiper motor is visible in the bottom right of the picture. The pipework between the wing valance and the power steering reservoir is for the heater and demister system.

high-compression cylinder head and the bigger carburettors are fitted to all Silver Cloud chassis.

The cylinder head changes were introduced in three stages on Bentley chassis. Cars destined for the US had the high-compression head from chassis B120EG, but on other models the bigger carburettors were introduced first at B1EG and the new 8:1 compression ratio cylinder head afterwards at B257EK.

All these six-cylinder engines have a two-piece inlet manifold, one half of which is integral with the cylinder head while the other carries the carburettors and is bolted to it. This arrangement allowed greater casting accuracy and better shaping of the inlet gallery than was possible with the earlier one-piece manifold.

The cast aluminium rocker cover should be finished in black, and should carry a Rolls-Royce or Bentley nameplate. The oil filler cap on it has a plain metal finish, but its cap has a black central section with maintenance instructions in white.

The pulleys at the front of the engine were finished by the Roto process from B627EK and probably from early SGE-series Rolls-Royces.

Carburettors & Fuel System

All engines have two SU carburettors (specially made for Rolls-Royce) and an automatic choke. The Rolls-Royce automatic choke is in circuit

The ignition coil is correctly installed on this 1955 Bentley engine. Note the different pipework for the heater/demister, the different wiper motor, and the plain Bentley chassis plate on the bulkhead. The vacuum-operated Trico washer bottle is visible, attached to the wing valance.

This is the inlet side of a 1955 Bentley engine. Note the linkages for the automatic choke on the pipe running from the air cleaner and, of course, the single brake fluid reservoir on this early car.

with the ignition switch and is turned off by a pressure switch (in the oil gallery) which operates when the engine oil pressure has reached a pre-set level. This differs from the R-type system, where the automatic choke is in circuit with the starter and cuts out when the starter is disengaged, leading sometimes to stalling.

The early engines are fitted with SU HD6 diaphragm-type carburettors with 1¾in chokes. Modified butterfly valves and countersunk screws were fitted very early on at SWA14/B270AN to facilitate slow-running adjustments. From chassis SDD136 and B1EG, cars for the US have HD8 carburettors with 2in chokes, and these carburettors are standard for all markets from SFE9/B1EK. The carburettors are always finished in black, with unpainted brass dashpot screws.

A mesh air cleaner is fitted to all cars except those destined for operation in dusty conditions, which have an oil-bath type. The standard air cleaner is a long cylindrical type, finished in black and fitted horizontally along the top of the engine. The oil-bath type is located on the left-hand side of the engine, and is also finished in black.

Cooling System

The cooling system is pressurised to 7psi, and has a belt-driven water pump with a black, five-bladed, cooling fan on its nose. On cars fitted with the optional power-assisted steering, there are double pulleys on the water pump and the rubber drive-belt is duplicated.

The Marston radiator is finished in black and at its top is a cowl which projects back over the fan. The radiator drain tap is unpainted. A modified radiator and drain tap, suitable for the splayed-end chassis frame, were introduced at SYB116/B60CK. Note that the frame itself was not modified until later, at SZB139/B27CM. From SKG119/B24GC in February/March 1959, there were modified heater and demister connections on the radiator.

Exhaust System

The exhaust system is a single large-bore type with two large expansion boxes. It emerges on the left-hand side of the engine, where the manifold is stove enamelled, and the pipework then runs outside the left-hand chassis rail to a centre silencer carried between the central and rear chassis outriggers. The rear pipe section joins the centre section just behind the rear body mounting, and curves up and inwards over the chassis rail to the rear silencer, which is just ahead of and above the axle. The tail pipe then curves up and over the axle, back under the chassis rail and finishes in a long straight section, which emerges beneath the left-hand end of the rear bumper. There is a mounting bracket on the chassis rail, and behind this the pipe has a chromed finish.

From SWA126/B257AP in late 1955, the exhaust fittings had modified flanges, and at SHF1/B338FA in summer 1958, the rear silencer mounting was modified to prevent exhaust heat burning the rubber.

Transmission

All the six-cylinder Silver Clouds and S-series have the Rolls-Royce-built Hydra-Matic four-speed automatic transmission with fluid flywheel as standard equipment. The gear selector is a lever mounted on the steering column. A very few standard steel cars and Bentley Continentals were fitted with manual gearboxes to special order but from 1957 all models were automatics.

Gearbox

The casing of the Rolls-Royce-built Hydra-Matic transmission is unpainted. It carries a maker's plate similar to the one fitted to Rolls-Royce-built transmissions for the R-type/Silver Dawn. The internal gear ratios (with overall ratios in brackets) are: First 3.819:1 (13.049:1), Second 2.634:1 (8.999:1), Third 1.450:1 (4.954:1), Fourth 1.000:1 (3.417:1), and Reverse 4.306:1 (14.712:1). For the few cars with a manual gearbox the ratios were the same as the final R-types with the 3.417:1 axle.

Propshaft

The propshaft is a divided type with a splined sliding joint in its centre. This sliding joint is provided with a grease nipple. The centre and rear Hardy Spicer universal joints have needle roller bearings and are also provided with grease nipples. The finish of all components should be black.

At chassis number SZB35/B352CK, the body of the ball and trunnion joint between gearbox output shaft and propshaft had a new spot facing, and a reach nut and washer were fitted to suit. The propshaft centring button was improved at B562EG and mid-way through the SED series.

Protracted trouble with the grease seal on the propshaft brought about three successive modifications. The original type was made of rubber, and was replaced by a neoprene type with detail dimensional changes at SGE160/B352FA in early 1958. Wire-type clips were added to it a few months later at SHF1/B438FA, and finally a new seal with an extended neck was specified at SMH3/B4GC in the early summer of 1959.

Electrical Components

The electrical system on the Silver Cloud and S-series has a negative earth. The wiring harness has an outer casing of black plastic, and there are variations in its configuration to suit the equipment fitted and to suit left-hand or right-hand steering.

The light-coloured bulkhead carries the fuse box and chassis lubrication reservoir on this 1955 Bentley. The separate fuse box for the horn circuit is to the left of the main fuse box.

Battery, Dynamo & Fuses

The 12-volt 57-amp/hour battery is carried in a special compartment at the right-hand rear of the chassis; original batteries were made by Dagenite. The dynamo, mounted on the engine and driven by the auxiliary drive belt (or both belts on cars with power-assisted steering), has a black body with unpainted end caps, and its mounting and adjustment brackets are unpainted metal. The dynamo type changed twice, first to a Lucas E-type at chassis SYB90/B188CK in 1956, and then to a Lucas C48 in summer 1959 at SHF43/B71FD. In 1957 a new dynamo pulley giving a 2:1 drive ratio was fitted from B628EG and at some time in SED series production.

The voltage regulator is mounted on the engine side of the bulkhead. Three different types were fitted on production; all made by Lucas and all with a black plastic casing. The first was an RB310 unit, which was replaced by an M-type at SYB90/B188CK when the E-type dynamo was fitted. There was a second change in 1956, this time to an H-type regulator with swamp resistance at SCC33/B25DE.

The main fuse box is fitted on the engine side of the bulkhead, ahead of the driver. It has a black cover and contains eight fuses. There is also a separate fuse box alongside, which contains a single fuse covering the horn circuit.

Starter Motor & Ignition System

The starter motor is on the left-hand side of the engine for right-hand-drive cars, and on the right-hand side for left-hand-drive cars. It is a Lucas component with an unpainted body and a black clamp ring at the end further from the mounting. From SED131/B530EG, the starter drive was

improved. The mounting for the starter relay was simplified at B649FD and during SKG-series Rolls-Royce production.

Delco-Remy ignition equipment is standard. The coil is mounted top downwards at the front of the engine and the distributor has twin contact breakers. Sparking plugs were supplied initially only by Champion (type N8BR), and their contact gap was set to 0.25in. Later recommendations were Lodge CLNP or Champion RN5 with a 14mm reach.

Horns, Windscreen Wipers & Washer

The twin horns are of Lucas manufacture and are located behind the left-hand front wing. The windscreen wiper motor is a two-speed Lucas unit with a self-parking feature. An improved DR3 type was introduced in late 1957 at chassis numbers SFE279/B635EK.

The windscreen washer is not electrical, but is included in this section for convenience. It is a vacuum-operated Trico type, with a glass bottle and a distinctive diaphragm unit on top of its metal lid. It operates by manifold depression, and owners were advised to ease off on the accelerator pedal when operating the washer, 'otherwise there may be insufficient depression to actuate the pump'! From chassis numbers SWA40/B492AN, the sealing between the windscreen washer and the wiper mounting and body was improved.

Lighting

There are three different types of headlamp fitted to the six-cylinder Silver Clouds. Standard models have Lucas R700 headlamps, which incorporate a small RR or B motif behind the glass in the centre of their lenses. These come in right-hand or left-hand dip forms, to suit the steering position of the car. From B22GC and early SMH series chassis in 1959, RL headlamp units are fitted. Cars exported to the USA were shipped without headlamps, and were equipped with sealed-beam units on arrival. These units do not have the motif behind the glass. Sidelamps are of Lucas manufacture and carry a small red tell-tale made of plastic.

All cars are fitted with twin Lucas foglamps, mounted behind the front bumper and just outboard of the air intakes on the front wings. These foglamps have twin filament yellow bulbs; the second filament enables the fog lamps to double as the front direction indicator flashers.

The rear lamps are sometimes known as 'cathedral' lamps and incorporate separate bulbs for the stop and tail lamps; early cars have red lenses, later changed to amber. The flashing direction indicators operate through the stop lamp bulbs and interrupt the stop lamp circuit; the rear wiring loom was modified early on, at

Headlamps on the S-series models once again carried a 'B' motif behind the glass; Rolls-Royce types, of course, carried an 'RR' motif.

Lucas foglamps with yellow bulbs doubled as front turn indicators.

SWA72/B155AP, to facilitate this. A circular red reflector is incorporated in the chromed lamp body, below the main lens.

Electric Windows

Electrically-operated windows were introduced as an optional extra in October 1958. At B118GC (and from some point in the early SMH series), there were modified clips and fuses for these in the fuse box.

Body

The main body structure is in 20-gauge steel, and the sills and bulkhead are zinc-plated in order to protect against corrosion. The doors are made of 18-gauge Birmabright lightweight aluminium alloy; the boot lid and bonnet are in the same material but of 16 gauge. All the bodyshells were made by Pressed Steel at Cowley, and were despatched to Crewe for painting and trimming. The body is mounted to the chassis on 12 Silent-bloc soft rubber mountings, adjustable via slotted bolt holes and tightened to a predetermined torque after the body had been floated on pneumatic jacks so that equal loading was applied to all of the body mountings.

The standard saloon bodyshell incorporates the double-skinned front bulkhead and the inner wings (engine compartment sides). Chassis for coachbuilt bodies were built at Crewe with a bulkhead and inner wing panels.

Front Wings, Radiator Grille, Bonnet & Scuttle

The front wings of the Silver Cloud and S-series Bentley are massive steel pressings, which incorporate cut-outs for the headlamps and the air intakes. There are mouldings for the sidelamps on

their crowns. The headlamps, sidelamps and air intakes have chrome-plated bezels; the air intakes have diagonal mesh grilles behind their chromed bezels. Up to the end of 1958 approximately, the front wings and valance panel are attached by fixing bolts with a diameter of 0.25in; from B359FD and some point in the SHF or SJF series, bolts with a larger diameter of 0.3125in are used.

The bonnet is hinged down its centre and is fastened by concealed catches, which are released from inside the car. When closed, its panels sit just below the sloping sides of the Rolls-Royce radiator grille, which is surmounted by a fixed mascot. The Spirit of Ecstasy mascot is completely different to the ones used on previous Rolls-Royce models. It is a 4⅝in tall standing version of Charles Sykes's original 1911 mascot but is cast in stainless steel by the 'lost-wax' process at Crewe. The Bentley's Winged-B mascot is made in the same way but is not mounted on a dummy radiator cap, as it was on the earlier models. However, a dummy radiator cap (part number UE1883) for special

The cars were identical from behind, except for the emblem carried at the centre of the rear bumper. Again, the shape appears beautifully balanced from this angle, which usually shows up styling flaws if there are any!

The bonnet lids on Rolls-Royce models sit just below the top of the radiator shell when they are closed. The Silver Cloud was the first Rolls-Royce to have a stainless steel Flying Lady mascot.

mascots could be supplied. Both Rolls-Royce and Bentley cars exported to Switzerland were supplied without radiator mascots, to meet local traffic regulations.

The radiator grille, front wings and bonnet lids of the standard Bentley saloon body all differ from the Rolls-Royce version. The Silver Cloud's radiator grille, with 20 fixed shutters, is fabricated by Rolls-Royce craftsmen in stainless steel. The shutter opening is 24.6in tall by 19.875in wide and the radiator shell is 4.3in deep from front to rear. The Bentley's slatted radiator grille is a chromium-plated brass pressing. Less obviously the Bentley bonnet tops and wings are shaped differently from the Rolls-Royce ones. The Bentley front wings are slightly curved at their inner edges

where they touch the sides of the radiator shell, whereas the Rolls-Royce wings are flat in that area. Bonnet tops follow the radiator shape at the front, so the Bentley panel is curved and the Rolls-Royce straight. As a result, front wings and bonnet lids are not interchangeable between the two.

The scuttle panel on both Rolls-Royce and Bentley cars carries the windscreen wiper mountings and the chromed washer jets. The two individual washer jets were replaced by a single twin-jet type, mounted in the centre of the scuttle, at SHF1/B472FA in summer 1958.

Doors

Both front and rear doors are hinged at their leading edges, and the hinges have Oilite bushes with stainless steel hinge pins. Stronger hinges were fitted at chassis numbers SFE75/B471EK in late 1957. The main door panels are made of aluminium alloy, and there are separate stainless steel window frames, which incorporate hinged quarterlights. The window channels were improved to ease opening at B556FA and on early SHF series chassis during 1958, and then again shortly afterwards at B607FD, when the aim of the change was to reduce winding loads under adverse weather conditions. This second change was made during SKG series Rolls-Royce chassis production.

Each door carries a chromed Wilmot Breeden exterior handle with a push-button release. These handles and push-buttons were modified at chassis number SXA51/B158BA and the buttons were sealed at SJF140/B433FD. The front doors both incorporate Yale private keylocks in the outer panels just below the push-button. The door locks can be operated by the ignition key (with a round head) or by the master key (with a rectangular head), but the ignition key will not operate any of the other locks except for the ignition itself. All locks are of the self-cancelling type, which unlock if the door is slammed.

Some improvements were made to the sealing rubbers, first of all those for the doors at B101EK (late SED series), and then those for the front quarterlights at B388FA (late SGE series).

Roof & Radio Aerial

The roof panel does not contain a sliding sunroof, as fitted to earlier models, because an additional stiffening cross-member is fitted to the roof at that point. However, some customers insisted on a sliding-steel sunroof so a factory-fitted version was installed on a few cars: 1958 Silver Cloud LSHF173 is one. A chrome-plated radio aerial, mounted above the centre of the windscreen, is standard equipment. It can be turned parallel to the top edge of the screen by a knob inside the car. A few cars have a radio aerial mounted underneath the car, supported by brackets.

All doors were hung at their leading edges. The paint missing from two nuts here suggests that this front door has been re-hung at some stage.

Door handles were neatly integrated with the side finishers; Yale private locks were mounted below them on the front doors.

Rear Wings

The steel rear wings are not separate panels, but part of the much larger rear-quarter body pressings, which extend up to roof level. They contain apertures for the rear lamp units, and the left-hand wing incorporates the fuel filler door. This is released electrically through a solenoid activated by a dashboard-mounted switch; there is a wire-pull release inside the boot for emergency use.

Boot Lid & Interior

The boot lid is top-hinged and counterbalanced so that it will remain in the open position without a support rod. It carries a mercury switch, which operates a boot lamp when the lid is open. The rear number plate is mounted on the outside of the boot lid in a chromed surround and is illuminated from below by bulbs in a separate chromed housing, which also incorporates twin reversing lamps; US models have a different square number-plate box. The fixing of the number plate and reversing lamp was changed to a four-point type at B133EK (and probably during the SED series) in summer 1957. Below the number-plate housing is a large horizontal handle with a keylock and press-button release in its centre. From chassis SJF168/B513FD at the end of 1958, the boot lock has a more secure freewheeling mechanism.

The boot lid opens to reveal the front of the spare wheel and tool compartment underneath a flat, carpeted floor. A lift-up flap in the front of the boot floor allows the tyre pressure to be checked without removing the spare wheel. Lifting the carpet on the right-hand side of the boot floor gives access to the lid of the battery compartment; export models from B649FD (early SLG series) in March 1959 have a special lid with improved sealing. Lifting the carpet on the left-hand side gives access to the lid covering the rubber-lined tool tray. This should contain the following items: screwdriver; adjustable spanner; pliers; two combined ring and open-ended spanners; tyre pressure gauge; tappet-adjusting spanner combined with 2, 3, and 5 BA open-ended spanner; exhaust tappet-adjusting lock; feeler gauges; distributor-adjustment spanner; sparking plug box spanner; drain-plug spanner for sump, gearbox, torus cover and rear axle; one tail/stop bulb; one headlamp bulb (except cars with sealed beams); two foglamp/flasher twin-filament bulbs; one sidelamp bulb.

Inside the spare wheel compartment, the wheel is offset slightly to the right, with the Smiths Bevelift jack and an inspection lamp stowed to its left. The other major tools are a socket spanner for the wheel nuts, a tommy-bar and a tyre pump. These are positioned in front of the spare wheel and should all be held in place by their own clips.

The Silver Cloud's boot was considerably larger than the Silver Dawn's. The large tools, laid out here, were fitted in clips alongside the spare wheel. There was no longer a starting handle. The boot floor was covered with haircord carpet. The small tools (left) are contained in a removable tray under the carpet on the left of the boot.

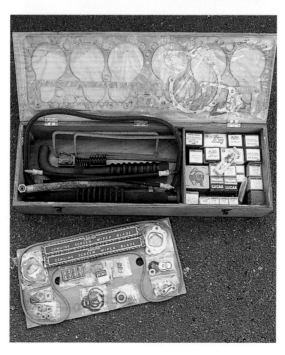

This is a rarity of a very special kind, an Isolated Territories Kit for the 1955 S-series Bentley. It contained a large selection of spares, which might be needed far from a Rolls-Royce dealer, all neatly packed into a wooden box.

Early cars had two washer jets on the scuttle, but the 1959 models had a single unit with twin jets.

The symmetrical instrument panel simplified manufacture of both left-hand-drive and right-hand-drive models. This one is on a 1955 Bentley with right-hand drive.

Bumpers

All standard saloon models are fitted with the same type of Wilmot Breeden bumpers, which carry massive and ornately curved overriders. The front and rear bumpers are single-piece castings. In the centre of the rear bumper, as appropriate, is a Rolls-Royce badge on a plinth or a Bentley badge attached directly to the bumper.

Windscreen & Glass

A ¼in thick laminated windscreen and heated rear window are standard; both are made by Triplex.

Interior

Facia, Instruments, & Steering Wheel

The facia, made of Bakelite plastic with a facing veneer of walnut, consists of several distinct sections. At the top is the capping rail, angled towards the occupants. Below this is a shaped central instrument panel, containing the dials and major switches. Behind that is a further section, with an open cubby on the driver's side and a lockable glovebox with drop-down hinged lid on the passenger's side. Below the central instrument panel is a further panel containing the radio. Underneath the dash in the centre is a pull-out, walnut-veneered table, with a sliding ashtray below it. The ashtray finisher was modified at B389EK (SFE series) in 1957. All the veneered woodwork is sprayed with several coats of synthetic lacquer and stoved to protect it from damage by sunlight or excess moisture.

The capping rail is veneered to match the facia with cross-banding on its front edge. Its front face carries a long chromed grab handle on the passenger side and there is a clockwork-timed self-cancelling direction indicator control switch on the driver's side. The rear view mirror is carried on a chromed stalk screwed to the centre of the capping rail.

The main instrument panel is laid out symmetrically with two large dials at the outside extremities and the traditional Rolls-Royce switchbox central between them. The dial nearest the driver is always the Smiths speedometer and the other is the Smiths four-in-one instrument. These large dials carry Rolls-Royce or Bentley motifs, as appropriate. The four-in-one dial contains the clock in its centre and (clockwise from top) gauges for fuel, oil pressure, amps and coolant temperature. A thermal conductor type of water temperature gauge is fitted from chassis number B637FD (SKG series) in early 1959. The switchbox has a dull black finish with white lettering and is simplified compared with earlier types because the key operates the starter as well as switching on all the electrical circuits. The lighting switch is above the keylock and has four positions: Off, S & T (side and tail lamps on), H, S & T (head, side and tail lamps on) and F, S & T (fog, side and tail lamps on). Flanking the keylock and lighting switches are warning lamps for ignition on/ dynamo not charging (red) and low fuel (green), the latter illuminates when three gallons remain in the tank.

Inboard of the main instruments are two black-finished recesses containing chromed knobs shaped like violin keys. These are for the demister (pull and twist), two-speed windscreen wiper (twist), panel lights, and heater (pull and twist). They are labelled in white lettering.

Immediately below the switchbox is a push-button which changes the fuel gauge into an oil level indicator; between the main dials and the switchbox are a cigar lighter and the release switch for the petrol-filler flap.

The radio should be an HMV Radiomobile Model 200X, a valve type with five push-buttons giving both Medium and Long wave reception.

There are no control levers on the hub of the black three-spoke steering wheel, which has a chromed horn button in its centre. The ride control is operated by a two-position switch on the left-hand side of the steering column, labelled 'N' for Normal and 'H' for Hard. On the right-hand side of the steering column is the selector quadrant for the automatic transmission. This is marked with five positions: N, 4, 3, 2 and R. There is no Park position as on more modern transmissions but the engine can be started only in Neutral, and first gear is selected only through the kick-down switch operated by the accelerator pedal. A button in the end of the selector lever releases the detent covering Neutral and Reverse.

The switch for the heated rear window is not fitted to the facia but is located on the rear parcels shelf. Not surprisingly, Rolls-Royce recommended that it should be left on permanently in cold weather!

The quadrant for the standard automatic transmission is mounted on the steering column, and the two-position ride control switch is fitted to the opposite side.

Pedals, Handbrake & Bonnet Releases

The accelerator pedal on right-hand-drive cars is rectangular and has a rubber pad. Left-hand-drive models have a larger, bare-metal, pedal like that on left-hand-drive MkVI, R-type and Silver Dawn. The brake pedal is oval on all models, and has a rubber pad with an R-R or B monogram, as appropriate. All models have a T-handle, twist-grip, handbrake under the facia, positioned outboard of the driver.

There is a foot-operated dipswitch inboard of the driver on right-hand-drive cars; this is finished in bare metal on some early cars but later a black rubber cover was added. On all left-hand-drive models, the dipswitch is mounted to the left of the pedals and always has a black rubber cover. The tiny pedal for the chassis lubrication pump is located on the toeboard, next to the steering column on all cars. There is a bonnet release lever in each footwell alongside the carpeted kick-panel. Pushing down on a lever releases the catch for one half of the hinged bonnet. The lever is pulled upwards to secure the bonnet once the lid has been closed. Pedal operation of the horns was an option, and an improved version of it arrived at B159FD (late SGE or early SHF series chassis) in summer 1958.

Seats

All upholstery is in top-quality Connolly Vaumol hide. The seats have foam rubber overlays on Intalok spring cases. The front seat is a bench type, which moves fore and aft on ball-bearing slides and is assisted in the forward direction by springs. The release lever is located centrally below the cushion. The two squabs are individually adjustable for rake (and to increase legroom slightly), and are released by a chromed lever on the outboard edge of the cushion at each side. The

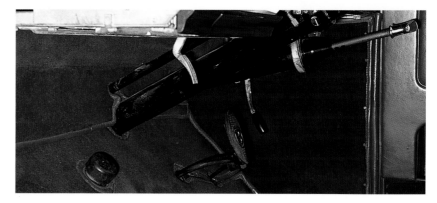

first cars have no central armrests, but folding armrests for each squab were added early in 1956, with effect from chassis numbers SXA137 and B210BA. The front seat backs contain walnut-veneered folding picnic tables, with an ashtray above each.

The rear bench seat on all cars has a folding central armrest with generous corner padding from wrap-around bolsters. There is a short, fixed armrest at each side.

Carpets

Deep-pile Wilton carpets can either tone in with the upholstery or contrast with it; the Connolly leather binding usually matches the upholstery as offcuts from the same hides are used. Matching lambswool rugs are an extra fitted to many cars.

Door Trims & Headlining

The door pads are trimmed with Connolly leather to match the seats. The front doors incorporate deep map pockets and have armrests which are adjustable both vertically and horizontally, or can be removed altogether. New trim pad clips and retainers were introduced at B544EG and during the SED series in 1957. All door trims carry

The T-shaped handbrake, bonnet-release handle, bare metal chassis-lubrication pedal and dipswitch with black rubber cover of a 1955 Bentley S-series.

Strangely, perhaps, the heated rear window switch was fitted to the rear parcels shelf rather than to the facia.

The front seat was always a bench type with individually adjustable backrests but later cars, like this 1959 Silver Cloud (above), were fitted with a pair of folding armrests to give additional support when cornering. Early cars, like this 1955 Bentley S-series (right), had no folding armrests for the front seat.

Wilmot Breeden chromed lock release handles and chromed winding handles for the windows; the winders were modified at B645FD and during the SKG series to remedy a foul on the trim pad. The wood veneer door fillets were sprayed with a synthetic lacquer and then stoved to prevent damage from sunlight and moisture.

The headlining is West of England wool cloth. There are two rigid cloth-trimmed sun visors above the windscreen; the one on the driver's side was modified to improve vision at B457FD (SJF or SKG series chassis) early in 1959. Between the visors is a Bakelite knob, which allows the roof-mounted aerial to be turned through 90° to give greater clearance when entering domestic garages. This knob is engraved with an arrow to show which way the aerial is pointing. There are two spring-loaded leather hand grips on chromed swivels above the rear quarterlights.

There are vanity mirrors in the rear quarters, with illumination. A second cigar lighter is fitted in the right-hand vanity mirror surround.

Heater

The heating and demisting system is complicated and reasonably effective, although early complaints of its inflexibility were never fully overcome. Fresh air enters the system through mesh-screened intakes and gauze filters in both front wings. Once the dashboard switch is turned to its first position to open a vacuum-operated

butterfly valve, the ducted air is fed to an axial-type fan, which forces the air through a water-heated radiator matrix on each side of the car. The facia heater knob uses a vacuum-operated water tap to admit hot water to the matrix. The left-hand duct and heat exchanger feed four demister slots at the base of the windscreen, whilst the right-hand duct and radiator serve as the passenger compartment heater. There is underfloor ducting to take heat for the rear seat passengers to an outlet at the back of the front seats.

A number of modifications were introduced on production. From February 1957, taps were added so that the heating side of the system could be turned off during summer in order to give a greater throughput of cold air without the need to open the windows. Two months later, a smaller-diameter vacuum pipe at the rear of the manifold was introduced to deal with complaints of a sucking noise when the vacuum-operated temperature and demister controls were used. Then the heater and demister taps were changed in June 1957; the earlier taps have an H (for Heater) and a D (for Demister) to assist in identification. From October that year, there was also a new heater matrix for use in extremely cold climates, which was said to be 11 per cent more efficient than the standard type. It carried part number UD3857 and was identified with a red paint mark.

Air Conditioning

In October 1956 air conditioning – refrigeration in Rolls-Royce language – became available at extra cost, initially for export only. The component parts of this original system were imported from the US, and it is characterised by a large evaporator and blower unit mounted in the boot, directly behind the rear seat and under the rear parcels shelf. The OMC Texas boot unit is purely recirculatory so it draws in air from the passenger compartment through a grille in the centre of the parcels shelf, and returns cooled air through ducts built into the cant rails. A blower unit on each side assists in air distribution. On maximum setting, this boot-mounted system can change the air inside the car at a rate of 300cu ft per minute, so that there is a complete change of air inside the car every 1½ minutes.

From April 1958, Rolls-Royce offered its own boot refrigeration unit, capable of providing 400cu ft of airflow per minute, for both home and export markets. The OMC Texas boot-mounted system remained available but was normally specified only for the US, being fitted to the cars on arrival there. The Rolls-Royce boot-mounted system is also recirculatory, drawing in air from a central grille in the rear parcels shelf and discharging cooled air through two Smiths centrifugal blower units to circular outlets at each end of

Rear seat passengers had pull-down picnic trays, veneered to match the rest of the interior wood.

Door trims remained unchanged during production of the six-cylinder models. These are on a 1955 Bentley S-series. As on the earlier post-war cars, the radio aerial (far right) was operated by a Bakelite knob inside the car. The leather-trimmed sun visors matched the upholstery and not the headlining.

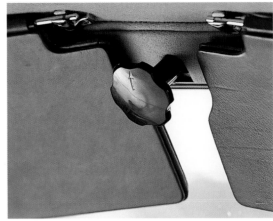

The hand grips were spring-loaded on these cars, and were finished to match the upholstery. The companion in the right-hand rear quarter again contained a cigar lighter and had its own lighting.

Summer and Winter heater and demister taps for the complicated system on a late six-cylinder Silver Cloud. Note also the instruction plate on the oil filler cap.

the parcels shelf. Dunlop developed special concentric pipes, with high-pressure copper tube inside a low-pressure Neoprene-lined rubber pipe, to carry the refrigerant in the Rolls-Royce system and Marston Excelsior made the aluminium evaporator in the boot.

The underbonnet components of both systems are the same. A twin-cylinder compressor is mounted on the right-hand front of the engine and driven by twin rubber belts from additional pulleys mounted behind the radiator fan, which has a faster speed and is cowled. (There are in fact three additional pulleys; the third is used for the power-assisted steering which is normally fitted.) To switch the air conditioning system on and off, the compressor incorporates a magnetic clutch, which is in turn operated by a three-position switch fitted just outboard of the driver on the dashboard. Ahead of the engine coolant radiator is a second, smaller radiator which acts as a heat exchanger for the system, and below it a receiver-and-drier unit is mounted to the chassis frame. Pipework carries the refrigerant towards the back of the car along the inside of the right-hand body sill, up to the boot-mounted evaporator and blower unit. Both systems originally used Freon 12 gas as the refrigerant medium. This gas is now

PAINT & INTERIOR TRIM

The standard or recommended paint and trim options for the Rolls-Royce Silver Cloud and Bentley S-series are listed below. It was normal (but not invariable) practice for the bonnet top on two-tone Rolls-Royce cars to be finished in the same colour as the upper portions of the body. On two-tone Bentley models, the bonnet top was usually finished in the lower colour.

1955
There were six standard paint finishes, four two-tone options and seven interior colours. Catalogues did not tie interior colours to exterior paint, although Rolls-Royce would probably have discouraged certain combinations if those had been requested! The six single colours were: Black, Black Pearl, Cellon Blue, Maroon, Midnight Blue and Velvet Green. The four two-tone options were: Shell

Grey over Tudor Grey, Sage Green over Smoke Green, Sand over Sable and Shell Grey over Black Pearl.
The seven interior colours were: Beige, Blue, Brown, Green, Grey, Red and Tan.

1956
There were six standard paint colours, five two-tone options, and seven interior colours. Five of the standard colours were carried over from 1955, and Lugano Blue replaced Cellon Blue. The same four two-tone options were available, with the addition of Shell Grey over Velvet Green. The interior colours were unchanged.

1957
There were 12 standard paint colours, which consisted of the six 1956 colours (but Lugano Blue was replaced by the

earlier Cellon Blue), plus the six other colours available in the two-tone combinations (Sage Green, Sable, Sand, Shell Grey, Smoke Green, and Tudor Grey). Any combination of colours could be ordered to make a two-tone finish. The same seven interior colours were available.

1958
There were 14 standard paint colours. These were the 12 listed for 1957 (except that Steel Blue replaced Cellon Blue), plus Pacific Green and Porcelain White, the latter two available for export only. Any combination of colours could be ordered to make a two-tone finish. The same seven interior colours were available.
Carpets normally matched the upholstery colour. Headlinings could be 'matched to individual taste' but were normally in Beige or Grey.

IDENTIFICATION, DATING & PRODUCTION FIGURES

The chassis number of a Silver Cloud or Bentley S-series will be found under the bonnet on a plate attached to the left-hand side of the bulkhead and on the left-hand chassis frame member forward of the bulkhead. There were 2238 Rolls-Royce Silver Cloud chassis, and 3072 S-series Bentleys.

CHASSIS NUMBERS

The chassis numbers for these cars are set out below, together with delivery dates.

Rolls-Royce chassis numbers consist of three letters and up to three digits. The final letter denotes the chassis series. Left-hand-drive cars have an L prefix before the chassis letters (eg LSWA250).

Bentley chassis numbers begin with B followed by up to three digits and two suffix letters, the first of which denotes the chassis series. Left-hand-drive cars have the letter L before the suffix letters (eg B500LAN).

Both Rolls-Royce and Bentley sequences beginning with 1 used odd numbers only and always excepted 13; sequences beginning with 2 used even numbers only.

Rolls-Royce Silver Cloud

SWA2 to SWA250	April 1955 to January 1956
SXA1 to SXA251	January to May 1956
SYB2 to SYB250	March to June 1956
SZB1 to SZB251	June to September 1956
SBC2 to SBC150	August to October 1956
SCC1 to SCC151	October 1956 to April 1957
SDD2 to SDD450	February to May 1957
SED1 to SED451	April to August 1957
SFE1 to SFE501	August 1957 to January 1958
SGE2 to SGE500	December 1957 to July 1958
SHF1 to SHF249	July to November 1958
SJF2 to SJF250	October 1958 to January 1959
SKG1 to SKG125	January to February 1959
SLG2 to SLG126	February to April 1959
SMH1 to SMH265	March to June 1959
SNH2 to SNH262	May to July 1959

Bentley S-series

B2AN to B500AN	April to November 1955
B1AP to B501AP	September 1955 to March 1956
B2BA to B250BA	December 1955 to March 1956
B1BC to B251BC	February to April 1956
B2CK to B500CK	April to July 1956
B1CM to B501CM	July to November 1956
B2DB to B350DB	September to November 1956
B1DE to B351DE	October 1956 to January 1957
B2EG to B650EG	January to July 1957
B1EK to B651EK	July to December 1957
B2FA to B650FA	November 1957 to June 1958
B1FD to B651FD	June 1958 to March 1959
B1GD to B125GD	February to April 1959
B2GC to B126GC	March to May 1959
B1HB to B45HB	May to June 1959
B2HA to B50HA	May to July 1959

ENGINE NUMBERS

Engine numbers are located at the front of the crankcase on the left-hand side, just above the engine mounting. The numbering sequences are consecutive, include 13, and are:

Rolls-Royce Silver Cloud

SA1 to SA250	A-series chassis
SB1 to SB250	B-series chassis
SC1 to SC150	C-series chassis
SD1 to SD450	D-series chassis
SE1 to SE500	E-series chassis
SF1 to SF250	F-series chassis
SG1 to SG125	G-series chassis
SH1 to SH263	H-series chassis

Bentley S-series

BA1 to BA500	A-series chassis
BB1 to BB250	B-series chassis
BC1 to BC500	C-series chassis
BD1 to BD350	D-series chassis
BE1 to BE650	E-series chassis
BF1 to BF650	F-series chassis
BG1 to BG125	G-series chassis
BH1 to BH47	H-series chassis

The chassis identification plate is attached to the engine side of the bulkhead with rivets; Bentley plates were attached with two rivets, while the Rolls-Royce type had four. Note that the bulkhead was always light-coloured, to make underbonnet work easier.

considered damaging to the earth's atmosphere and is illegal in many countries, but modern equivalents give satisfactory results.

Cars with refrigeration have a fast engine-idle speed of 900-1000rpm so that the car can be left parked with the air conditioning system operating – as then permitted in the US. Extra insulation was fitted to the exhaust system and ½in of thermal insulation was added inside the roof. Customers were recommended to specify Sundym tinted glass (a no-cost option with refrigeration) and choose light-coloured paintwork.

The Rolls-Royce underwing unit adds a pair of evaporator units to the main heater complex, and draws in fresh air (upper system) from the same wing-mounted vent as the heater, or recirculated air (lower system) from an intake on the floor behind the right-hand front seat. Switches and valves allow the air from either source to be passed across the heater matrix or across the evaporator unit, and then into the car in the usual way, boosted by the fans if required. Both upper and lower systems can be operated simultaneously.

There were three changes to the air conditioning system over the years. At the end of 1957, a 6in drive pulley was fitted to the compressor clutch of the Rolls-Royce type system from B186FA (early SGE series). The capacity of the boot-mounted system was increased with effect from B579FD (late SJF series) in early 1959, and a Purolator air filter was added to the system at B126GC (SMH or SNH series) in May 1959.

Long-Wheelbase Silver Cloud & S-series, 1957-59

The Rolls-Royce Silver Cloud and Bentley S-series long-wheelbase versions were announced in September 1957. They were intended to bridge a gap between the standard saloons and the coach-built Silver Wraith, by providing a car which could be used as a chauffeur-driven limousine during the working week and as an owner-driver saloon when required: an early sales brochure described the Rolls-Royce version as 'The Dual Purpose Silver Cloud'. The 127in wheelbase was just enough to make room for a division.

The long-wheelbase models have a chassis frame that is 4in longer than the standard type. It was supplied in this condition by the manufacturer, John Thompson Motor Pressings. The mechanical elements of the long-wheelbase cars

are the same as those of the standard-wheelbase models, except for a longer propeller shaft and a longer exhaust centre section. All the long-wheelbase cars have power-assisted steering as standard, although theoretically it was an optional extra, and all of them also have the dual hydraulic circuit for the front brakes. At 17ft 11¼in long, the long-wheelbase version was also 170lb heavier at 4750lb. The Silver Cloud LWB's UK price at introduction in 1957 was £6,893 17s (£6,893.85) compared with a total of £5,693 17s (£5,693.85) for the standard-wheelbase model. In November 1957 a Bentley LWB version was made available at the same price as the Rolls-Royce.

The bodies of the long-wheelbase cars all started life as standard saloons, which were sent

Externally the long-wheelbase model could be distinguished by the 4in longer rear door with bigger window and no quarter-light. This is Gerald Bonner's 1959 Silver Cloud (CLC35).

to the Rolls-Royce-owned Park Ward coachworks for conversion. They were cut in two behind the B/C-post, an extra 4in were inserted in the roof and floor, and longer rear doors were fitted. The lines of the standard car were retained; the most obvious change being that an additional front-hinged opening quarter-light window was inserted in the rear quarter panel behind the door. The bodyshells were then shipped to Crewe for finishing, trimming, and assembly to their chassis.

The long-wheelbase cars are identical to the standard-wheelbase models except where noted in the following text, which also gives production change details. All references are to cars with the converted standard steel bodywork, unless otherwise noted. All Bentley LWB chassis numbers have the prefix ALB; Rolls-Royce LWB versions are prefixed ALC, BLC or CLC.

Chassis

Chassis Frame
The long-wheelbase chassis has 127in between axle centres.

Chassis Lubrication System
The changes from centralised lubrication to grease lubrication in the steering elements of the front suspension took place in three stages. The first change was to the idler lever at BLC1; on the Bentley chassis, this change took place at approximately ALB6. The second change affected the track rod ends, at BLC18/ALB14, and the third affected the centre steering lever at chassis numbers BLC28/ALB17.

Front Suspension
The first type of modified stub axles was introduced in May 1958 at ALC25/ALB4. The second, strengthened type, arrived at BLC11/ALB6, and the stronger hubs came in at BLC38/ALB17. The seal between front bearing housing and damper was added at ALB30 and at or about CLC26.

Rear Axle & Rear Suspension
The stronger damper link bushes were introduced at ALC19, and were probably standard on all Bentley chassis.

Brakes
The improved expander wedges in the rear brakes were introduced at BLC18/ALB6. Two changes occurred at ALB17 (and somewhere between BLC28 and LBLC38). These were the enlarged shakeback stop slots in the brake shoe webs, and the re-routing of the handbrake cable. Plain washers were fitted to the pivot distance piece of the brake linkage at ALB25 and during the BLC series, and the modified front brake shoe links

came in at ALB31 and at some point after CLC26. The check valve was deleted from the brake fluid supply pipes at CLC31 and probably also late in the ALB series.

Engine

All the engines in the long-wheelbase chassis have the 8:1 compression ratio, big-valve cylinder head, and SU HD8 carburettors.

Cooling System
The heater/demister connections on the radiator were modified at BLC38/ALB29.

Exhaust System
This is lengthened to suit the increased wheelbase. The modified rear silencer mounting was fitted from BLC1.

Transmission

Propshaft
The three modifications made to the propshaft grease seal all affected long-wheelbase models as well. The first improved seal was introduced at BLC1 followed by the wire clip retainer at BLC5. The retainer reached Bentley chassis at ALB6, and the improved seal must have been fitted at or before that chassis. The second improved seal, with its longer neck, was introduced at chassis numbers CLC26/ALB30.

Electrical Components

Dynamo, Starter Motor Relay & Fuses
The Lucas C48 dynamo was fitted from BLC39/ALB21. The simplified starter relay mounting was introduced at ALB30 and at around CLC26. Modified clips and fuses for the electric windows, as well as modified fuses in the main fuse box, came in at ALB32 and late in the CLC series.

Body

The differences from the body on the standard-wheelbase cars are all behind the B/C pillar. The roof and floorpan are lengthened, and there are longer rear doors without separate quarter-lights, which are let into the rear quarter panels instead.

Front Wings
The larger-diameter fixing bolts for the front wings and valance panel came in at ALB21 and probably at around BLC39.

Scuttle
The twin-jet, centrally-mounted windscreen washer was fitted from BLC11/ALB11.

The extra 4in added in the Silver Cloud's wheelbase behind the centre pillar gives room for a glass division with folding tables and central console with radio speaker, cigar lighter, heater controls and division switch.

Doors

The front doors on the long-wheelbase models are the same as those on the standard-wheelbase car. The rear doors are longer. The door on the kerb side has a Yale lock and is locked with a key.

The improved door seals were introduced at ALC15 and were probably fitted to all Bentleys with the standard bodywork. Modified window channels arrived on ALB24 and probably early in the CLC series. From CLC8/ALB26, the modified door handles with button sealing were fitted.

Boot Lid

The freewheeling lock mechanism arrived at ALB26 and probably early in the CLC series.

Interior

Instruments

A black switch to operate the glass division from the driving seat was added to the facia panel just above the steering column. The thermal conductor type of water temperature gauge was fitted from ALB29 and during the BLC series.

Heater

Intermediate heater and demister controls were added to Rolls-Royce models at BLC1 and were probably fitted to all Bentleys.

Air Conditioning

This was an option but was fitted to most cars; the Rolls-Royce boot unit was specified for this model, except for the US where an American-supplied OMC unit was fitted. The first car fitted on production with the Purolator filter was Bentley chassis ALB35. The filter was probably fitted to Rolls-Royce models from mid-way through the CLC series.

Division

The majority of long-wheelbase models were fitted with an electrically-operated division between front and rear seats. This has a one-piece glass upper section, and the lower section has a deep capping of cross-banded veneered wood, with a grab-handle on either side. Below it are drop-down picnic tables with small chromed handles, similar to those in the seatbacks of the standard saloon. In the centre is a wood-veneered console, with various controls on its upper surface and a radio speaker low down on its rearward-facing side. The number and details of the controls vary, depending on the equipment fitted. The controls normally include those for the rear compartment heating, a switch to raise and lower the division, a radio volume control and a switch for the roof lamps in the rear compartment. On cars with air conditioning, the controls for this are also fitted in the console.

Sun Visors

The improved driver's sun visor arrived with chassis number ALB24 and was probably fitted from late in the BLC series.

Seats

The front seat squab is a fixed, single-piece unit with a fold-down central armrest. The bench front seat is adjustable, but only forwards from the division. The rear seat is identical to the standard saloon type.

Door Trims

The trim pads for the longer rear doors are obviously different from those fitted to the standard saloons, but they have a similar pattern. There is a long, chromed grab-handle on the vertical face of the wooden capping on each rear door.

The modified window winder handles were introduced on ALB26 and probably early in the CLC series.

PAINT & INTERIOR TRIM

Long-wheelbase cars had the same range of exterior colours and interior trim combinations as the standard steel cars.

IDENTIFICATION, DATING & PRODUCTION FIGURES

The chassis identification plate and chassis number on the frame for long-wheelbase models are found in the same place as on standard-wheelbase cars.

There were 121 long-wheelbase Rolls-Royce Silver Cloud chassis, to which must be added one prototype which was renumbered as a production vehicle and sold off. There were just 35 long-wheelbase chassis with Bentley badges. The lengthened standard steel body was fitted to 83 Rolls-Royce and 23 Bentley chassis; the remainder were coachbuilt models.

CHASSIS NUMBERS

The chassis number sequences for Rolls-Royce and Bentley long-wheelbase cars are set out here, together with delivery dates. All chassis numbers consist of three letters and up to two digits. The first letter denotes the chassis series. Cars with left-hand drive have an L before the prefix letters (eg LBLC46). Both odd and even numbers were used in all Rolls-Royce and Bentley sequences, but 13 was always omitted.

Rolls-Royce Silver Cloud Long Wheelbase

ALC1 to ALC26[1]	November 1957 to June 1958	
BLC1 to BLC51	February 1958 to January 1959	
CLC1 to CLC47	December 1958 to July 1959	

Bentley S-series Long Wheelbase

ALB1 to ALB36	November 1957 to July 1959	

[1] In addition, experimental chassis 28B was renumbered before sale as ALC1X.

ENGINE NUMBERS

Engine numbers are located at the front of the crankcase on the left-hand side, just above the engine mounting. The numbering sequences are consecutive, include 13, and are:

C1A to C25A	Rolls-Royce A-series chassis
C1B to C50B	Rolls-Royce B-series chassis
C1C to C46C	Rolls-Royce C-series chassis
B1A to B35A	Bentley chassis

Bentley Continental S-series, 1955-59

John Blatchley at Crewe was responsible for the styling of the Park Ward Continental S-series drophead coupé (above), which provided close-coupled seating for four people and 120mph performance. The H. J. Mulliner fastback body (left) on the S-series Continental chassis was one of three bodies available when the car was introduced and was enlarged from the R-type Continental body to fit the longer-wheelbase S-series chassis. This 1957 car is BC88BG.

The Continental derivative of the Bentley R-type had proved such a success that the eventual introduction of a successor on the S-series chassis was a foregone conclusion. The first Continental S-series chassis left Crewe for the coachbuilder on 29 March 1955, but the existence of a Continental derivative of the new Bentley was not announced until September that year. As before, the Continental chassis was designed for high speed motoring, with a more powerful engine and

Park Ward built open and closed versions of the same style for the Continental chassis, both of them derivatives of the company's offerings on the later R-type Continentals. This 1957 car (BC51CH) is one of the 89 drophead coupés. Note that the hood cover on this car matches the upholstery, but that the hood itself matches the body colour.

taller gearing. A reduced frontal area (to lessen aerodynamic drag) was a further characteristic of these cars, which all had coachbuilt bodies, and approved Continental bodywork was of lightweight construction.

Although the original R-type Continental had been available initially with only one body style, the number of approved styles had increased towards the end of production. So the Continental S-series was introduced with a choice of three body styles, and this number quickly increased. From 1957 there were four-door saloon bodies available on the Continental chassis as well as two-door sports saloon and drophead coupé types.

Fuller details of Continental S-series bodies are provided at the end of this chapter.

The mechanical and electrical elements of the Continentals are identical to those of the standard saloons except where indicated in the following text, which also details the production changeover points. The various bodies available are dealt with separately.

Chassis

The Continental chassis is essentially the same as the chassis used on other S-types. However, it has higher axle gearing of 2.923:1, and early cars have

Although similar to the H. J. Mulliner fastback body for the earlier Continental chassis, the S-series version has straighter wing lines and more pronounced fins at the rear.

a 7.25:1 compression 4887cc engine instead of the standard 6.6:1 ratio.

Chassis Frame
Welded stiffeners were added on either side of the jacking brackets at BC27BG, and the front ends of the side rails were splayed at BC37BG.

Chassis Lubrication System
The switch to grease lubrication was made in a single change at BC1FM, when the one-shot system was withdrawn from the idler lever, the track rod ends and the centre steering lever.

Front Suspension
At chassis BC11AF, a thick washer was added to the front suspension fulcrum bracket to spread the load over a larger area and to compensate for distortion of the lugs on the front pan. The stronger fulcrum bracket was introduced at BC3BG, and stronger fulcrum pins on the axle yoke at chassis BC41CH. From BC1FM, there were extended bearing blocks for the lower triangle lever – a suspension modification which affected only the Continental chassis.

The first strengthened drag links arrived at BC81AF, and the further modified links at BC36DJ. Strengthened spring support plates came in at BC96AF. The damper bodies were strengthened with a sleeve in the mounting bolt bore at BC1CH, stronger damper casings came in at BC7CH, and the dampers with larger end cover studs were fitted from BC47DJ. From BC16GN, a seal was fitted between the front dampers and the bearing housings.

Modified stub axle yoke seals were fitted from

BC8DJ, and strengthened front hubs were specified at BC14FM. From BC20EL, the radius of the stub axles immediately behind the inner hub bearings was modified.

Rear Axle & Rear Suspension
All Continental chassis have higher axle gearing of 2.923:1. Modified bosses increased the strength of the rear axle tube at BC12AF, and there are stronger Z-bar clamps from BC69AF. The rear axle tube with additional fixing holes was introduced at BC1BG, and there are additional fixing holes in the centre casing from chassis BC62BG.

The Flying Spur body by H. J. Mulliner was the first four-door style approved for the Continental chassis, and was once again of lightweight alloy construction. This 1959 left-hand-drive example (BC44LFM) shows off the sporting yet eminently practical lines of the body.

The facia of the Mulliner Continental body for the S-series was different. This detail shows the centre section, which of course uses the standard instruments and switches but with a re-arranged layout. This radio is not original.

H. J. Mulliner's Flying Spur four-door saloon, design 7443, had a six-light configuration although there were some four-light cars.

The facia of the Flying Spur is different again, but the vertical pairing of the switches on either side of the central switchbox reflects the style chosen for Mulliner's fastback body on the S-series Continental chassis. Only Continentals had a rev counter.

The extra pair of doors, increased rear legroom and bigger boot were the main attractions of the Flying Spur body. Access to the rear seats could be achieved with some elegance, whereas agility was required on the two-door bodies! Note the matching loose cushions supplied with this car.

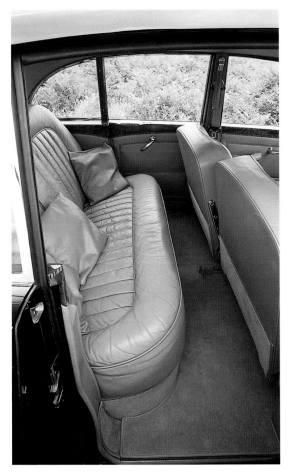

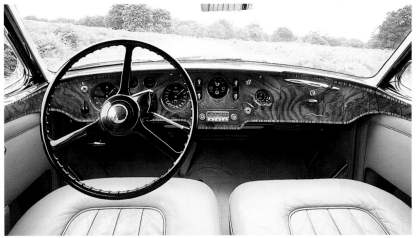

From this angle, the Flying Spur facia looks busy. By 1957 the vogue for plain cushions with pleated seat backs had passed. The seat belts are a later addition.

Modified axle shaft flanges arrived at BC10DJ and the larger-diameter axle shaft splines at BC1FM. There were three damper modifications: oil deflector plates were added at BC92BG, stronger damper bushes were fitted from BC3EL, and dampers with larger end cover studs were introduced at BC47DJ.

From BC101BG, the Z-bar on the rear axle is fitted with rubber bushes and no longer has an anti-roll function, but instead serves only as a radius rod to counter spring wind-up under torque. This was found to improve directional stability and to increase understeer.

Brakes

The brakes of the Continental chassis are the same as the standard car. The twin master cylinders for the front brake dual hydraulic circuit are fitted to Continental chassis beginning with BC16BG, and chassis from BC44FM have no check valve in the fluid supply pipes. The brake fluid reservoir has a filter from chassis number BC70AF. The aluminium brake master cylinder was introduced at BC88AF. On BC28BG and all later chassis, the pipes run uphill from the twin master cylinder to the supply reservoirs.

The servo sealing was improved at BC16AF, and again at BC4CH, and the load on the servo return spring was increased at BC21AF. At BC1FM, the handbrake cable was re-routed, and from BC31FM the distance piece on the direct and intermediate brake linkage was fitted with plain washers.

As far as the braking components at the wheels were concerned, there were aluminium wheel cylinders until BC68AF, and the cast iron type were fitted from BC69AF. The friction on the brake shake-back stops was increased at BC21AF, and the modified stops were introduced at BC6BG. Then from BC11FM there were enlarged shake-back stop slots in the brake shoe webs. The modified front brake shoe links were introduced at BC28GN. At the rear, chassis number BC1FM brought improved expander wedges with more side clearance to prevent them sticking.

Steering

Castle nuts with larger bearing surfaces were fitted to the ball joints at BC19AF, and taper roller bearings replaced bushes on the steering lever at BC2BG. From BC44DJ there is a stronger adjusting sleeve on the steering cam.

Power-assisted steering became optional from early in the B-series. The first chassis built with PAS appears to have been BC21BG. Many later BG-series chassis were converted to PAS before

The Park Ward interior has an appealing air of restrained elegance. Note the seat belts, a later addition coloured to tone in with the upholstery. The Park Ward facia was different yet again, although there are similarities to the Mulliner designs. Note the vertically-paired switches flanking of the central switchbox. This steering wheel is not original.

delivery, presumably as word got around to customers about it. The last Continental with manual steering was BC33EL in February 1958. The sealing ring on the centre steering lever was modified at BC23BG, and the power cylinder mounting bolt was reversed at BC70BG.

Fuel Pipes & Pumps
Copper petrol pipes arrived with chassis BC28BG, and the improved stone guard for the fuel pumps at chassis BC29BG.

Wheels & Tyres
The standard tyres are narrower than the saloon type at 7.60-15, but some cars were fitted with an intermediate size of 8.00-15 to suit heavier bodywork. The normal tyre pressures are 27psi at the front and 30psi at the rear, but the owners of Continentals with 7.60-15 tyres were advised to lower the pressures to 22psi and 24psi respectively for better comfort, except for high-speed motoring. For sustained speeds of 100mph or more, 30psi front and 35psi rear were recommended.

Engine

Block, Head & Fittings
Early Continental engines up to chassis BC19BG have a 7.25:1 compression ratio (instead of the 6.6:1 of the standard engine) and two 1¾in SU HD6 carburettors. From BC21BG, Continentals have the same big-valve, twin-HD8 carburettor engine with 8:1 compression as the standard cars.

The engine modifications on production were otherwise the same as those for the standard cars. Internally, setscrews replaced studs on the main bearing caps at BC16AF. The combined inertia and starter ring on the flywheel, together with the stiffened clutch casing, came in at BC31CH, and the Roto-finished pulleys at BC42DJ.

There is a discrepancy in Rolls-Royce records over the introduction of the modified rear engine mounting and bracket. According to Service Bulletins, it arrived at BC28AF, but the Rolls-Royce Chassis Numbers Booklet gives BC79AF. A further modified bracket and larger-diameter rear mounting bolts were fitted at BC96AF.

Carburettors
Modified butterfly valves and countersunk screws were introduced together at BC11AF.

Cooling System
A modified radiator to suit the splayed frame was fitted from BC30BG. As on the standard chassis, this was before the frame itself was modified.

Exhaust System
The modified rear silencer mounting was introduced at BC1FM.

The engine compartment of the Continental is laid out in much the same way as that of the standard S-series saloons. Note, however, the Vokes air cleaner on this example. Cream paint is used on all flat surfaces around the engine bay, to facilitate maintenance.

Transmission

Automatic transmission was always standard on the Continental S-series, and it featured different governor settings from the standard saloon in order to give higher upchange speeds consistent with the Continental's more sporting pretensions. The Continental retained the same internal automatic gearbox ratios as the standard saloon but the overall gearing was higher. Overall gear ratios were: First 11.164:1, Second 7.699:1, Third 4.238:1, Fourth 2.923:1 and Reverse 12.587:1.

Nevertheless, between September 1956 and March 1957, 17 chassis were built to special order with the synchromesh gearbox fitted to R-type Continentals coupled with the higher 2.923:1 final drive ratio. This gave overall gear ratios of: First 7.804:1, Second 4.501:1, Third 3.554:1, Fourth 2.923:1 and Reverse 8.363:1. All these cars were RHD and their chassis numbers were: BC56BG, BC59BG, BC60BG, BC62BG, BC63BG, BC64BG, BC65BG, BC66BG, BC71BG, BC72BG, BC73BG, BC74BG, BC75BG, BC76BG, BC79BG, BC81BG and BC95BG.

Propshaft

From BC28BG, the ball joint and trunnion body between gearbox output shaft and propshaft was spot-faced and fitted with a reach nut and washer. The propshaft grease seals were altered at BC1DJ (neoprene seal), BC1FM (wire clip fasteners) and BC25GN (seal with longer neck).

Electrical Components

Dynamo & Voltage Regulator

The E-type dynamo and M-type voltage regulator are fitted to chassis from BC21BG. The H-type regulator arrived with chassis BC96BG.

Starter Motor & Relay

The longer starter drive was fitted at BC31CH, and the simplified mounting for the starter relay at chassis BC1GN.

Windscreen Wiper Motor

The Lucas DR3 type of windscreen wiper motor was fitted from chassis number BC1EL in 1957.

Body

The Continental chassis was supplied to coachbuilders from Crewe with inner wing panels and bulkhead attached. The bulkhead is shorter than the standard type to mate up with the radiator grille which is 1½in lower than the type fitted to standard saloons. The steering column is more steeply raked, to suit these modifications and to give a more sporting driving position.

There were 432 Continental S-series cars, of which 430 were production models and two were prototypes sold off by the factory. H. J. Mulliner bodied 217 of them, Park Ward 187, James Young 20, Hooper 6, and Graber and Franay one each. Chassis numbers of cars bodied by individual coachbuilders are given on the facing page.

Just two production modifications were made which are (at least theoretically) common to all body types. These were the introduction, at BC1FM, of larger-diameter front wing and valance fixing bolts, and the fitting of a single central twin-jet windscreen washer nozzle.

A small number of other changes also affected all Continentals. At BC1FM, the intermediate type of heater and demister controls were fitted, and the capacity of the optional boot-mounted air conditioning system was increased. A Purolator filter was fitted with this system from BC30GN. From BC9GN, the thermal conductor type of water temperature gauge was fitted.

PAINT & INTERIOR TRIM

As the Continental was always seen as a coachbuilt car, which was built to individual order, there were no standard paint finishes or trim colours. Customers could – and did – choose from the range offered on the standard saloons, but also cars were painted or trimmed in other colours to the individual customer's choice.

IDENTIFICATION, DATING & PRODUCTION FIGURES

The chassis identification plate and chassis number on the frame for Continental models are found in the same place as on cars with the standard chassis. There were 430 production Bentley Continental S-series chassis, plus two prototypes which were later sold off by the factory

CHASSIS NUMBERS

The chassis number sequences for these cars are set out here, together with delivery dates. Bentley Continental chassis numbers have the prefix BC followed by up to three digits and two suffix letters, the first of which denotes the chassis series. Left-hand-drive cars have an L before the suffix letters (eg BC46LEL). Both odd and even numbers were used in all sequences, but 13 was always omitted.

BC1AF to BC101AF[1]	March 1955 to February 1956
BC1BG to BC101BG	February 1956 to January 1957
BC1CH to BC51CH	January to July 1957
BC1DJ to BC51DJ	July 1957 to January 1958
BC1EL to BC51EL	October 1957 to June 1958
BC1FM to BC51FM	June 1958 to January 1959
BC1GN to BC31GN	December 1958 to April 1959

[1] To this sequence must be added BC102AF, renumbered from experimental car 27B.

Experimental chassis 26B was also sold off by the factory in 1962, but retained its original chassis number. It was fitted originally with a Park Ward drophead coupé body but following an accident in 1956 was rebodied as a Park Ward two-door saloon.

ENGINE NUMBERS

Bentley Continental engine numbers are located at the front of the crankcase on the left-hand side, just above the engine mounting. The numbering sequences are consecutive, include 13, and are:

BC1A to BC100A	A-series chassis
BC1B to BC100B	B-series chassis
BC1C to BC50C	C-series chassis
BC1D to BC50D	D-series chassis
BC1E to BC50E	E-series chassis
BC1F to BC50F	F-series chassis
BC1G to BC30G	G-series chassis

CONTINENTAL S-SERIES BODIES

Bentley Continental S-series chassis were fitted with coachbuilt bodies from the companies listed below.

H. J. MULLINER & CO LTD

All the bodies built by H. J. Mulliner on the Continental S-series chassis were closed types, except for one. The exception was a drophead coupé built on chassis number BC37FM in 1958. Mulliner's major designs were the two-door sports saloon derived from the fastback body on the R-type Continental, and the magnificent Flying Spur, which was the first four-door style to be fitted to a Continental chassis.

The two-door sports saloon, design 7400, was one of the three bodies available at the beginning of Continental S-series production. It is very similar to the R-type Continental body, but is modified to suit the longer wheelbase of the S-series chassis, and has a higher, straight-through wing line with scallops on the rear wings. It also has no rear wheel spats, which were no longer fashionable. The rear wings have special tail lamps, which are the same as those used on the contemporary Alvis body built by Park Ward, and there are two round reversing lamps above the rear number plate box. The facia design is very similar to its R-type counterpart, but the seats are much heavier and have a pleated and bolstered style.

This body style was developed in later years to have a closer resemblance to the Flying Spur. The later version is design 7466, and it has a higher swage line (scallop) on the rear wings, sidelights in nacelles on top of the front wings and a slight flare to the wheelarches. There are also detail interior changes. A total of 20 cars had this later body style.

Mulliner's 7500 design is another two-door, four-light style. Its rear wings carry fins intended to give stability at speed. The windscreen and standard heated rear window are both laminated. Between the front seats is a lidded box, and there are transparent tinted sun visors. The spare wheel is carried flat on the boot floor, under a loose cover.

The Flying Spur, design 7443, was announced in 1957. It was named after the family crest of Arthur Johnstone, Mulliner's Managing Director, and set out to be more practical than existing Continental bodies with its four doors and larger boot. Initially Rolls-Royce would not allow the association of the Continental name with a four-door body and the earliest advertising makes no mention of the fact that the chassis is that of the Continental!

The overall lines of the Flying Spur were derived from a four-door Mulliner saloon on the standard chassis. This body was discontinued when the Flying Spur was introduced. The new body offered more headroom and legroom for rear seat passengers than Mulliner's existing fastback two-door Continental body.

The lightweight construction which made this six-light design suitable for the Continental chassis was achieved by a framework of light alloy with the pillars and main floor in steel. The exterior panels are all aluminium, and the windscreen and rear window are of Triplex laminated glass, while other windows are in Triplex toughened glass. Upholstery was available in either leather or West of England cloth, and the rear seat has a single bench-type cushion but a divided backrest.

There were a number of extra options: electric windows in the front doors only, an electric radio aerial, fitted suitcases, Sundym tinted glass (made by Triplex), seat covers, extra floor covers and rugs, and picnic and cocktail fittings. Both single colours and two-tone paintwork were available.

There is a rare four-light variant of the Flying Spur body with blind rear quarters, and a small number of cars were bodied with a two-door derivative of the Flying Spur style in 1959. The 217 Continental chassis bodied by H. J. Mulliner were:

A series: BC3AF, BC6AF, BC8AF, BC9AF, BC11AF, BC12AF, BC14AF, BC18AF, BC20AF, BC32LAF, BC36LAF, BC38AF, BC40AF, BC41AF, BC43AF, BC45AF, BC47LAF, BC49AF, BC50AF, BC51LAF, BC53AF, BC55AF, BC58AF, BC60AF, BC62AF, BC64AF, BC65AF, BC66AF, BC69AF, BC71AF, BC73AF, BC77AF, BC79AF, BC81AF, BC82AF, BC84AF, BC85AF, BC87LAF, BC88AF, BC90AF, BC92AF, BC93AF, BC94AF, BC96LAF, BC97AF, BC98AF, BC99AF, BC100AF, BC101AF and BC102AF.

B series: BC1BG, BC2BG, BC4LGB, BC5LGB, BC6BG, BC9BG, BC10BG, BC11BG, BC12BG, BC14BG, BC15LBG, BC16BG, BC17BG, BC19LBG, BC21BG, BC28BG, BC29BG, BC37BG, BC38BG, BC39BG, BC41BG, BC42BG, BC46BG, BC51BG, BC53BG, BC54BG, BG55BG, BC56BG, BC58BG, BC60BG, BC62BG, BC64BG, BC65BG, BC66BG, BC69BG, BC70LBG, BC71BG, BC72BG, BC74BG, BC75BG, BC76BG, BC79BG, BC81BG, BC83BG, BC86BG, BC87BG, BC88BG, BC89BG, BC90BG, BC92BG, BC95BG, BC96LBG, BC97LBG, BC99BG and BC101LBG.

C series: BC2CH, BC4LCH, BC6LCH, BC7LCH, BC8LCH, BC9LCH, BC14CH, BC15CH, BC16CH, BC19CH, BC24CH, CB28CH, BC29LCH, BC32LCH, BC33CH, BC34CH, BC36LCH, BC37LCH, BC45CH, BC46CH, BC47CH and BC50LCH.

D series: BC4LDJ, BC6DJ, BC7DJ, BC12DJ, BC14DJ, BC16DJ, BC22DJ, BC23LDJ, BC24DJ, BC28LDJ, BC29LDJ, BC30DJ, BC31DJ, BC32LDJ, BC33DJ, BC34DJ, BC37DJ, BC39DJ, BC40DJ, BC41DJ, BC43DJ, BC45DJ, BC49DJ and BC51DJ.

E series: BC1EL, BC2EL, BC3EL, BC5EL, BC6EL, BC8EL, BC10EL, BC11LEL, BC12EL, BC14LEL, BC17EL, BC19EL, BC22LEL, BC26EL, BC28LEL, BC31EL, BC33LEL, BC34LEL, BC35EL, BC36EL, BC37EL, BC38LEL, BC42EL, BC44EL, BC45EL, BC46LEL and BC51LEL.

F series: BC2FM, BC8FM, BC9FM, BC14FM, BC16FM, BC17FM, BC19FM, BC21FM, BC24FM, BC26FM, BC27FM, BC28FM, BC30FM, BC31FM, BC32LFM, BC35FM, BC37FM, BC41LFM, BC43LFM, BC44LFM, BC45FM, BC46FM, BC47FM, BC50FM and BC51LFM.

G series: BC1GN, BC2LGN, BC3LGN, BC8GN, BC11GN, BC17GN, BC19GN, BC21GN, BC22GN, BC25GN, BC26GN, BC27GN, BC29GN and BC30LGN.

PARK WARD & CO LTD

The other two body styles available from the beginning of Continental S-series production were from Park Ward. These were a two-door sports saloon and a drophead coupé. Both had been introduced on the later R-type Continentals, and were variants of the same design. They differed only in small details from the R-type Continental bodies, mainly to accommodate the longer wheelbase of the S-series.

By about 1957, the design had been modified to incorporate fins on the rear wings, which sales literature claimed aided stability at speed. A later variant of the two-door sports saloon has longer rear quarter-lights and a three-piece, wraparound rear window.

Of the 187 Continental chassis bodied by Park Ward, 89 are known to have drophead bodies. Not included in this latter total or the following lists is experimental chassis 26B, which started life with a Park Ward drophead body and was rebodied as a saloon before being sold by the factory.

TWO-DOOR SALOONS:
A series: BC10AF, BC16LAF, BC21AF, BC24AF, BC25AF, BC26LAF, BC27LAF, BC29LAF, BC30AF, BC31LAF, BC33AF, BC35AF, BC37AF, BC39AF, BC44AF, BC46AF, BC48LAF, BC52AF, BC56LAF, BC59AF, BC61AF, BC67AF, BC68AF, BC70AF, BC72AF, BC74AF, BC78AF, BC80AF, BC89AF and BC91AF.

B series: BC3BG, BC8BG, BC18BG, BC20LBG, BC23LBG, BC30BG, BC31BG, BC32BG, BC34BG, BC36BG, BC43BG, BC44BG, BC45BG, BC47BG, BC48LBG, BC49LBG, BC50BG, BC57BG, BC59BG, BC61BG, BC63BG, BC67BG, BC68BG, BC73BG, BC80BG, BC82BG, BC84BG, BC85BG and BC94LBG.

C series: BC1CH, BC3LCH, BC11LCH, BC22LCH, BC23LCH, BC27CH, BC31LCH, BC35LCH, BC38LCH, BC39LCH, BC44LCH, BC48LCH and BC49CH.

D series: BC1LDJ, BC5DJ, BC19LDJ, BC26LDJ, BC35LDJ, BC36DJ and BC38DJ.

E series: BC15LEL, BC16EL, BC21EL, BC24EL and BC48LEL.

F series: BC3LFM, BC4FM, BC5FM, BC11FM, BC20FM, BC33LFM, BC38FM and BC49LFM.

G series: BC7GN, BC9GN, BC12LGN, BC23GN and BC24GN.

DROPHEAD COUPÉS:
A series: BC1AF, BC2AF, BC4AF, BC5AF, BC7AF, BC15LAF, BC19AF, BC22AF, BC23LAF, BC28AF, BC34AF, BC42AF, BC54LAF, BC57AF, BC63AF, BC75AF, BC76AF, BC83LAF, BC86AF and BC95AF.

B series: BC7LBG, BC22LBG, BC24LBG, BC26LBG, BC27BG, BC33BG, BC35BG, BC40BG, BC52BG, BC77BG, BC78BG, BC91LGB, BC93BG, BC98BG and BC100BG.

C series: BC5LCH, BC10LCH, BC12CH, BC18LCH, BC20LCH, BC21LCH, BC30LCH, BC40LCH, BC41LCH, BC42CH, BC43LCH and BC51CH.

D series: BC2LDJ, BC3LDJ, BC8DJ, BC9DJ, BC10DJ, BC15LDJ, BC20LDJ, BC25LDJ, BC27LDJ, BC42LDJ, BC44DJ, BC48DJ and BC50DJ.

E series: BC4EL, BC7EL, BC9EL, BC18LEL, BC20EL, BC27EL, BC32LEL, BC39EL, BC40EL, BC41EL and BC50EL.

F series: BC1FM, BC10FM, BC12LFM, BC15FM, BC22FM, BC25LFM, BC29FM, BC34FM, BC39FM and BC40LFM.

G series: BC4GN, BC10GN, BC14LGN, BC15GN, BC18GN, BC20LGN, BC28GN and BC31GN.

JAMES YOUNG LTD

James Young built 20 Continental bodies, beginning in 1957 with a four-door saloon on BC17CH. Most of the remaining bodies also had four doors, but some were two-door versions of the same style. The James Young bodies are quite similar to the contemporary Park Ward offering, but appear rather longer. They can be recognised easily by their distinctive door handles with square push-buttons. Chassis are: BC17CH, BC25CH, BC26CH, BC11DJ, BC17DJ, BC21DJ, BC46DJ, BC47DJ, BC23LEL, BC25LEL, BC29EL, BC30EL, BC47LEL, BC49EL, BC6FM, BC18FM, BC23FM, BC36FM, BC42LFM and BC48FM.

HOOPER & CO (COACHBUILDERS) LTD

There were six Hooper-bodied Continentals, all to four-door Design 8512. They were on chassis BC18DJ, BC43EL, BC7FM, BC5LGN, BC6GN and BC16GN.

CARROSSERIES GRABER & FRANAY

Just two cars were bodied outside Britain, both during 1957. Graber's effort was a drophead coupé on BC25BG, delivered in March and displayed on the coachbuilder's stand at that year's Geneva Show. The Franay body was a saloon, delivered in November on chassis BC17LAF.

Rolls-Royce Silver Cloud II & Bentley S2, 1959-62

The main distinguishing feature of the Silver Cloud II and Bentley S2 ranges, introduced in September 1959, is their new 6230cc V8 engine. This gives them appreciably better performance than the six-cylinder models which preceded them, with a maximum speed of about 115mph (as against 105mph for the final six-cylinders) and 0-60mph in 11.5sec (as against 13sec).

The cars are visually indistinguishable from the six-cylinder types, although there are several hidden specification differences. This time, the Rolls-Royce badged version of the standard chassis

outsold the Bentley equivalent by a factor of almost four to three, with 2417 production cars against 1863. The cars were more expensive in standard form than the six-cylinder models which they replaced. At £5660 14s 2d (£5660.70) in the UK, the Bentley S2 cost £259 more and the Silver Cloud II at £5802 7s 6d (£5802.37) was £269 more than the models they replaced when those were fitted with the optional power-assisted steering, standard on the V8-engined cars.

The Rolls-Royce and Bentley models are identical in all respects except where indicated. The

The Bentley S2 was indistinguishable from the six-cylinder S-series cars. This beautiful 1960 two-tone model (B395BR) in Sage Green over Smoke Green belongs to Frank Parkin.

The Silver Cloud II was equally indistinguishable from the earlier model. This 1962 Dawn Blue car is owned by Geoffrey Bates.

Two-tone paintwork always made the cars look longer, as demonstrated by this rear view of the 1960 S2.

starting-point for all specifications, unless otherwise stated, is the final production specification for the six-cylinder models. Chassis numbers for Rolls-Royce Silver Cloud IIs have a sequence of three letters and up to three numbers (eg SPA326). Bentley S2 chassis numbers start with the letter B followed by one, two or three digits and two letters (eg B325AA); Bentley Continen-

tals have the prefix BC. Left-hand-drive cars are identified by an L before the chassis letters.

Chassis

Chassis Frame

The engine mountings are different, to accommodate the wider V8 engine.

Chassis Lubrication System

There is no centralised chassis lubrication system. Instead, there are 21 long-life grease lubrication points for the front suspension and steering.

Front Suspension & Steering

The load-carrying elements of the front suspension on these cars are all stronger than those fitted to the earlier Silver Clouds and S-series Bentleys. This is not because the V8 engine is significantly heavier than the six-cylinder type, but because the same suspension components are used for the bigger and heavier Phantom V limousine chassis which was contemporary with the Silver Cloud II and S2. The wishbones, for example, are forged rather than pressed, and the anti-roll bar is stiffer.

The basic design of the front suspension remained unchanged throughout the production life of these cars. However, the dampers were changed twice during 1960. They were first given stronger casings with new mounting plates at SWC44/B1CT, and then were further strengthened with new bodies at SXC623/B392CU.

Power-assisted steering is standard on the Silver Cloud II and Bentley S2. The wider V8 engine made it necessary to relocate the steering box outside the frame, and the steering column is more steeply raked than on the six-cylinder models. A pair of pinions links the column to the steering box, so that the column remains in its original place relative to the centre line of the chassis. The pump for the power-assisted steering is a Hobourn Eaton type, and is driven by a vee-belt from the crankshaft pulley.

The steering was lightened on left-hand-drive cars with effect from LSAE441/B192LDW in June 1962 (although Silver Cloud LSAE443 had the earlier, heavier, type).

Rear Axle & Rear Suspension

The final drive ratio on the Silver Cloud II/S2 is 3.077:1 (13/40), this higher ratio being permitted by the greater power and torque of the V8 engine as compared to the older six-cylinder.

The final drive was modified twice during the early months of production in 1959. Stepped fixing bolts improved the attachment of the crown wheel at SPA260/B186AA. Further improved bolts were introduced at chassis numbers SRA181/ B258AM.

The Z-bar on the rear axle is rubber-bushed and, as on the final six-cylinder Bentley S-series Continentals, it no longer has an anti-roll function but serves only as a radius rod.

Brakes

The brake servo was modified in May 1960, to increase the internal working clearances between the pressure plate and the ends of the friction plate drive pins. The change took place at chassis numbers SVB351 and B166BS. Retrospective modification of earlier cars (by shortening the pins) was advised if the servo had to be removed, and retailers were instructed to put a spot of blue paint on the gearbox rear extension to show that the modification had been carried out.

The brake servo cam angles were modified yet again (to 47°) in late 1960 to alter the ratio of braking effort between front and rear. The change took place at B576CU and during late SWC-series or early SXC-series production. Further back along the braking system, and on left-hand-drive chassis only, the bell crank lever of the intermediate brake system was fitted with an additional washer. This modification was introduced on LSAE379 and B154LDW.

The front brakes were fitted with improved clevis pins from November 1961. These had a bronze-coloured finish rather than the cadmium-plated finish of the older pins, and retailers were recommended to fit them to earlier cars as and when work was being done on the front brakes. The modification was introduced on production at chassis numbers LSZD503 and B554CU.

All service replacement brake linings after October 1964 were of the shortened type introduced on Silver Cloud III production in October 1963 to alleviate brake squeal.

Fuel Tank, Filters & Pumps

The tank is the same type as fitted on the earlier six-cylinder chassis, and the layout of the pipes, filters and pumps is the same. Larger-capacity pumps are fitted to Bentley chassis from B28DW in late 1961; the first Rolls-Royce chassis to have them was SAE 103.

Air locks could prevent the fuel tank from being filled to the brim, and so a vent pipe was added on production during May 1961 at SYD408/B81DV, and Rolls-Royce retailers were instructed to fit it as a retrospective modification. This pipe is connected by a rubber hose to a second vent pipe in the filler tube assembly.

Bumpers

The bumper supports were the same as on six-cylinder models until summer 1961, when new support springs were fitted at B231DV. The change probably affected Rolls-Royce chassis from early in the SZD series.

Tyres

Tyre recommendations differed over the years of Silver Cloud II and Bentley S2 production. The recommended size was always 8.20-15, and all recommended types were available with either white or black sidewalls. Original equipment tyres were either Dunlop Fort C or Avon Safety, except for

From this angle the 1961 Silver Cloud II H. J. Mulliner convertible coupé (SZD43) looks like a saloon which has been decapitated, which is exactly what it is. Door and rear-quarter windows can be lowered completely but the hinged quarter-light remains. A modified chromed waist moulding is fitted. The folded hood's detachable cover stands proud. The convertible coupé's hood (right and below) has a PVC backlight, measuring 35in by 11½in, and the rear quarters are very blind with only small quarter-lights.

the US where Firestone tyres were usually fitted. Tyre pressures were 22psi at the front and 27psi at the rear for all conditions.

The replacement tyre types recommended in February 1960 were: Dunlop C Rayon WH2 (UK, US, Canada and Europe), Dunlop Fort C Rayon WH2 (other territories). From December 1961, the recommendations were: Avon HM Ribbed Airseal Safety, Dunlop Elite C40 (tubeless), Dunlop Fort C WH4, Firestone P345 (with either rayon or nylon casing), India Super Nylon WH4. The recommended winter tyres (on the rear wheels only) were 8.00-15 or 8.20-15 Dunlop Heavy Duty Weathermaster or 8.00-15 Firestone Town and Country tyres, running at 30psi and restricted to sustained speeds below 80mph.

Engine

The 6230cc V8 is an all-alloy engine, with press-fit cast-iron wet liners. It has oversquare dimensions (with the bore of 104.14mm being greater than the 91.44mm stroke) and was the first such engine to come from Rolls-Royce, being designed by Jack Phillips and his team at Crewe. They decided on LM8 silicon/aluminium alloy for good corrosion resistance, so the V8 weighs around 30lb less than the six-cylinder B60 despite being around 25 per cent more powerful than the last of the earlier engines. Its output has been estimated at over 200bhp, with torque of around 325lb ft. The compression ratio is 8:1 for all engines.

The V8 engine has a five-bearing crankshaft and a single gear-driven camshaft in the centre of the vee. The overhead valves have self-adjusting hydraulic tappets. The twin SU carburettors are on a pent-roof manifold which allows each carburettor to feed cylinders one and four on one bank and cylinders two and three on the other. The sparking plugs are underneath the exhaust ports, and those on the right-hand side can be reached only through an inspection panel in the wheelarch when the engine is installed in the car; the road wheel also has to be removed first! However, in July 1961 Rolls-Royce overcame this major inconvenience by making available to their retailers a ratchet-type plug spanner (part number RH7327) which allowed sparking plug changes to be made from above.

From chassis numbers SRA321 and B288AM in December 1959, a vibration cushion was fitted under the engine.

Block & Timing Case

For the first time on any Rolls-Royce there was a pressed steel sump, for ease of repair if it was damaged in some far-flung corner of the world.

In November 1961, at B457DV and during the SZD series, the starter ring on the flywheel was modified. Unfortunately, this supposed improvement was not satisfactory and the original type of ring was substituted a few months later at B208DW and during the SAE series.

From LSAE91 and some point in the DW series, left-hand-drive cars were fitted with a fully-enclosed crankcase breather system. This was never fitted to the engines of right-hand-drive cars during production.

Cylinder Heads

The cylinder heads are interchangeable and the gaskets between their joint faces and the cylinder block are made of corrugated steel.

Valvegear & Camshaft

It is quite clear from the number of changes made to the valvegear during the first two years of production that this was a weak point on the V8 engine. The problems were mainly associated with excessive wear and consequent noise. The valves, rockers, rocker shafts, camshaft and hydraulic tappets were all changed – in some cases, more than once – and special attention was paid to lubrication of the camshaft.

It was camshaft lubrication that first received attention, shortly after the V8-engined cars had entered production. A solid camshaft replaced the hollow type from SPA314/B80AM (but not on B322AM), although the new camshaft had been fitted on several chassis from SPA272 and B35AA. This second type of camshaft could not be fitted retrospectively to earlier engines. A third scheme was introduced at SRA5/B325AA, with a slightly modified camshaft, which was interchangeable with the second type. However, the second type of camshaft continued to be fitted on several SRA-series and AM-series chassis, and the third scheme did not become standard until approximately SRA105/B74AM. To be on the safe side, the oil level in the camshaft trough was also increased during November 1960 by a modification to the crankcase at B562CU/SWC320. Early 1962 then brought improved camwheel lubrication from a revised oil jet fitted at chassis numbers SAE507/B222DW.

Several improvements were made to valvegear components in 1960 and 1961. Although Rolls-Royce service literature provides precise changeover points for most of them, this was clearly a period of quite rapid change on the production lines and the chassis numbers given here should be regarded with some caution. June 1960 brought modified hydraulic tappets, initially bought in from Chicago Screw in the US but by this stage being manufactured by Rolls-Royce. The revised tappets incorporated flats and were introduced at SVB431/B246BS. Then valves and valve mechanism were modified at B2CU in November 1960; the equivalent change on Rolls-Royce chassis may have been made at SXC1. A second modification that month brought packing for the valve stems at SXC19/B52CU. Not long afterwards at SXC389 and B398CU, bushless rockers were fitted. These were hardened all over and came with a flatted rocker shaft. The rockers appear to have been modified further during 1961 at B142DW and probably on SAE series Rolls-Royce chassis.

Sparking Plug Caps

From June 1961, at chassis numbers SZD39 and B231DV, waterproof sparking plug adaptor caps are fitted. They are made by Champion and have the HT lead bonded into the adaptor with an adhesive compound.

The Bentley (or Rolls-Royce) name is carried on both tappet covers of the V8 engine. Accessibility is not a strong point: the sparking plugs (below the manifold) on the right-hand cylinder bank are only just visible in this picture.

The air cleaner can be swung out of the way when the left-hand bonnet lid is raised. Also visible here are the Lucas electric windscreen washer with its glass reservoir, and the high-mounted dynamo alongside the reservoir for the standard power-assisted steering. Once again, the bulkhead is finished in a light colour to aid maintenance.

The radiator on the V8-engined cars was fitted with a fan shroud to aid cooling. Note the twin belt drives to the dynamo and steering pump.

Carburettors & Automatic Choke

The V8 engines have two SU type HD6 1¾in carburettors mounted on a pent-roof inlet manifold. Each carburettor feeds two cylinders on its own side of the engine and two on the opposite bank. A Rolls-Royce automatic choke is standard, and incorporates a Scintilla thermal delay switch. This is mounted to the bulkhead by a single 3BA screw. From SRA33/B192AM in December 1959, a neoprene washer was added between the switch and the bulkhead to seal the switch against water.

The carburettors remained largely unchanged throughout the production life of these cars. Just one modification is recorded, when the jet assemblies were changed at chassis numbers LSWC130 and B452BS in July 1960 in an attempt to overcome hot-starting problems. Some earlier cars were fitted with the new jets on production, and these had an M stamped on the carburettor flange adjacent to the serial number.

Problems with the automatic choke gave rise to a number of modifications over the years. High under-bonnet temperatures could cause the choke to close, and the hot-spot could become chilled at high speeds in cold weather and partially prevent the choke from closing. So in late 1959, at B112LAM and late in the SPA series, an Otter switch was wired in series with the thermal delay switch to cure the first problem. The Otter switch was fitted to the bulkhead with two self-tapping screws. The second problem was cured in two stages. First of all the hot air pipes were lagged with asbestos from chassis number B409BR, and then a shield was fitted over the bi-metal coil housing at chassis number B437BR. The corresponding changeover points on Rolls-Royce chassis were somewhere in the STB series.

Not long after these changes, B471BR became the first chassis with a modified choke butterfly valve. This had a radiused section on its leading edge, designed to maintain the valve in a stable position when the throttle was fully open. This new valve was almost certainly the otherwise unidentified modification to the choke carried out on Rolls-Royce chassis at STB282. A further change – the last for some time – came in June 1960 at SWC184/B462BS when the mounting of the fast-idle cam on its bracket was revised.

The next round of changes to the automatic choke started in autumn 1961, when cars destined for the UK and for Europe were fitted with an aluminium heat sink. This was designed to retain heat and to allow a greater flow of heat over the bi-metal coil. The first car to have it was SYD486; the corresponding change was made on Bentley engines at B193DV. Earlier cars had two bi-metal coils; with the heat sink came a single, longer coil. This modification improved the initial drive-away with a cold engine, and prevented the choke closing with hard driving and coming on too quickly after stopping. Fitting the heat sink and single coil was a recommended service modification for earlier cars.

The final modification was a two-step fast-idle cam in place of the original three-step type at SZD369/B445DV, to give more progressive closing of the throttle. (Nevertheless, SZD373 and SZD385 had the old component.) Rolls-Royce retailers were instructed to fit the new cam to all earlier cars which had the heat sink.

The air silencer on cars built in 1959-1961 has a metal body, but a glass fibre type was introduced in early 1962 at LSAE371 and during DW-series production. The air filter was originally an oil-wetted mesh type (part number UE9513), but this was found to restrict air flow under certain conditions. Rolls-Royce retailers were therefore instructed to destroy their stocks of the original filter and to use a dry paper filter (UE5801) as an interim measure. From January 1962, a dry wire mesh filter (UE9813) was made available.

Cooling System

The cooling system is pressurised, and has a five-bladed fan, mounted on the front of the water pump and driven by belts. Normal operating temperature is 90°C, and the standard thermostat starts to open at 66-70°C. However, there were some complaints of poor heating on the early cars, and so a new thermostat (RE23713) was introduced as an optional modification in June 1961. This thermostat started to open at higher temperatures of 70-75°C, and was recommended for use all the year round.

Some early cars suffered from coolant loss because of poor sealing of the header tank filler, so there was a service recommendation to sweat a brass ring into the filler aperture to give firmer seating for the rubber sealing washer. A modified washer was later introduced, at SWC232 and B223CT. However, this could not be used with the modified header tank, and so another new washer with a wider lip was introduced to suit these modified header tanks.

Early examples of the pressure relief valve in the radiator header tank sometimes leaked, and so a new valve was introduced on production at chassis numbers SAE149/B42DW in March 1962. Re-worked examples of the original type supplied by Crewe were marked with a spot of yellow or green paint.

The tips of the fan blades sometimes fouled the cowl on early cars, so the fan was moved closer to the engine in May 1961 by shortening the extension cone on which it was mounted. The first cars to have the short cone were SVB17 and B326AM, but it did not become standard on production until SWC246 and B498BS. In the meantime, it was fitted to the following chassis: SVB series: 239, 385, 391, 427, 441, 463, 467 and 475; SWC series: 20, 38, 42, 46, 116, 146, 148, 216 and 230 to 242; BS series: 182, 184, 220, 282, 288, 300, 316, 326, 354, 400, 434 and 488. One later car (B79CT) had the early type of long cone.

There was a consequent modification to the radiator bottom outlet pipe, which was extended rearwards, and a new bottom water hose was also introduced. The new bottom hose (part UE8446) was standardised at SWC246/B81CT but before that was also fitted independently of the new radiator and fan mounting, to the following chassis: SVB series: 17, 239, 373 to 401, and 405 to 501; SWC series: 20 to 38, 42, 46, 116, 146, 148, 216, 230 to 242; BS series: 104, 180 to 416 and 420 to 500; CT series: 3 to 77.

Improved hoses with new internal reinforcement were introduced for the whole cooling and heater system at LSAE85 and B22LDW.

Exhaust System

The exhaust system of the Silver Cloud II and Bentley S2 is broadly similar to that of the six-cylinder models, except that there are two down-pipes from the manifolds. The right-hand pipe is routed under the engine and meets the pipe from the left-hand manifold at a Y-junction just ahead of the main exhaust silencer outside the left-hand chassis rail. The pipe then runs back and over the top of the chassis rail to a long tubular silencer, and then to the tail pipe. On cars fitted with air conditioning, the exhaust system is fitted with additional insulation where it passes under the passenger compartment.

Early exhausts suffered from a noise problem known as 'exhaust pipe titter', which was cured on production during June 1960 by fitting asbestos lagging in aluminium cover sleeves on the two exhaust pipes just ahead of their meeting at the Y-junction. Service kits were also made available so

The headlamps on these cars never had the 'RR' or 'B' motif behind their lenses, but were standard Lucas types. Sealed-beam units were not standardised until 1962, but this one is on a 1960 model. The sidelamps, also by Lucas, have red tell-tales.

that this lagging could be fitted to earlier cars. Later that same month, at STB370 and B418BS, the six-cylinder pattern front silencer, modified with twin inlet pipes, was adopted. Then all the exhaust silencers were redesigned in November 1960 at B280CU and near the end of SWC series or the start of the SXC series. There was a further modification at SXC393 when the exhaust pipe was lowered; the same modification on Bentleys presumably took place during the BW series.

Transmission

Some transmission components are strengthened as compared to the six-cylinder models.

Automatic Gearbox
The gearbox ratios (with overall ratios in brackets) are: First 3.819:1 (11.752), Second 2.634:1 (8.105), Third 1.450:1 (4.462), Fourth 1.000:1 (3.077), and Reverse 4.306:1 (13.249).

From B576CU in about March 1961, a gearbox throttle valve control was added to right-hand-drive chassis. This change was reflected on Rolls-Royce chassis during the SYD series.

Some cars have a yellow paint mark around the drain plug socket. This indicates that the fluid put into the transmission at Crewe was drained and replaced with Mobilfuid 200 type AQ-ATF-752A after a service instruction dated May 1962.

Propshaft
The split propshaft has a universal joint at each end and a flexible centre bearing. The front universal joint is a Detroit type, and the rear is a Hardy Spicer type with needle roller bearings.

Manufacturing improvements introduced during early production resulted in the introduction of a seamless propshaft in November 1959 at chassis SPA272/B2AM.

Electrical Components

The electrical system of the Silver Cloud II and Bentley S2 models is a 12-volt type with negative earth. The wiring harness is encased in a black

The early rear lamps on V8 models are the same as those on the previous six-cylinder cars.

plastic sheath. As on six-cylinder models, there are variations in the detail of the harness to suit right-hand drive, left-hand drive and coachbuilt cars. Much of the electrical system is similar to its equivalent on the earlier six-cylinder models.

Dynamo
A modified mounting bracket for the dynamo is fitted from chassis number B52CU. This modification was probably made at SXC1 on Rolls-Royce chassis production.

Voltage Regulator
The voltage regulator was always a Lucas RB310, but from mid-1968 approximately a Lucas type 6GC was sometimes supplied as an alternative. This has part number 37470 (with 35-amp rating) or 37469 (with 30-amp rating).

Starter Motor & Relay
The starter motor on the V8 engine is a pre-engaged type made by Lucas. Four different types are found on Silver Cloud II and Bentley S2 chassis. The first change came in June 1960 at B422BS (late SVB series or early SWC series on Rolls-Royce chassis), and the second in October that year. The final change was to a new motor (part number UD5692) in November at SXC1/B417CT and B372CU.

Chassis numbers SXC351 to SYD306 and B252CU to B738CU were fitted with a starter relay (Lucas 33226B) just below and outboard of the flasher relay on the engine side of the front bulkhead. This was intended to prevent use of the starter when the engine was running. However, it did not always work correctly, and Rolls-Royce retailers were advised to remove faulty examples. Evidence that a relay has been removed is now provided by the two pairs of redundant wires connected together by double-ended Lucar terminals, and by the two redundant fixing screws for the relay in the bulkhead.

Horns
The horns are underneath the left-hand wing on the first cars, but from B362CU/SXC1 in November 1960 are found on the front apron. This change was made to allow a revision of the air intakes for the heater and demister.

Lighting
Sealed-beam headlamps were standardised on all cars from SAE407 and from some point in the DW series in August 1962.

The final cars (from SAE389/B148DW in May 1962) have larger rear lamps with a bigger base area. There are in fact three different types of lamp: one for France, one for the USA and Canada, and one for the rest of the world.

Electric Windows

There is a panel of master switches for the optional electric window lifts on the driver's door. There are usually either two or four switches, depending on whether fitment is to the front windows only or all four, but some cars had electric operation of the driver's window only. Each of the other doors also carries its own chromed switch for window operation.

From SYD496/B167DV, the top mounting bracket assembly for the electric window motors was improved. Then from SZD341 in December 1961, cars with electric windows have a plastic duct fitted into the doors just below the quarter-light, to shield the window switches from water coming in through the quarter-light pivots. It was possible to fit these ducts to earlier cars if necessary. This change was made on Bentley models at or around chassis B415DV.

Body

The body of the Silver Cloud II and S2 models is identical to that of the six-cylinder cars in all major respects.

Front Wings

These differ between Rolls-Royce and Bentley models and are not interchangeable. At some point during production, the intake grilles in the front wings changed from black rubber mouldings to plated wire gauze to improve airflow.

Doors

Modified door seals were fitted at chassis number B497DV in December 1961 and at some point during the early SAE series.

Roof

The Silver Cloud/Bentley S-series cars were not intended to have a sliding sunroof but some customers insisted and a factory-fitted sliding steel roof was installed on a few cars. Silver Cloud IIs STB130 and LSTB226 and Bentley S2 B429CT are known to have had this feature.

Rear Wings

There are two different types of rear wing fitted to the Silver Cloud II and S2 models. The early type is the same as that fitted to the six-cylinder cars. The later type, fitted from chassis numbers SAE389 and B148DW, has provision for the larger rear lamps introduced towards the end of production in May 1962.

Boot & Fitted Luggage

From May 1961, the profile of the boot locking cams (one on each side) was modified to prevent jamming. The new cams are fitted to chassis from

The bonnet lids on Bentley models always fitted more closely to the profile of the radiator grille than their Rolls-Royce equivalents. Compare this with the Silver Cloud picture on page 87.

A different style of rear lamp was used after May 1962. This view of the boot interior also shows the cover plate over the spare wheel compartment that was standardised in November 1960.

The boot lid carries an ornate but sturdy handle, together with twin reversing lamps. The centre of the bumper is adorned with an 'RR' or 'B' logo, as appropriate, but only the 'RR' is on a plinth. All items are the same as on the six-cylinder cars.

B59DV and early in the SYD series and have triangular profiles at the top as opposed to the flat profile of the old ones. They were an authorised service replacement.

Fitted luggage became available as an option during October 1960. There were two different sets, one of nine pieces and the other (for cars with a boot-mounted air conditioning unit) of six pieces. All suitcases were made by Antler and had timber frames, quilted taffeta linings and Arlinghide light or dark tan outer coverings. The handles were soft and flexible, and the cases and bags had brass locks and other fittings. The two sets were:

Case size	Nine-piece set	Six-piece set
24in x 18in x 7½in	3 off	2 off
21in x 15in x 7in	3 off	2 off
16in x 13in x 6½in (soft bag)	2 off	2 off
13in x 13in x 5½in (hatbox)	1 off	–

Spare Wheel Compartment
A light alloy cover plate is fitted over the exposed end of the spare wheel compartment from SXC1 and B592CU. This production change was made in November 1960.

The cam profile on the spare wheel clamp was modified and the spare wheel stop at the rear left-hand side of the compartment was no longer fitted from chassis numbers SZD139/B279DV in September 1961. This was to allow room for certain modern tyres with increased tread width, and became an authorised service modification.

Interior

Facia, Instruments & Steering Wheel
The layout of the facia is subtly different from the six-cylinder Cloud and S-series type, with face-level adjustable louvred openings in the facia capping rail. Cars fitted with the new Rolls-Royce underwing air conditioning (see later section) have a pull-out drawer which directs refrigerated air to the rear seat passengers. The steering column is more raked than on the earlier cars, and the steering wheel is both an inch smaller in diameter than before and located nearer to the facia. The direction indicators are operated from a stalk on the steering column, rather than a switch on the capping rail.

A number of changes were introduced all together in November 1960 on Rolls-Royce chassis at SXC1. However, these changes were introduced progressively on Bentley chassis and not at a single point. The features of the modified facia are air direction controls for the face-level vents, an amber glow ring for the cigar lighter, a concealed map light (under the capping rail), revised switching for the interior and capping rail lights, a new switchbox and a radio balance control for the rear speaker. On Bentley chassis, the map light and modified switch are fitted from B2CU, and the radio balance control from B556CU. The air direction control handles were added at B2CU after trial on B429CT, but are not fitted to B120CU and B178CU. The remaining features are fitted from B180CU.

A second group of changes to the facia and switchgear was made in October 1961 at SZD347. This time, a handbrake warning lamp was added to the facia, and the heated rear window switch was relocated there from its earlier position on the rear parcels shelf. The instrument lighting was now tinted, with blue filters and instrument picture plate backs, plus additional bulbs and lenses. The indicator stalk on the steering column

As on the six-cylinder cars, the driver was provided with a deep open-fronted cubby, and the handbrake was a twist-grip type. The right-hand bonnet release lever is visible alongside the handbrake.

The facia was broadly similar to that of the six-cylinder cars, but there were two major differences. The first was the installation of the radio and speaker, and the second was the addition of louvred face-level air vents at the outer ends of the capping rail. Also the clock was no longer within the four-in-one instrument. This is a 1960 Bentley.

This 1962 Rolls-Royce facia displays the 'RR' motifs on the instruments. By this time, a rear radio speaker was fitted, and its balance control can be seen here above the front speaker. The push-button Radiomobile set is original.

was made to double as a headlamp flasher, and the rear view mirror stem was changed from brass to steel and a stiffer mounting bracket fitted to eliminate mirror vibration at speed. Three-position heater and demister switches were fitted, to give the option of ram-air demisting and ventilating. All of these changes took place on Bentley chassis at B415DV.

Two other modifications were made to the instrument lighting. A new two-position switch was fitted from SRA235/B212AM in November 1959. The instrument illumination bulbs in the speedometer and four-in-one dial are 2.2 watt types on cars built before March 1960, when they were changed for 3.6 watt bulbs, accompanied by a modified panel switch. The lighting switch on early cars has both a fixed and a variable resistor, but it can be used with the more powerful bulbs if the fixed resistor is removed. (In practice, it was most commonly taken out of circuit by removing its wire and soldering it to number 3 terminal on the switch.)

From April 1962, an improved speedometer cable was made available for replacements under warranty. It is identifiable by two white plastic wrappings, approximately one-quarter and one-half of the way along the cable from the gearbox end. These markings coincide with a clip on the chassis frame and with the lower of the two clips on the bulkhead.

Transistor type radios replaced the earlier valve types in January 1962. The standard equipment was a Radiomobile 622T with Medium Wave only, or a model 620T with Medium and Long Wave reception.

Pedals

The throttle linkage on left-hand-drive cars gave some trouble and was modified twice. The first time was in March 1960, when the throttle shaft

The original Rolls-Royce key fob was made of black impact-resistant plastic, and was supplied on new cars well beyond the end of the Silver Cloud era.

From late 1960 this chromed operating lever was added to the face-level vents.

The steering column on this 1962 Silver Cloud II carries the ride control switch and indicator/headlamp flasher stalk on its left side, while the automatic transmission quadrant is on the right. Visible on the door is the master switch for the electric windows.

operating lever and the carburettor throttle and stop lever were modified to prevent slipping and consequent damage. Rolls-Royce retailers were recommended to fit both modified levers to earlier cars. It is not clear whether this change was made at chassis LSPA230/B303LAA, or at LSRA315/B310LAM; Rolls-Royce service literature quotes both as changeover points.

The linkage could still foul against the bulkhead, however, although for some reason the

Ashtrays and picnic tables were once again provided in the backs of the front seats. This 1960 model also has a special-order headrest on the front passenger seat. The front seat (right) remained a bench with split squabs, adjusted via the small chromed lever on the outer edge of the seat base.

problem seemed to be confined to left-hand-drive cars for European countries. So from LSYD46/B492LCU, an extra washer was added between the lever and its flanged Metalastik bush, and the lever itself was bent to give additional clearance. This change was also recommended as a service modification when necessary.

A split throttle valve lever, which gave easier adjustment, was fitted from March 1961. At the same time, an adjustable stop was fitted below the accelerator pedal on right-hand-drive cars to make kick-down easier. These changes took place at Bentley chassis B576CU; the changeover point on Rolls-Royce production was somewhere within the later SYD-series chassis.

There was also a change to the brake pedal, when a gap plate was added at B1CT and during production of the Rolls-Royce SWC series.

Seats, Seat Belts & Rear Picnic Tables

In early 1961, modified backs for the front seats were introduced, with ashtrays for the rear seat passengers. These arrived during SZD series and at B556CU. That autumn, adjustable rear footrests arrived with B415DV and during late SZD-series production. Then from B467DV (and probably from SAE1), smaller ball catches and

The H. J. Mulliner convertible coupé uses the standard Silver Cloud facia and bench front seat with split squabs. The latter are modified to fold forwards for access to the rear and have rake adjustment by chromed levers. Note the wide door aperture provided by the two-door configuration. A door-operated courtesy lamp is fitted beneath the facia and the tumbler switch for the (optional) power operation of the roof is positioned beneath the facia on the driver's side.

striker plates were fitted to the rear picnic tables.

Seat belts were introduced as an optional extra in April 1961, and were made by Irvin. These early belts have U-shaped shackles, and there are stiffening plates on the underside of the floor where they are bolted through. The front belts are full lap-and-diagonal fixed belts; the rear belts are lap-type only.

Door Trims, Headlining, Rear Companions & Parcels Shelf

There is an additional half an inch of insulation under the roof lining of cars which are equipped with air conditioning.

The front door trims were modified in October 1961 by the addition of sliding doors for their stowage cubbies at SZD347/B415DV. Shortly afterwards, a larger cigar lighter was fitted to the right-hand rear companion at SAE1/B493DV.

A radio speaker was fitted to the rear parcels shelf at SXC1/B556CU. This is concealed below the shelf and is covered by a metal grille.

Heater & Air Conditioning

The Silver Cloud II and Bentley S2 models have a completely different heating and ventilating system from the one used in six-cylinder models. This is a split-level type and its main components are mounted under the right-hand front wing. In addition, there are no fewer than three different types of air conditioning system. Cars for the US retain the OMC Texas boot-mounted system seen on earlier models. Other standard-bodied cars and Mulliner 'convertible coupé' conversions have a new Rolls-Royce air conditioning system integrated with the under-wing heater, but coachbuilt

cars have the Rolls-Royce-built unit mounted in the boot (as fitted to previous models).

The standard heating system draws air in from the vent in the right-hand front wing and delivers it through polythene ducting to the heater matrix which is mounted under the wing behind the wheel. On early cars, this ducting could foul the tyre, and from August 1960 it was fitted with an additional B-shaped clip to hold it in place. In the Upper system, fresh air passing through the top part of the matrix can be heated if required and is then directed to three windscreen demisting outlets and the face-level louvres on the facia capping rail outlets. The Lower system is purely recirculatory and draws air from a floor-level duct behind the right-hand front seat. The air passes through the heater matrix, being heated if required, and into the car via floor level vents below the facia on each side of the car and into

The well behind the rear seat to accommodate the hood (left) means the seat cushion is 4in narrower between the armrests than on the standard saloon. The rear seat is also further forward so there is only 9½in, instead of 13in, of rear kneeroom. The folding hood sticks, partly visible here, are normally concealed by the detachable leather cover.

One of the two chromed over-centre catches (below) which secure the hood to the windscreen.

Bentley S2 models had a cast metal chassis number plaque, similar to that traditionally used on Rolls-Royce models.

the rear compartment via an outlet under the front seats. The Upper and Lower systems have their own variable-speed fans and air and water control valves. Reinforced heater hoses are fitted from May 1962.

The Rolls-Royce underwing unit adds a pair of evaporator units to the main heater complex, and has the great advantage that cooled air is available in the front of the car. Switches and valves allow Upper system fresh air or Lower system recirculated air to be passed across the heater matrix or across the evaporator unit, and then to be passed into the body of the car in the usual way, boosted by the fans if required. Both upper and lower systems can be operated simultaneously. A 'Texas duct' drawer below the facia can be opened to allow the refrigerated air to be circulated to the rear compartment.

There were two major modifications to the heating and ventilating system. The first was made in November 1960 at SXC1/B362CU, when a second cold air intake was provided. This drew in air from the grille in the left-hand front wing (and the horns had to be moved to make room for it), in order to give a ram-air option. It was not fitted to all the subsequent coachbuilt cars, however; LSXC173 and LSXC359, for example, did not have it. In addition, certain earlier CU-series Bentley cars have it. Service literature lists it as fitted from B2CU but as absent from chassis numbers B18CU, B102CU, B120CU, B132CU, B136CU, B154CU, B164CU, B178CU and B360CU.

The second major change was made in October 1961, when a twin-matrix heater was fitted at SZD347/B415DV. This brought with it an additional water tap and a series of extra hoses, and a new central heater duct to the rear compartment was fitted at the same time. The Lower system air inlet was also moved to underneath the outer edge of the right-hand front seat.

The compressor for the air conditioning system is a Tecumseh type HH on cars built up to September 1960. Subsequent examples have a York Shipley A209 compressor. The York compressor is fitted to Rolls-Royce models from SXC639 and to Bentley models from B570CU. However, the York compressor was also fitted to the following chassis: SWC series: 78, 270, 310, 396, 474, 478, 480, 482, 486, 500, 502, 516, 558, 560, 636, 638, 652, 664 and 678; SXC series: 1, 9, 11, 87, 89, 145, 149, 151, 159, 213, 239, 259, 335, 339, 359, 375, 381, 405, 437, 455, 471, 491, 513 and 547; CT series: 151, 155, 187, 217, 273, 285, 305, 363, 367 and 415; CU series: 8, 70, 72, 172, 312, 340, 348, 364, 386, 390, 396, 406, 466, 490, 498, 534 and 536.

The undersheets for the underwing air conditioning unit were initially in glass fibre but were changed to steel at B504CU and during SXC-series production in late 1960 or early 1961.

PAINT & INTERIOR TRIM

The standard or recommended paint and trim options for the Rolls-Royce Silver Cloud II and Bentley S2 are listed below. It was normal practice on two-tone Silver Clouds for the bonnet top to be finished in the same colour as the upper portions of the body; on Bentleys the bonnet top was normally finished in the lower of the two colours. Sales literature boasted that bodies carried at least 14 coats of paint.

1959
There were 17 standard paint finishes, and two-tone cars could be ordered in any combination of these colours.

Seven interior colours were offered, but these were not tied to exterior colours. Headlinings and carpets could be ordered to individual taste, although most headlinings were in beige or grey and carpets normally matched the upholstery colour.

The paint options were: Black, Black Pearl, Blue Grey, Maroon, Metal Grey, Midnight Blue, Opal, Pacific Green, Porcelain White, Sable, Sage Green, Sand, Shell Grey, Smoke Green, Steel Blue, Tudor Grey, and Velvet Green.

The seven interior colours were the same as on the six-cylinder Silver Clouds: Beige, Blue, Brown, Green, Grey, Red, and Tan.

1960-1962
The options remained the same throughout production of the Silver Cloud II, except that for 1960 Maroon was deleted, leaving just 16 exterior colours available.

IDENTIFICATION, DATING & PRODUCTION FIGURES

The chassis numbers of these cars are in the same position as on the six-cylinder models.

There were 2417 Rolls-Royce Silver Cloud II chassis, and 1863 Bentley S2 types. In addition, one Silver Cloud II prototype was renumbered with a production chassis number before sale by the factory.

CHASSIS NUMBERS
The chassis numbers for these cars are set out on the right, together with delivery dates.

Rolls-Royce chassis numbers consist of three letters and up to three digits. The final letter denotes the chassis series. Left-hand-drive cars have an L prefix before the chassis letters (eg LSPA326).

Bentley chassis numbers begin with B followed by up to three digits and two suffix letters, the first of which denotes the chassis series. Left-hand-drive cars have the letter L before the suffix letters (eg B325LAA).

Both Rolls-Royce and Bentley sequences beginning with 1 used odd numbers only and always excepted 13; sequences beginning with 2 used even numbers only.

Rolls-Royce Silver Cloud II

SPA2 to SPA326	September to December 1959	
SRA1 to SRA325	November 1959 to March 1960	
STB2 to STB500	February to April 1960	
SVB1 to SVB501	April to September 1960	
SWC2 to SWC730	June to December 1960	
SXC1 to SXC671	November 1960 to February 1961	
SYD2 to SYD550	February to August 1961	
SZD1 to SZD551	June to December 1961	
SAE1 to SAE685[1]	December 1961 to August 1962	

[1] Plus SAE687, which was re-numbered from experimental chassis 30B.

Bentley S2

B1AA to B325AA	September to December 1959
B2AM to B326AM	November 1959 to January 1960
B1BR to B501BR	January to May 1960
B2BS to B500BS	May to August 1960
B1CT to B445CT	September to November 1960
B2CU to B756CU	November 1960 to May 1961
B1DV to B501DV	April to December 1961
B2DW to B376DW	December 1961 to August 1962

ENGINE NUMBERS
Engine numbers are stamped on the rear of the crankcase (just below the air cleaner trunking) on the left-hand side of the engine. The numbering sequences are consecutive, include 13, and are:

Rolls-Royce Silver Cloud II

2AS to 325AS	A-series chassis
1BS to 500BS	B-series chassis
1CS to 700CS	C-series chassis
1DS to 550DS	D-series chassis
1ES to 342ES	E-series chassis

Bentley S2

1AB to 325AB	A-series chassis
1BB to 500BB	B-series chassis
1CB to 600CB	C-series chassis
1DB to 438DB	D-series chassis

Long-Wheelbase Silver Cloud II & S2, 1959-62

The long-wheelbase versions of the Rolls-Royce Silver Cloud II and the Bentley S2 were announced in September 1959, although Bentley deliveries did not start until January 1960. They have exactly the same relationship to the standard-wheelbase cars as did their six-cylinder predecessors. Like those cars, they have a longer 127in-wheelbase chassis, and the bodies of the standard cars were converted from ordinary saloon shells to the 4in longer six-light configuration by Park Ward.

These cars are identical in every detail to their standard-wheelbase sisters, except where noted in the following text. Details of production changeover points are also given here; for fuller details of the nature of these changes, see the relevant sections on the standard-wheelbase cars.

Chassis

Front Suspension & Steering
New mounting plates for the front dampers were specified from LCB1/LBA18, and stronger damper bodies from LCB81 and probably late in LBA-series production.

The lighter steering for left-hand-drive cars was introduced at chassis LLCD11/LLBB30.

Rear Axle
The improved crown wheel fixing bolts were fitted from LCA19 and LBA2. All cars had the standard saloon's 3.077:1 gearing.

Brakes
The bronze-coloured clevis pins for the front

The long-wheelbase cars retained their well-balanced proportions, despite the extra length. This is Alfred Gooding's 1962 left-hand-drive example (LLCC90) in Sage Green over Velvet Green. It conforms to the usual Rolls-Royce two-tone practice with the upper colour on the bonnet.

From the rear, the appearance still remains balanced. The aerials for radio and radio telephone on the boot saddle panel were a special fitment.

The extra 4in of length was all inserted in the rear passenger area, and the longer rear door makes this readily apparent.

brakes replaced the cadmium-plated type at chassis numbers LCC71 and LBB25.

The modified brake servo pins were fitted at chassis number LLCA66 in May 1960. Left-hand-drive chassis were fitted with an additional washer on the bell crank lever of the intermediate braking system at LLCD7/LLBB29.

Fuel Pumps & Tank
A breather was added to the fuel tank at LCC16 and LLBB11. The larger-capacity fuel pumps were introduced LBB25 and at LCC84.

Engine

A vibration cushion was fitted under the engine at LCA2 and from the beginning of Bentley chassis production at LBA1. The modified crankcase with deeper oil trough for the camshaft was introduced at LCB29/LBA21, and the 'improved' starter ring was introduced at LLBB19. This modification probably arrived at or about LCC49; the original starter ring was fitted again from LLBB30 and at or about LLCD11. Fully enclosed crankcase breathing for left-hand-drive cars came in at LLCC74 and at or about LBB24.

Camshaft & Valvegear
The solid camshaft was fitted from chassis numbers LCA11 and LBA1, and the tappets with flats were introduced at LCA69/LBA17. The subsequent changes to valves, valve mechanism and tappets are difficult to chronicle exactly, and so the changeover points given here should be

treated with some caution. The modified valves and valve mechanism arrived at LLBA22 and at LCB40 approximately, and valve stem packing was introduced at LCB48 (and probably some time around LBA20). From LLBA23 there were further modifications to the cylinder head and valves, and the bushless hardened rockers and flatted rocker shaft were first fitted at chassis LCB67/LBA26, with further improved rockers at LLBB29 and during LCB-series production. Cars from LCD19 and LLBB30 have the improved camwheel lubrication.

Three different camshaft and oil feed schemes affected the A-series Rolls-Royce chassis. The Stage 1 scheme applied to engines in chassis LCA1 to LCA10 and LCA23. The Stage 2 scheme was used on LCA25 and LCA26, and the Stage 3 scheme on LCA11 to LCA22, LCA24 and LCA27. Chassis numbers for the equivalent changes on Bentley models are not available, but all of them were probably before LBA20.

Sparking Plug Caps

The waterproofed plug caps are fitted from LCC28/LLBB15.

Carburettors, Choke & Air Silencer

The carburettor jet assemblies were changed at chassis numbers LCB8 and LBA19.

The automatic choke appears to have been equipped with both an Otter switch and a sealed thermal delay switch from the beginning of long-wheelbase chassis production. A further choke modification (probably the radiused butterfly valve) was made at LCA31 and early in the LBA series. From LCB8/LBA19 the fast idle cam bracket mounting was altered, and the heat sink and single bi-metal coil for the automatic choke were fitted to cars destined for the UK and for Europe from chassis LCC24 and LBB11. The Rolls-Royce Chassis Numbers Booklet, however, gives the change points here as LCC1/LBB10.

The two-step fast-idle cam on the automatic choke replaced the original three-step type at chassis number LCC54. The equivalent change on the Bentley probably took place before LBB25.

The air silencer changed from metal to glass fibre at LCD5 and probably at or about LBB27.

Cooling System

The shortened fan mounting extension was fitted as standard to C-series Rolls-Royce chassis and from Bentley chassis LBA18. It was also fitted to several earlier chassis: LCA70, LCA72, LCB4, LCB11, LCB14 to LCB101, and LBA16.

The extended radiator bottom outlet pipe and the new bottom hose were fitted from LCB14 and LBA16; they were also on the following chassis: LCA67 to LCA76, LCB4, LCB11 and LBA9.

The improved radiator cap seal was introduced at LCA76 and LBA19. Improved coolant and heater hoses came in with LLCC83/LBB25.

Exhaust System

The modified six-cylinder front silencer was fitted to all chassis from LCA57 and LBA18. The lowered exhaust pipe was introduced at LCB63 and during LBA-series production, and the new silencer assemblies were on Bentleys from LBA25 and on Rolls-Royce chassis from about LCB73.

Transmission

Gearbox

The gearbox throttle valve control is on Bentley chassis from LBA25 and on Rolls-Royce chassis probably from some point late in the LCB series.

Propshaft

The seamless propshaft was fitted from chassis LCA29 and LBA4.

Electrical System

Dynamo

The modified dynamo-mounting bracket is fitted to Bentley chassis from LLBA22 and to Rolls-Royce chassis probably early in the LCB series.

Starter Motor

The modified starter motor was introduced at Bentley chassis LBA18 and on Rolls-Royce

The arrangement of instruments on this left-hand-drive car differs from that on right-hand-drive models; compare with the picture on page 116. The car was originally delivered in France, and is fitted with a speedometer marked in kilometres per hour. The Voxson stereo radio/cartridge player is not original; the car would have been fitted with a Radiomobile 620T push-button set.

models probably somewhere between LCA57 and LCA70. Then from LCB42/LBA26, the improved motor with part number UD5692 was fitted. The Lucas 33226B starter relay was fitted to Rolls-Royce chassis between LCB66 and LCC6, and to Bentley chassis between LBA25 and LBB12.

Lighting

Sealed-beam headlamps are standard on all cars from LCD8. The changeover on Bentley chassis probably took place at or around LLBB30. The larger rear lamps are fitted to Bentley models from chassis number LLBB30. They were fitted to all Rolls-Royce models from LCD14, but were also fitted earlier to LLCC65, LLCC101 and LCD1.

Electric Windows

These were an optional extra. The improved top mounting brackets for the electric window motors are fitted from LCC21 and LLBB11. There are plastic water shields over the motors in the front doors from LCC51 and from some point in the LBB series.

Body

Doors

The electric window switches in the front doors were protected by a plastic duct from chassis numbers LLC51 and LLBB19. The improved door seals were introduced on Bentley chassis at LBB24, and at or around LCC70 during Rolls-Royce production.

Rear Wings

The modified rear wings to suit the enlarged tail lamp clusters are fitted to Bentley models from chassis LLBB30. They are fitted to all Rolls-Royce models from LCD14, but were also on LLCC65, LLCC101 and LCD1.

Bumpers

The modified rear bumper support springs are fitted from LLBB15 and from about LCC28.

Boot & Spare Wheel Compartment

The modified boot lock cam was fitted to Bentley chassis at LLBB11 and to Rolls-Royce chassis early in the LCC series. A cover was fitted to the spare wheel compartment from LCB42/LLBA23. The cam profile on the spare wheel clamp was modified and the spare wheel stop was deleted from chassis numbers LCC34 and LLBB15.

Interior

Facia & Instruments

The air direction control on the capping rail air louvres was added at LCD2 and LLBB28. It was also fitted to chassis LLC57, LLC92, LLC94, LLC96 and LLC100. The two-position lighting switch was fitted at chassis LCA20 and LBA4.

The improved facia with new switchbox and amber glow ring for the cigar lighter was introduced at LCB42. On Bentley chassis, the new map lamp and the modified switching for the instrument and capping rail lights arrived at LLBA22 but the amber glow ring for the cigar lighter was introduced at LLBA23. The radio balance control was fitted from LCB73 and LBA25. The rear window demister switch was relocated on the facia at LCC48/LLBB19, and the blue instrument lighting, handbrake warning light and stiffened mirror stem all arrived with LCC49/LLBB19. The combined headlamp flasher and indicator stalk on the steering column was standard from LCC49/LBB20, but was also fitted to Rolls-Royce chassis LCC46 and LCC47.

Pedals

All left-hand-drive long-wheelbase chassis had the first-stage improved throttle control linkage. The modified throttle control linkage on left-hand-drive cars for Europe was introduced at chassis numbers LLCB87 and LLBB5.

The brake pedal gap plate was introduced at LBA18 on Bentley chassis and probably early in the LCB series of Rolls-Royce chassis. An accelerator pedal stop was fitted to right-hand-drive

The black vertical switch on the facia enables the driver to operate the electric division. Note the handbrake warning lamp on this 1962 Silver Cloud II.

The lower section of the division had a wood-veneered capping rail and was equipped with picnic tables. The division glass has been lowered in this picture, but the fixed wraparound ends are still visible. The front compartment was the same as the standard saloon except that the seat squabs did not recline (far left).

The rear seat (left) on the long-wheelbase cars was exactly the same as the standard saloon.

The lengthened rear doors have special trim pads and veneered cappings. Note the angled armrest and the electric window switch in its chromed escutcheon.

Some forward seat adjustment (right) was available for the driver and front seat passenger, even on cars fitted with a division.

The ashtray (above) has its own mounting at the top of the division, while the console beneath carries controls for the radio volume, heater and division, as well as a cigar lighter. Hand grips (right) were still on the cant-rail above the doors, but there was no rear companion. Instead, reading lights were let into the roof.

PAINT & INTERIOR TRIM

Long-wheelbase cars had the same range of exterior colours and interior trim combinations as the standard steel cars.

Bentley models from LBA25 and to Rolls-Royce chassis probably from somewhere towards the end of the LCB series.

Seats

On cars without a division, the modified front seat backs incorporating ashtrays were fitted from LLBA23. It is not clear if the modification was ever applied to Rolls-Royce chassis but, if so, the change would have taken place probably some time around LCC1.

Door Trim

Sliding doors for the front cubby boxes are fitted from LCC49/LLBB19.

Rear Parcels Shelf

On non-division cars a second radio speaker was fitted under the parcels shelf at LCB73/LBA25.

Heater & Air Conditioning System

The twin-matrix heater is fitted to long-wheelbase saloons from chassis numbers LCC83 and LLBB28. From chassis LLCC92 and LLBB28, the heating and demisting systems on the long-wheelbase models are commonised with the standard-wheelbase cars.

The York compressor for the air conditioning system was fitted to all Rolls-Royce chassis with air conditioning from LCB90 and to Bentleys from LBA21. In addition, it was fitted to certain other LCB-series cars: 15, 18, 28, 31, 41, 44, 45, 46, 48, 50, 52, 53, 73, 82 and 87.

Division

As with the six-cylinder cars, most of the long-wheelbase Silver Cloud II and Bentley S2 models have an electrically-operated division between front and rear seats. This is unchanged from its earlier form.

The picnic tables in the division were fitted with the same smaller ball catches and striker plates as those in the front seat backs of standard cars from LBB24. The changeover probably occurred on Rolls-Royce chassis at about LCC70.

IDENTIFICATION, DATING & PRODUCTION FIGURES

The chassis identification plate and chassis number on the frame are in the same place as on standard-wheelbase Rolls-Royce and Bentley models.

There were 299 long-wheelbase Rolls-Royce Silver Cloud II chassis, and 57 long-wheelbase chassis with Bentley badges. The chassis number sequences for these cars are set out here, together with delivery dates.

All long-wheelbase chassis numbers consist of three letters and up to three digits. Sequences begin with L, followed by C for Rolls-Royce versions and B for Bentley models. The third letter of the prefix denotes the chassis series. Cars with left-hand drive have an L before the

prefix letters (eg LLCA1). Both odd and even numbers were used in all sequences, but 13 was always omitted.

Rolls-Royce Silver Cloud II Long Wheelbase

LCA1 to LCA76	September 1959 to August 1960
LCB1 to LCB101	August 1960 to May 1961
LCC1 to LCC101	April 1961 to July 1962
LCD1 to LCD125	June to September 1962

Bentley S2 Long Wheelbase

LBA1 to LBA26	January to December 1960
LBB1 to LBB33	January 1961 to September 1962

ENGINE NUMBERS

Engine numbers are stamped on the rear of the crankcase (just below the air cleaner trunking) on the left-hand side of the engine. The numbers include 13, and are:

Rolls-Royce Silver Cloud II Long Wheelbase

LC1A to LC75A	A-series chassis
LC1B to LC100B	B-series chassis
LC1C to LC100C	C-series chassis
LC1D to LC24D	D-series chassis

Bentley S2 Long Wheelbase

LB1A to LB25A	A-series chassis
LB1B to LB32B	B-series chassis

Bentley Continental S2, 1959-62

The chassis of the Bentley Continental S2 is essentially the same as that of the contemporary Bentley S2 standard saloon, although some cars were fitted with a 'heavy gauge' frame. Its engine is identical to that of the standard car, but the rear axle has a higher final drive ratio of 2.923:1 for the first 248 chassis numbers (with four exceptions), switching to the standard 3.077:1 gearing thereafter. There are narrower tyres, and the front brakes have four shoes. The radiator shell is 3in lower than the standard type, leans slightly forward (whereas the standard type is raked slightly towards the rear) and is mounted 2in further forward than on the Continental S1.

The text which follows highlights the differences between the Continentals and their standard saloon contemporaries. In addition, it contains details of production changes. For further details of the nature of these changes, see the corresponding section on Bentleys with the standard chassis.

Chassis

Front Suspension & Steering
New mounting plates for the front dampers were specified from BC1BY, and stronger damper bodies from chassis BC92BY. The lighter steering for left-hand-drive cars was introduced at chassis number BC135LCZ.

Rear Axle
The first change to the crown wheel fixing bolts took place at BC45AR, when stepped bolts were fitted. The second change, to an improved type of bolt, was at BC52AR.

The first cars had 2.923:1 (13:38) gearing, but it appears that the 3.077:1 (13:40) gearing was

H. J. Mulliner no longer offered a fastback sports saloon body for the Continental S2 chassis. Instead, there was a two-door derivative of the popular Flying Spur style, which from the front nevertheless looked very much like the fastback style available on the six-cylinder S-series chassis. This design was built on 96 chassis.

optional and it was specified for chassis BC98AR, BC5LBY, BC7BY and BC87LBY. This lower gearing became standard at BC100LBY.

Brakes

The front brakes of the Continental S2 have four cast aluminium shoes instead of the two shoes of the standard chassis. The four self-adjusting shoes increased the brake swept area from 240sq in to 300sq in. At chassis number BC95CZ, the original cadmium-plated front brake clevis pins were replaced on production by clevis pins with a bronze finish, and these later pins became a recommended service modification.

On left-hand-drive cars only, an additional washer was fitted to the bell crank lever of the intermediate brake system from BC135LCZ.

Brake Servo

The modified brake servo pins were fitted at chassis BC128AR.

With effect from chassis BC93BY, the braking ratio between front and rear was reduced to improve heavy braking on greasy roads. This was effected by fitting servo-operating levers with 47° cams, which could also be fitted to existing cars as a service modification. The presence of the modification was indicated by a spot of yellow paint on each of the operating levers.

Wheels & Tyres

The wheels on the Continental chassis are identical to those on the standard saloon, but the lighter overall weight of the cars allowed narrower tyres to be fitted. These were of 8.00-15 size instead of the 8.20-15 size fitted to standard chassis. When the cars were new, all the recommended types were available with the option of black or white sidewalls.

In the beginning, the recommended tyres for the Continental chassis were 8.00-15 India Super Speed Specials, running at 20psi on the front wheels and 25psi on the rears (or 25psi and 30psi respectively for high-speed use). For winter use, 7.00-15 or 7.60-15 Dunlop Weathermaster or Firestone Town and Country tyres were recommended for the rear wheels only, running at 30psi. An 85mph maximum speed was recommended.

From September 1960, the tyre pressure recommendations for the Park Ward drophead coupé (the so-called 'Koren' body) were changed to 20psi at the front and 28psi at the rear (or 25psi and 33psi respectively for high-speed use).

In January 1962 recommended 8.00-15 tyres were: Dunlop Road Speed C, Firestone Sports or Firestone Super Sports 170 ORB.

Fuel Tank & Pumps

The tank was fitted with a breather at chassis number BC28CZ, and larger-capacity fuel pumps came in at BC112CZ.

Engine

All the Continental S2 chassis have a vibration cushion under the engine.

The modified crankcase with a deeper camshaft oil trough is fitted from BC74BY, but BC97BY had the earlier type. The 'improved' starter ring was introduced at BC85CZ and the original type was reinstated at BC137LCZ.

Camshaft & Valvegear

The solid camshaft was fitted from chassis number BC38AR, and the tappets with flats were introduced at BC139AR. The subsequent flurry of changes to valves, valve mechanism and tappets is rather easier to follow on the Continental

H. J. Mulliner's Continental S2 two-door saloon body was built in aluminium alloy. The low-drag design featured slim roof pillars and a wrap-around rear window. Although it was still a four seater, there was less rear knee and head room than on the four-door Flying Spur. This is actually the prototype body on Continental S-series chassis BC27GN. It has a more sloping boot and slightly higher bonnet line.

chassis than on the standard type, and begins with modified valves and valve mechanism at chassis BC46BY. Service literature does not record the introduction of valve stem packing, but this would probably have occurred during the later BY series. From BC51BY there were further modifications to the cylinder head and valves. With BC78BY came the bushless hardened rockers and flatted rocker shaft, and further improved rockers followed at BC134CZ. Cars from BC139CZ have the improved camwheel lubrication.

Three different camshaft and oil feed schemes affected the AR-series chassis only. The Stage 1 scheme applied to engines in chassis BC1AR to BC33AR. The Stage 2 scheme was used on BC34AR to BC38AR, and the Stage 3 scheme was fitted on BC39AR.

Sparking Plug Caps
The waterproofed sparking plug caps are fitted from BC43CZ.

Carburettors & Automatic Choke
The carburettor jet assemblies were changed at chassis BC149AR.

The changes to the automatic choke and associated components did not take place in the same order as on the standard chassis. A sealed thermal delay switch was fitted from BC11AR and an Otter switch from BC106AR. Lagged air pipes were introduced at BC112AR and the radiused butterfly valve at BC114AR. The bi-metal coils were shielded from BC137AR, and the heat sink and single bi-metal coil were fitted to cars destined for the UK and for the rest of Europe from

chassis BC37CZ. The modified mounting for the fast idle cam bracket was introduced at chassis BC3BY and the two-step fast-idle cam replaced the three-step type at chassis BC76CZ.

Cooling System
The modified fan cone and bottom hose were fitted as standard from chassis BC10BY, but earlier chassis BC133AR to BC151AR also had these modified items.

The improved radiator cap seal was introduced at BC21BY, and the improved pressure relief valve in the radiator header tank at BC86CZ. The reinforced coolant and heater hoses came in with chassis BC109CZ.

Exhaust System
A modified six-cylinder type front silencer is fitted from BC16LBY, and the redesigned silencers from BC76BY.

Transmission

Gearbox
The gearbox throttle valve control is fitted to Continental chassis from BC99BY.

Chassis up to BC99BY have a higher 2.923:1 (13:38) axle ratio, although the saloon axle ratio of 3.077:1 (13:40) was optional. From BC100LBY onwards the 3.077:1 (13:40) axle ratio was fitted as standard. Gearbox ratios with the 2.923 axle (with the overall ratios in brackets) were: First 3.819 (11.164), Second 2.634 (7.699), Third 1.450 (4.238), Fourth 1.000 (2.923) and Reverse 4.306 (12.587).

Park Ward introduced a new drophead coupé style for the S2 Continental chassis. Designed by Vilhelm Koren, it featured straight-through wing lines and a most attractively styled front end. As the number plate suggests, this is indeed BC58LCZ, a left-hand-drive example. The narrow-band whitewall tyres add an appropriate period feel to the car.

Park Ward's Continental S2 drophead coupé body was particularly distinctive from the rear with a cowled circular rear lamp treatment that was quite different from other Bentleys. The body was a steel and alloy composite structure and the fully-lined power-operated hood had a zipped PVC rear window. Facia styling of the H. J. Mulliner Continental two-door saloon (right) was borrowed from the Flying Spur design. Note the four small instruments directly ahead of the driver — a Mulliner characteristic of the period. The driver's heel mat proudly displays the HJM initials, and the central armrest doubles as a lid for the cubby box.

Propshaft
Chassis from BC66AR are fitted with the seamless propshaft.

Electrical System

Dynamo
The modified dynamo mounting bracket is fitted from chassis BC51BY.

Starter Motor
The modified starter motor is fitted from BC1BY, and the improved type from BC40BY. Continental chassis between BC72BY and BC19CZ have the Lucas 33226B starter relay.

Lighting
Service literature does not record the introduction of sealed-beam headlamps on Continental

The Park Ward cars have a distinctive aircraft-style instrument nacelle, which stands proud of the main facia and is surrounded by black trimming which is padded for safety. The four small dials are situated directly ahead of the driver, in the style pioneered by H. J. Mulliner.

chassis, although they probably arrived at or after BC78CZ. The larger rear lamps are fitted to all cars from chassis BC78CZ, but were also on BC55LCZ, BC59CZ, and BC62CZ to BC76CZ.

Interior

Facia & Instruments

The design of the dashboard varies from coach-builder to coachbuilder, but certain elements were supplied by Rolls-Royce and remain constant. Thus the speedometer, for example, differs between cars with the 2.923:1 axle ratio and those with the lower 3.077:1 ratio, and a transistorised rev counter is fitted to CZ-series Continentals built after May 1962.

Several changes were introduced together at BC72BY. These were the addition of a map lamp, modified switching for the instrument and capping rail lights, and the amber glow ring for the cigar lighter. The blue instrument lighting and associated modifications were on all chassis from BC66CZ, but nine earlier CZ-series chassis also had them. These were BC34CZ, BC38CZ, BC40CZ, BC41CZ, BC44CZ, BC45CZ, BC47CZ, BC50CZ and BC53CZ. The headlamp flasher became standard at BC70CZ, but had been fitted to 15 earlier chassis: BC34CZ, BC38CZ, BC40CZ, BC41CZ, BC44CZ, BC45CZ, BC47CZ, BC50CZ, BC51CZ, BC53CZ, BC62CZ, BC64CZ, BC66CZ, BC67CZ and BC68CZ. The handbrake warning lamp was not fitted until BC78CZ, when it became standard.

Pedals

The first-stage improved throttle linkage for left-hand-drive cars was fitted to all Continental chassis (of which the first was B2LAR). The second modification, which affected left-hand-drive cars for Europe, was introduced at chassis number BC100LBY.

A brake pedal gap plate is fitted from chassis number BC1BY and an accelerator pedal stop and

Paint & Interior Trim

As the Continental was always seen as a coachbuilt car, which was built to individual order, there were no standard paint finishes or trim colours. Customers could – and did – choose from the range offered on the standard saloons, but also cars were painted or trimmed in other colours to the individual customer's choice.

Identification, Dating & Production Figures

The chassis numbers of these cars are in the same positions as on the standard steel S2 models. There were 388 Continental S2 chassis.

BC1AR to BC151AR	July 1959 to June 1960
BC1BY to BC101BY	June 1960 to July 1961
BC1CZ to BC139CZ	February 1961 to August 1962

Chassis Numbers

The chassis number sequences for these cars are set out here, together with delivery dates. All Continentals have the chassis number prefix BC, followed by up to three digits and two suffix letters, the first of which denotes the chassis series. Cars with left-hand drive have an L prefix before the suffix letters (eg BC74LBY). Both odd and even numbers were used in all sequences, but 13 was always omitted.

Engine Numbers

Engine numbers are stamped on the rear of the crankcase (just below the air cleaner trunking) on the left-hand side of the engine. The numbering sequences are consecutive, include 13, and are:

A1BC to A150BC	A-series chassis
B1BC to B150BC	B-series chassis
C1BC to C138BC	C-series chassis

a gearbox throttle-valve control to right-hand-drive chassis from BC99BY in July 1961.

Heater & Air Conditioning System

Continental chassis have the same heater unit as the standard chassis, but their reduced frontal area made it impossible to fit the under-wing refrigeration unit. Air-conditioned cars therefore have a boot-mounted unit, of Rolls-Royce manufacture.

The engine-driven compressor is a Tecumseh type HH on early cars, and changes to a York Shipley A 209 at chassis BC90BY.

Body

The radiator grille supplied to all coachbuilders by Rolls-Royce is 3in lower than the type fitted to the standard saloons. All of the Continental S2 chassis were fitted with coachbuilt bodies which were to standardised designs.

Of the 388 Continental S2s, 222 were bodied by H. J. Mulliner, 125 by Park Ward, 40 by James Young and one by Hooper. Chassis numbers of cars bodied by individual coachbuilders are given in the section below.

CONTINENTAL S2 BODIES

The most popular of H. J. Mulliner's Continental bodies was the Flying Spur four-door saloon, to design 7508. Compared with the original version fitted to six-cylinder Continentals, the bonnet was lowered at the front to suit the lower radiator grille. The boot lid was also extended downwards so that there was no longer a loading lip, and the number plate and reversing lights moved from this lip onto the boot lid. H. J. Mulliner built 124 Flying Spur bodies on the Continental S2 chassis, and nearly as many (96) of a two-door style. This was no longer the classic fastback style but was a clever adaptation of the Flying Spur design. In addition, there were two bodies recorded simply as 'saloon' on BC4LAR and BC5LAR.

The framework of these bodies is light alloy and the panelling is all aluminium. Standard Bentley bumpers are fitted at both front and rear, and the windscreen is laminated while the other glass is toughened. The twin front seats each have a folding centre armrest, which doubles as a stowage box and has a hinged lid.

The full list of 222 Mulliner-bodied chassis is:

A series: BC2LAR, BC3LAR, BC4LAR, BC5LAR, BC7LAR, BC11AR, BC12AR, BC14LAR, BC16AR, BC18LAR, BC19LAR, BC20LAR, BC21AR, BC22LAR, BC24LAR, BC26AR, BC29LAR, BC31LAR, BC32AR, BC33LAR, BC36AR, 39LAR, BC40AR, BC41LAR, BC42AR, BC43LAR, BC44LAR, BC47AR, BC48AR, BC49AR, BC50AR, BC51AR, BC52AR, BC55AR, BC56AR, BC58AR, BC59AR, BC63AR, BC65AR, BC66LAR, BC69AR, BC70AR, BC71LAR, BC76AR, BC81AR, BC83AR, BC84LAR, BC85AR, BC86AR, BC87AR, BC89AR, BC90AR, BC92LAR, BC98AR, BC99AR, BC100AR, BC102LAR, BC104AR, BC106AR, BC115AR, BC116LAR, BC118AR, BC122AR, BC124AR, BC126AR, BC127AR, BC129AR, BC130LAR, BC131AR, BC132AR, BC133AR, BC134AR, BC135LAR, BC136AR, BC137LAR, BC138AR, BC139AR, BC140LAR, BC141AR, BC142LAR, BC143AR, BC144AR, BC145AR, BC146AR, BC147AR, BC148LAR and BC150AR.

B series: BC1LBY, BC3BY, BC7BY, BC9BY, BC11LBY, BC14LBY, BC15LBY, BC16BY, BC18LBY, BC19LBY, BC21BY, BC23LBY, BC25BY, BC28LBY, BC31BY, BC33LBY, BC35BY, BC37BY, BC39BY, BC40BY, BC42BY, BC43BY, BC44LBY, BC46BY, BC47LBY, BC48BY, BC49BY, BC52BY, BC54LBY, BC56LBY, BC58BY, BC60LBY, BC62BY, BC64LBY, BC68LBY, BC70LBY, BC71BY, BC73BY, BC75BY, BC76LBY, BC78BY, BC83BY, BC85BY, BC87LBY, BC88BY, BC90LBY, BC91BY, BC93BY, BC94BY, BC97BY, BC99BY and BC101LBY.

C series: BC2CZ, BC5CZ, BC7CZ, BC10LCZ, BC12CZ, BC15CZ, BC16LCZ, BC17CZ, BC18CZ, BC19LCZ, BC20CZ, BC21CZ, BC22LCZ, BC24LCZ, BC26CZ, BC27LCZ, BC29CZ, BC30LCZ, BC33CZ, BC35LCZ, BC36CZ, BC38CZ, BC39CZ, BC41CZ, BC42LCZ, BC43LCZ, BC46CZ, BC47CZ, C48CZ, BC49LCZ, BC53LCZ,

BC54CZ, BC55CZ, BC56CZ, BC59LCZ, BC60LCZ, BC62LCZ, BC63CZ, BC64LCZ, BC65CZ, BC66LCZ, BC67CZ, BC68CZ, BC69CZ, BC71CZ, BC72CZ, BC73CZ, BC75CZ, BC76LCZ, BC80CZ, BC82CZ, BC83CZ, BC85CZ, BC87CZ, BC88CZ, BC90CZ, BC91CZ, BC93CZ, BC94CZ, BC97CZ, BC98CZ, BC100CZ, BC101LCZ, BC103LCZ, BC104CZ, BC106LCZ, BC107CZ, BC109CZ, BC110CZ, BC112LCZ, BC121LCZ, BC122LCZ, BC123CZ, BC124CZ, BC125CZ, BC126CZ, BC129LCZ, BC132CZ, BC133LCZ, BC134CZ, BC135LCZ, BC137LCZ and BC139CZ.

PARK WARD & CO LTD

The Park Ward drophead coupé bodywork for the Continental S2 chassis was constructed using aircraft techniques, with extensive use of welded lightweight steel and alloy pressings for the framework. Both steel and alloy panels were used, the front wings, bonnet, doors and boot being aluminium. The steel rear panels were formed using Kirksite dies and a stretch press.

The styling, by Norwegian designer Vilhelm Koren working under John Blatchley, features straight-through wing lines and slab sides with a single chromed styling strip on the sills. At the front are peaked headlamp surrounds, while there is a reverse-slope trailing edge on the rear wings, with circular indicator, stop/tail and reversing lights in a vertical row within a cowled area at the rear. The number plate is deeply recessed into the boot lid.

The convertible top has electro-hydraulic power operation, and features a zipped PVC rear window. It is lined with cloth to match the upholstery and has a leather hood cover which also matches the upholstery. The leather-covered seats are bolstered and padded, with pleated centre sections. At the front are individual bucket seats, while the rear squab folds forward to provide an additional luggage platform. It is released by means of a metal catch in the centre of the parcels shelf, and there is a leather loop on its top horizontal surface. Electric windows were optional on these bodies, and all the windows disappear fully into the bodywork.

The facia is distinctive, with the main instruments grouped in a hooded nacelle ahead of the driver. Standing proud of the main instrument board, this nacelle has the switchgear in two vertical groups at right and left, with the radio inboard of the driver at the bottom, while the speedometer and rev counter flank the four smaller dials grouped in the centre. The capping rail and nacelle surround are in padded black leather, and this treatment is carried through to the veneered door cappings and side quarter-trims as well.

Among the colours available was a light blue metallic called Alice Blue, which was generally accompanied by Beige upholstery and hood.

There were 124 Continental S2 chassis with Park Ward drophead bodies. Just one chassis, BC9LAR, was bodied as a four-door saloon.

The full list of 125 Park Ward-bodied Bentley Continentals is:

A series: BC8AR, BC9LAR, BC10AR, BC15LAR, BC17LAR, BC23AR, BC25AR, BC30AR, BC34AR, BC37AR, BC54AR, BC57AR, BC60AR, BC61AR, BC64AR, BC67LAR, BC72AR, BC73LAR, BC74AR, BC75AR, BC77LAR, BC80LAR, BC82AR, BC88AR, BC91AR, BC93AR, BC107LAR, BC108LAR, BC109AR, BC111AR, BC112AR, BC114AR, BC117AR, BC119AR, BC120AR, BC123LAR, BC125AR, BC149AR and BC151AR.

B series: BC2BY, BC4LBY, BC6LBY, BC8BY, BC10BY, BC12LBY, BC20LBY, BC22LBY, BC24LBY, BC27BY, BC30BY, BC32BY, BC34LBY, BC36BY, BC38BY, BC50LBY, BC51BY, BC53LBY, BC55LBY, BC57LBY, BC59LBY, BC61LBY, BC63LBY, BC65LBY, BC66LBY, BC67BY, BC69BY, BC72BY, BC74LBY, BC77BY, BC79LBY, BC81BY, BC82LBY, BC84BY, BC86BY, BC92BY, BC96LBY, BC98LBY and BC100LBY.

C series: BC1CZ, BC4LCZ, BC6CZ, BC9LCZ, BC11LCZ, BC14LCZ, BC23CZ, BC25CZ, BC28LCZ, BC31LCZ, BC32LCZ, BC34LCZ, BC37CZ, BC40CZ, BC45LCZ, BC52LCZ, BC57LCZ, BC58LCZ, BC61LCZ, BC70CZ, BC74CZ, BC78LCZ, BC79LCZ, BC81CZ, BC84CZ, BC86LCZ, BC89LCZ, BC92LCZ, BC95CZ, BC96CZ, BC99CZ, BC102CZ, BC105LCZ, BC108CZ, BC111CZ, BC113CZ, BC114LCZ, BC115CZ, BC116LCZ, BC117LCZ, BC118LCZ, BC119LCZ, BC120CZ, BC127LCZ, BC128LCZ, BC131LCZ and BC136LCZ.

JAMES YOUNG LTD

All the James Young bodies on the Continental S2 chassis were saloons, and the majority had four-doors although a few two-door bodies were also built. Young's four-door body had a steel framework and light alloy panels. There were individual front seats and the wood trim was in figured walnut.

The full list of the 40 James Young-bodied Bentley Continentals is:

A series: BC6LAR, BC27AR, BC28AR, BC35AR, BC38LAR, BC45LAR, BC46AR, BC53AR, BC62AR, BC68AR, BC78AR, BC79AR, BC94AR, BC95AR, BC96AR, BC97AR, BC101AR, BC103LAR, BC105AR, BC110AR, BC113AR, BC121AR and BC128AR.

B series: BC5LBY, BC17BY, BC26BY, BC29BY, BC41BY, BC45BY, BC80BY, BC89BY and BC95BY.

C series: BC3CZ, BC8CZ, BC44CZ, BC50CZ, BC51CZ, BC77LCZ, BC130CZ and BC138CZ.

HOOPER & CO (COACHBUILDERS) LTD

Just one Continental S2 chassis was bodied by Hooper, using the same four-door style (number 8512) as the company had offered on the six-cylinder Continental chassis. This was on the very first chassis, BC1AR, and the car was exhibited at the 1959 Earls Court Motor Show.

Rolls-Royce Silver Cloud III & Bentley S3, 1962-66

The third-generation Silver Cloud and its Bentley S3 equivalent were introduced in October 1962. They retained all the well-liked features of the previous two holders of the name but added a number of modernising touches. Most noticeable were the twin-headlamp installation and built-in sidelamps/indicators at the front, while interior changes on the standard saloons included individual front seats as standard. There was also more power from an uprated version of the V8 engine, which gave a top speed approaching 120mph.

The Rolls-Royce version of the design was once again more popular, and 2556 chassis were sold as against 1286 of the Bentley. One reason for this was that the Rolls-Royce chassis remained available for coachbuilt bodywork, while the Bentley did not; just one Bentley chassis was coachbuilt, and that to special order. During this period, coachbuilt bodies on the standard wheelbase were exclusively sporting in nature, and formal bodies were confined to the long-wheelbase chassis. This demand for sporting body styles persuaded Crewe to make the Rolls-Royce chassis available with certain features of the Bentley Continental, and the distinction between a Continental and a coachbuilt Rolls-Royce became less clear-cut during this period. While production of the standard steel saloon ended in the summer of 1965, the last coachbuilt Silver Cloud III was not delivered until well into 1966.

The Silver Cloud III and Bentley S3 were of course continuations of the Silver Cloud II and Bentley S2 designs, and the starting-point for their specification is the final production specification of the earlier models. Chassis numbers for Rolls-Royce Silver Cloud IIIs have a sequence of three letters and up to three numbers (eg SCX877). From the SGT series in mid-1964, coachbuilt Silver Cloud III chassis have the suffix B or C following the number (eg SGT565C). Bentley S3 chassis numbers start with the letter B followed by one, two or three digits and two letters (eg B828CN); Bentley Continentals have the prefix BC instead of B. Left-hand-drive chassis are identified by an L in front of the chassis letters. Service records are remarkably imprecise about the introduction points for certain modifications

on Rolls-Royce chassis, although the records for Bentley models are as good as ever.

Chassis

Steering

The power-assisted steering is lighter at low speeds than on the Silver Cloud II and Bentley S2, and makes the car easier to park. This was achieved by providing power assistance when the steering wheel rim load exceeded ½lb (instead of 1lb) and supplying much more assistance when the rim load reached 6lb (previously 8-10lb). The power assistance provided between these two rim loadings was also increased. Service literature claimed that a certain amount of squeal from the drive belts was acceptable on full lock, and warned that over-tightening the belts in an attempt to eliminate this was likely to lead to engine roughness.

Steering hoses clearly gave some trouble, and on left-hand-drive cars from B30LDF the hose was re-routed and protected by a heat shield fitted to the steering box mounting arm. On Rolls-Royce

Twin headlamps modernised the appearance of these third-generation models and made them distinctively different from the earlier types. The radiator grille was also 1½in lower than before. This Silver Cloud III (SCX303) with Sand coloured paintwork belongs to Max Brown.

The Silver Cloud III's, and S3's, side profile was different, too, thanks to a more steeply raked bonnet and wings with a lower crown line.

It is arguable that the more streamlined styling suited the Bentley grille better than the Rolls-Royce type. This 1964 Sable over Sand two-tone S3 (B56FG) belongs to Peter Baines.

chassis, this change took place during SEV-series production. The hoses were then re-routed on right-hand-drive chassis at B348FG and during the SHS series.

Air locks in the steering could result in steering judder, and an air bleed was added to the steering box at B420CN and during the SCX series. Service literature offered two cures for earlier cars with this problem. One was to move the front ram feed from the side of the ram to the top so that air could bleed back to the reservoir. The alternative was to fit restricted banjo bolts in each of the ram feed pipes at the spool valve end.

Other production modifications began with a change to the steering box spool valve and

housing at B116FG and during the SFU series. The head of the power cylinder was then altered at B222FG and during SGT-series production in 1964. On a few cars built around the middle of 1965, the side steering lever (drag link) was fitted with waisted set screws. By October that year, however, a service bulletin recommended replacing these with ordinary set screws and fitting new locking plates, so it is unlikely that any cars survive with these waisted screws.

Brakes
The brake fluid reservoirs were moved and bolted to the enclosed crankcase breather during SCX-series (and presumably CN-series) production.

There was also an improved handbrake from August 1963.

Shorter brake linings were fitted to all cars built from SEV471/B92EC in October 1963, to prevent squeal. Complete shoe and lining assemblies could also be fitted to older cars, or the new shorter linings could be fitted to existing shoes, when it was necessary to drill two new rivet holes in the shoe.

The brake servo pressure plate was changed in October 1964 to counter glazing of the linings caused by frequent but light use of the brakes in town driving. The revised type has 16 slots machined at 45°angles across the friction face to provide scraping edges which keep the lining clean, and became a recommended service replacement in cases of rapid lining wear. It was fitted on production from chassis numbers SHS251 (standard saloon), SJR561C (coachbuilt) and B88GJ.

Wheels & Tyres
The wheel cover discs obviously differ between Rolls-Royce and Bentley models, in exactly the same way as on earlier cars. The detachable ring painted in the body colour carries a fine line, as before. The cover discs themselves are chromium-plated steel on the first cars, but from April 1963 they are made of stainless steel. This change took

This is the 1963 Earls Court Motor Show chassis, now owned by the RREC. The basic lines of the frame had not changed since 1955, although many details had done so. This view (left) of the front cross-member, taken from just ahead of the right-hand front wheel, shows the lower wishbone front pivot, the power steering ram and its associated pipework.

As on earlier cars, the wheel discs carry appropriate badging in their centres. Note how the trim ring is painted in the upper body colour on this two-tone Bentley, with the fine line in the lower body colour. This is the later stainless steel wheel trim.

The wishbone and coil spring front suspension (left) is seen on the right-hand side, looking rearwards. The anti-roll bar mounting is clearly visible. The view (middle left) of the front suspension on the left-hand side, taken from behind, shows the upper wishbone and hydraulic damper plus the twin brake lines to the wheel. The view (bottom left) of the rear end of the chassis shows the fuel tank (shaped to fit around the spare wheel), the shackles for the rear springs, and the body mounting points. Note also the fuel tank breather hose and the straps that hold the tank in place. This view of the demonstration chassis (below) shows the gearbox-driven brake servo, the mechanical brake linkages and the dual circuit hydraulic brake master cylinder and pipework. Seen from a different angle (bottom), this is the master cylinder for the braking system.

place with effect from chassis number B404CN and during the SCX series.

The standard wheel is a 6J-15 well-base type, but from SFU675/B484EC in May 1964 wider 6.5J rear wheels were fitted to cars for the home market and for Europe. These wider wheels carry a spot-welded plate which reads 'Rear wheel only', and were introduced to improve handling and steering, especially in blustery conditions at speed. They should be fitted with the standard-size tyres.

The standard tyre size is 8.20-15, and the recommended tyre pressures are 22psi at the front and 27psi at the rear. Coachbuilt models have 8.00-15 tyres at 20psi and 25psi respectively.

When new, the cars could be fitted with any one of the following tyre types, all of them available with white or black sidewalls: Dunlop Elite C40 (to August 1963, when production ceased), Dunlop Fort C WH4, Firestone ORB De Luxe, Avon Turbospeed R/R-B or India Super Nylon WH4. Winter tyres, for use on the rear wheels only, were Dunlop Weathermaster or Firestone Town and Country.

Coachbuilt chassis had one of the three following types: Dunlop Road Speed RS5, India Super Speed or Firestone Sports ORB P345, plus

A general view of the 6230cc V8 engine, in this case badged as a Rolls-Royce unit. Note the sparking plugs positioned below the exhaust manifold. The detail (left) of the 2in HD8 carburettors and their linkages can be seen in this view taken from the back of the engine, looking forwards.

The air cleaner is made of glass fibre, and is seen here in its normal position. Note the two hinges, which allow it to be swung up out of the way during maintenance.

The shielded Lucas distributor is positioned at the rear of the engine. Note the long dipstick tube and power steering hoses.

the same two winter tyre options for the rear wheels only.

Fuel Tank, Filters & Pumps

From April/May 1963, a small additional condenser was fitted to the fuel pump, and this was recommended as a service modification. The new fuel pump carried the SU part number AUA149, and retailers were instructed to alter the identification tag of modified pumps to carry this number. The condenser was connected directly across the contact points to reduce arcing and consequent failure of the points; the existing radio suppressor condenser was retained. The change became standard at chassis numbers SCX863/B466CN, but a number of earlier SCX- and CN-series chassis were also built with the extra condenser. These chassis were: SCX513, SCX567, SCX571, SCX615, SCX621, SCX623, SCX649, SCX655, SCX657, SCX671, SCX673, SCX679, SCX683 to SCX687, SCX691, SCX693, SCX697 to SCX717, SCX721, SCX725, SCX729 to SCX761, SCX765 to SCX771, SCX777 to SCX787, SCX795 to SCX807, SCX811 to SCX819, SCX823 to SCX833, SCX839, SCX843, SCX849, SCX857, B304CN, B328CN, B350CN, B354CN to

B368CN, B372CN to B448CN and B454CN.

Flexible pipes for the fuel pumps were introduced during the SDW series and probably during late CN-series production. Barrier-type nylon diaphragms were then incorporated in the pumps to improve their performance at chassis numbers B226HN, LSJR513 (standard saloon) and LCSC378 (coachbuilt) in May 1965. This was a short-lived modification, however, because the AUA149 fuel pumps were replaced by SU type AUF400 pumps late in production. The change affected Bentley chassis from B36JP and home market Rolls-Royce chassis from some time during the SKP series and in the CSC series for cars with coachbuilt bodies. At about the same time, the fuel filter was relocated.

Engine

The 6230cc V8 engine is essentially the same as the one in the Silver Cloud II and Bentley S2 chassis, but there are important modifications which give a power increase which Rolls-Royce claimed at seven per cent. This probably means that the engines put out around 215bhp. The Silver Cloud III and S3 engines have a higher compression ratio of 9.0:1, bigger carburettors, and a vacuum advance capsule on the distributor. These changes required the use of 100-octane petrol, but these high compression engines can be run on lower-grade fuel if the ignition timing is retarded to compensate. The forged molybdenum steel crankshafts are nitride-hardened and there are larger-diameter gudgeon pins than on earlier versions of the engine. There is also a sealed crankcase ventilation system.

An 8:1 compression version of the engine was introduced in late 1962 or early 1963 for some export territories where high-octane petrol was not available, and this is slightly less powerful than the standard type.

The engine was generally less troublesome than during its early production life, and in consequence there were fewer production changes.

Block, Pistons, Flywheel & Bellhousing

From B2JP and some point in SKP-series production during 1965, the cast iron cylinder liners have an interference fit. Modified scraper rings were introduced for the pistons during SKP-series production and are also fitted to the CSC-series chassis for coachbuilt bodywork.

During SCX- and CN-series production in 1962-1963, the tips of the starter ring teeth were hardened for longer life.

There were two modifications to the bellhousing, the first being made in mid-1964 when an underpan was fitted to all cars except for those destined for dusty or tropical territories. This change was made at B12FG and during the SFU series, but the underpan was not fitted to B18FG. The second modification was the addition of air vent holes to the bellhousing during SJR-series production early in 1965 and at B190GJ.

Cylinder Heads & Tappet Covers

The original diameter of the bronze exhaust valve guides was 0.3755in ± 0.0005in. However, the guides on later engines were reamed to 0.373in ± 0.0005in diameter. These later guides were also supplied as service replacements for all Silver Cloud II/Bentley S2 and Silver Cloud III/Bentley S3 engines from March 1968.

Valve sealing on these engines was effected by a wick-type grommet. However, from December 1966 a more efficient silicone rubber valve seal was supplied for service replacement in cases when oil consumption had been high.

There were some problems with leaks from the tappet cover joint, and a service recommendation was to machine the tappet cover set screw bosses down to allow the gasket to seal properly. In October 1964, an improved tappet cover joint made of Dermatine rubber-based compound was introduced to prevent oil leaks.

Valvegear & Camshaft

The camshaft bushes were deleted during SCX- and CN-series production, and there were further minor camshaft modifications in 1965 at B34HN and during the SJR series.

Heat-treated chilled iron tappets were introduced during SKP- and CSC-series Rolls-Royce production, and presumably also on Bentley chassis in the JP series. New castings for the tappet blocks and tappet block assemblies arrived on B136GJ and during SJR-series production.

Carburettors & Automatic Choke

The carburettors are 2in HD8 SUs rather than the 1¾in HD6 types of the Silver Cloud II and Bentley S2 engines. These HD8 carburettors were a special Rolls-Royce version, which was finished in stoved black enamel with cadmium-plated external screws and levers, and the float chamber had extra thermal insulation to prevent fuel vaporisation. Normally SU carburettors had brass throttle spindles but this material did not meet Rolls-Royce's durability criteria and was replaced by stainless steel.

The float lever and needle valve tended to stick and cause flooding, and so a modified float chamber lid was introduced at chassis numbers LSDW65/B508CN to prevent this. Then in December 1963, larger-bore vent pipes were introduced to allow the engine to run while the carburettor was flooding. These were fitted from

The five-bladed fan, the fan cowl, and the multiple auxiliary drive belts can be seen in this view.

The bellhousing, gearbox and gearbox linkages are all seen here. The brake servo is visible on the far side of the gearbox, at its rear, and the speedometer drive cable is in the foreground.

The rear axle Z-bar or torque reaction linkage and the brake pipe runs are seen here. Note the tight-fitting Wefco leather spring gaiter, which has dried out and torn, and is partially exposing the spring's leaves.

The rear brake pipes and linkages can also be seen in this view of the final drive unit. Note the traditional Rolls-Royce ring of small bolts securing the aluminium alloy differential casing.

B340EC and during SFU-series production, but were not on B368EC, B412EC or B491EC. Finally in September 1964, a service bulletin advised retailers that the new type of lid was not necessary in cases of flooding, but that fitting the new nylon-encased needle and seat (CD3514) to the old type of lid was just as effective.

The automatic choke was fairly trouble-free during Silver Cloud III and Bentley S3 production, but one problem which did come to light was that oil could block the stove pipes and cause the

choke to remain on. So modified stove pipes were introduced in July 1965 at B308HN, SKP139 (standard) and CSC71 (coachbuilt chassis).

Cooling System

A number of minor changes were made on production. A wax-filled thermostat was fitted from some point in SCX-series production, and presumably on CN-series chassis at the same time. The thermostat was switched to one which opened at 88°C during the SFU series and presumably for the EC-series Bentleys which were then in production. After production had ended, and from August 1968, new thermostats were supplied with a label which was to be fitted in a conspicuous position on the engine. The label (part number RH8147) reads: 'Replace thermostat assembly every two years. Next change due: (date to be added by hand). Rolls-Royce Limited'.

There was an improved radiator pressure relief valve at B176CN, and modified top and bottom hoses arrived at B388CN. Both changes were introduced on Rolls-Royce chassis during the SCX series. A new water tap and steady post were added during SCX-series production and at B10CN to cater for the twin matrix heater.

Exhaust System

A steady bracket was added to the downpipe from the left-hand bank of cylinders during SAZ-series production, and presumably to the AV-series Bentleys, which were being built at the time. Then from B210EC in January 1964, and during SEV-series Rolls-Royce production, a heat shield was added to the right-hand exhaust manifold.

Transmission

Gearbox

Stronger torus cover springs were fitted at B712CN and during the SDW series, but they were not fitted on B724CN.

Propshaft

During SFU-series Rolls-Royce production, and presumably during contemporary EC- or FG-series Bentley production, the propshaft centre bearing was pre-loaded on assembly to prevent it squealing when cold. Cars so fitted were marked with a yellow paint stripe on the centre bearing spring plates and mounting assembly. From January 1964, pre-loading the bearing was also recommended as a service modification.

Electrical Components

There are no major differences from the electrical system of the Silver Cloud II and Bentley S2 models. The battery was a special 67 amp-hour

Dagenite, built to a Rolls-Royce specification with 11 plates fitted into a nine-plate case. From B290FG, and some time during the SGT series, copper-cored battery cables were fitted.

Dynamo & Voltage Regulator
A Lucas RB340 voltage regulator was fitted from chassis number B38EC and during SEV-series production in late 1963. The dynamo bracket was modified at B8FG and during the late SFU series in mid-1964.

Starter Motor
The original starter motor suffered a number of failures, and so from SEV287 in October 1963 a Lucas 26209A starter motor was fitted. Rolls-Royce recommended that all earlier starter motors should be modified with new brushes, and that altered starter motors should be identified with a light blue mark painted on the rear end of the starter solenoid casing, so that it was visible from under the bonnet when looking down past the rear of the exhaust manifold.

Other modifications affected the starter relay, which was given a longer cable during the SAZ series and at B16AV and then had its positive cable re-routed during SDW-series Rolls-Royce production and presumably during CN-series Bentley production. The starter solenoid cable was replaced by a link strip at B152FG and during the SGT series.

Distributor, HT Leads & Sparking Plugs
The distributor on these engines is a Lucas type with a vacuum advance capsule rather than the Delco-Remy type fitted to earlier V8 engines. Most were fitted with a contact breaker cam lubricating pad, which tended to wear. In December 1967 a Service Bulletin recommended that the pad should be cut off when no longer serviceable, and that the cam should be lubricated with a silicone-based compound.

New HT leads with resistive cores were specified from B10GJ and during the SHS series.

The spark plugs were changed to Champion N16Y during the SEV series and presumably during the contemporary EC series. This change was not made on chassis destined for the US.

Lighting
The four headlamps are all Lucas 5¾in-diameter sealed-beam types. The inner pair has a single filament, which provides the long-range lighting on main beam. The outer pair has twin filaments, of which one is for the dipped beam and the second is slightly out of focus to add spread to the main beam. Total main beam wattage with the twin-headlamp system is 150 , compared with the 120 watts of the earlier single-lamp system, and the

dipped beam output is raised from 90 to 100 watts.

The fog lamps on these cars no longer do duty as flashers as well, so have single filament yellow bulbs, except for the US and Canada where the bulb is white. Instead, there is an oval lamp unit in the nose of each front wing, which combines an amber upper segment (for the flashers) with a smaller clear segment (for the sidelamps).

At the rear, the larger rear lamps introduced on the later Silver Cloud II and Bentley S2 models are fitted. Early cars have relays for the stop and flasher lamps, but these were discontinued from B152FG and during the SGT series. The reversing lamps are on the boot lid as before, and a choke was added to their circuit at B222EC and during SEV-series production. At B412EC and during the SFU series, a modified reversing lamp and rear number plate lamp unit was fitted.

Windscreen Wipers
Stops were added for the wipers at B496LCN and during the SDW series.

Electric Windows
Electrically-operated windows remained an optional extra on these cars, though most customers specified them. At the model's introduction the extra cost for UK customers was £84 11s 8d (£84.38). Stop brackets were added to them at B126GJ and during SHS-series production.

Body

Front Wings, Bonnet & Grille
The front wings on these cars differ between Rolls-Royce and Bentley versions in the vicinity of the radiator shell and are similar in shape to those on the earlier Silver Cloud and S-series cars. However, they are not single-piece pressings but are made of two parts joined along the swage line. Their crown lines are lower to suit the more sloping bonnet line, and their fronts are modified to accommodate the twin headlamp installation. The headlamps are carried in chromed surrounds,

The twin 5¾in Lucas headlamps are mounted in a neat chromium-plated fairing, which carries a small rectangular 'RR' or 'B' motif, as appropriate. The Lucas fog lamp still has a yellow bulb, but does not double as a flasher on these cars. Instead, there is an orange flasher segment in the wing-mounted sidelamp.

These cars had the larger style of rear lamps with modified plinth, as used on the later Silver Cloud II and S2 models.

which were restyled in March 1964 but continued to incorporate a small RR or B monogram, as appropriate. There is no separate housing for the sidelamp on the top of the wing, but instead there is a cut-out in the nose of the wing for a combined sidelamp/flasher unit.

There were no modifications to the wings themselves during Silver Cloud III and Bentley S3 production, but a tensioner was added to the wing stays during the SCX series and presumably during the contemporary CN series.

These cars were given a lower radiator grille and a more steeply raked bonnet than earlier Silver Clouds and S-series Bentleys. This was

done partly to give a slightly more modern, streamlined look, and also to improve forward visibility for the driver. Both Rolls-Royce and Bentley grilles stand 1½ in lower than on earlier models. The Rolls-Royce radiator shutter opening is 22.75in tall and imperceptibly wider at 19.90in, though the thickness of the shell (front to back) remains at 4.3in. The frontal changes mean the bonnet lids are also different from those on earlier Silver Clouds and Bentleys. The lids themselves differ between the two marques to accommodate differences in the shape of the grille.

Bentley models prior to B14EC suffered from vibration of the radiator shutters which set up a moaning noise. This could be cured by removing a triangular blanking plate behind the grille at the bottom, and by removing some metal in that area.

Doors

The only recorded production change to the doors is the arrival of new door seals during SDW-series production. These were presumably fitted to Bentley CN-series models at the same time.

Rear Wings

The fuel filler compartment is in the left-hand rear wing, as on earlier Silver Cloud models. At the bottom right-hand side of its base should be a small plate indicating the requirement for 100-octane fuel, and this plate is fitted even to cars with the lower-compression (8:1) engine. It was fitted to some cars on production before becoming standard at SCX129/B118CN, but was a recommended retro-fit in service. Cars built with it were: SAZ5, SAZ19, SAZ23, SAZ53, SAZ61, SCX35, SCX41 to SCX45, SCX49, SCX61, SCX65, SCX67, SCX75 to SCX89, SCX93, SCX95, SCX99 to SCX103, SCX107, SCX111 to SCX123, B26AV, B14CN, B20CN, B24CN, B28CN to B32CN, B38CN, B48CN to B58CN, B62CN to B100CN, B104CN, B108CN, B112CN and B114CN.

Boot Lid

There is a chromed 'Silver Cloud III' or 'S3' motif at the bottom right-hand corner of the boot lid, although this was not fitted to some of the first cars. Owners of cars without the badge could have it fitted from December 1962. Of the A-series Rolls-Royce cars, it was fitted only to SAZ5, SAZ19, SAZ23, SAZ37, SAZ49, SAZ53 and SAZ61. The first C-series car to have the motif fitted on production was SCX35. Thereafter, it was fitted to SCX39 to SCX49, SCX55 to SCX67, and SCX75 to SCX95, and became standard at SCX99. On Bentley models, the boot badge was fitted to chassis numbers B26AV, B14CN, B20CN to B32CN, B38CN to B40CN, and became standard at chassis B44CN.

Rolls-Royce models carried this identification on their boot lids; Bentleys had a simpler S3 badge. They were the first Rolls-Royce and Bentley cars ever to carry model identification.

For markets other than the USA, smaller and less ornate over-riders were fitted.

The re-profiled wings and lowered bonnet line are seen here on Max Brown's 1963 Silver Cloud III (SCX303).

Glass & Heated Rear Window

Sundym tinted glass was an optional extra and was usually specified on cars with air conditioning, on which it was a no-cost option. All cars had a heated rear window, but the heated area was increased in size (to 30in width) from B126DF and during SEV-series production in November 1963.

Bumpers

The overriders are of a smaller and neater design than on earlier models, and reduce the overall length by 1½in to 17ft 6¼in. Cars for the US retained the larger type fitted to Silver Cloud II and S2 models.

Interior

Rolls-Royce and Bentley variants share the same interior, except that the small monograms on the instrument faces and the brake pedal rubber are RR or B as appropriate. The most obvious difference between the interior of these cars and that of their predecessors is the separate front seats.

Facia, Instruments & Steering Wheel

The facia is broadly similar to the type on Silver Cloud II and Bentley S2 models, except that the top face and front edge of the capping rail is lightly padded and is covered in black leather. This was

Individual front seats and a black padded facia top with an ashtray at each end are unique to these third-generation models. The facia layout is similar to earlier V8 models but with blue instrument lighting. The heater controls have two anti-clockwise positions that admit ambient air.

a concession to new awareness about safety issues, particularly in the US, and was intended to reduce the injuries of an occupant thrown forward onto the facia in a collision. For similar reasons, the rear

The air vents in the capping rail are the same as those on late Silver Cloud II and S2 models. Note also the trimmed filler panel containing the map-reading lamp between the capping rail and the lower dashboard.

The side padding on the rear seat is less prominent than on earlier cars and the cushion is further back with a more upright squab.

view mirror is hung from above the windscreen on some export models and later cars, although its normal position is on a stalk mounted to the capping rail.

Other changes from the earlier facia layout are an ashtray let into each end of the capping rail and a redesigned radio panel. On these cars, the radio is offset towards the driver, and there is a speaker in a matching panel on the passenger side of the facia. When an electrically-operated telescopic radio aerial is fitted to the wing, its switch is fitted between the radio and speaker panels. Three types of radio were available, all of them made by Radiomobile: 620T (Medium and Long wave), 230R (Medium and Short wave) and 622T (Medium wave only). Many of the chassis supplied for coachbuilt bodywork had a steering column more steeply raked than standard, but this is less immediately noticeable because most of the coachbuilt bodies have their own facia layouts.

There were relatively few production changes. The handbrake warning lamp was modified during SCX-series production (and presumably on Bentley CN-series chassis), and then from B506EC and some time during the SFU series, additional cold air intake controls were fitted to suit the revised ventilating system.

An improved speedometer cable was fitted on production from SCX453 in April 1963, although some later cars had the earlier type. The improved cable is recognisable by two white wrappings around its casing, which coincide with the position of two mounting clips. The new cable was introduced on Bentley chassis at B232CN. The speedometer itself was changed in late 1964 at B206FG and during the SGT series. The new speedometer was made by Nemag and has its zero at the conventional 7 o'clock position instead of the 1 o'clock position Rolls-Royce previously favoured. A new drive cable accompanied it.

Handbrake
A pulley-type handbrake is fitted to right-hand-drive chassis from SDW485/B738CN.

Pedals
Left-hand-drive chassis have a larger rectangular-shaped brake pedal instead of the oval one fitted to right-hand-drive models.

Seats & Seat Belts
There are two individual front seats in place of the bench type (now a no-cost option) fitted to earlier Silver Clouds. The rear seat is also different, with the cushion moved back 2in so that it no longer protrudes over the heelboard. The squab is more upright and less prominent side padding allows more seat width. Seat piping on the front and rear armrests was repositioned for greater comfort. The

rear seat and side armrests were modified in January 1964 at B70EC and during the SEV series to give further room.

Seat belts were available for all Silver Cloud III derivatives. The early type was made by Irvin and was attached to the car by means of U-shaped shackles. From February 1964, a revised type with a single bolt fixing was specified for the US and Canada, and either lap only or lap-and-diagonal types were made available for both the front and rear seats. These later seat belts were available in grey, fawn, red or green to tone in with the colour of the upholstery.

Door Trim

The door trims are the same as those on the final Silver Cloud II and Bentley S2 models. Many cars had the optional electric windows, with either two or four master switches on the driver's door depending on the number of windows operated. Other doors each have an individual window switch in a circular chromed plate.

Heater & Air Conditioning System

The water control taps on these cars were all operated electrically. A service modification introduced in March 1964 involved moving the lead on the number three terminal of the upper water tap actuator to the number two terminal. This countered customer complains that it was impossible to maintain an even interior temperature without rotating the upper control switch between its second and third clockwise positions.

Cars for the US have an OMC air conditioning unit in the boot, but for other countries the refrigeration is incorporated with the under-wing heater unit. Coachbuilt cars, except for the US, have a Rolls-Royce boot unit. There were two production modifications. The first affected the water taps and their mounting plates, and was made at B10CN. The second, at B260CN, was the installation of an additional sight glass on the C61 refrigerated units, together with re-routed hoses on right-hand-drive chassis. Both changes were made during SCX-series Rolls-Royce production.

PAINT & INTERIOR TRIM

The standard or recommended paint and trim options for the Rolls-Royce Silver Cloud III and Bentley S3 are listed below. It was normal practice on two-tone Silver Clouds for the bonnet top to be finished in the same colour as the upper portions of the body. Sales literature boasted that bodies carried approximately 12 coats of paint – two fewer than the minimum promised on the Silver Cloud II!

Five new standard colours were introduced and four colours discontinued (although still available as special colours at extra cost), thus bringing the total up to 17.

Two-tone options could be created by combining any of these colours to taste. Eight interior colours were offered, but these were not tied to exterior colours. Headlinings and carpets could be ordered to individual taste, although most headlinings were in Fawn or Grey and carpets normally matched the upholstery colour.

The five new paint options were: Antelope, Astral Blue, Dusk Grey, Garnet, and Pine Green. The other standard colours were: Black, Black Pearl, Burgundy, Dawn Blue, Porcelain White, Sable, Sage Green, Sand, Shell Grey,

Smoke Green, Steel Blue, and Tudor Grey.

The eight interior leather colours were: Beige (VM3234), Black (VM8500), Green (VM3124), Grey (VM3393), Light Blue (VM3244), Scarlet (VM3171), Red (VM3086), and Tan (VM846). Headcloth colours, with normal upholstery combinations in brackets, were: Grey (Black, Grey or Light Blue), Light Fawn (Beige, Black or Tan), Fawn (Black, Red or Scarlet), and Green (Green). Carpet choices were: Blue, Black, Cumberland Stone, Green, Grey, Maroon, Red, and Sandringham Beige.

IDENTIFICATION, DATING & PRODUCTION FIGURES

The chassis number of a Silver Cloud III or Bentley S3 will be found on a plate attached to the engine side of the bulkhead and on the left chassis frame member ahead of the bulkhead. There were 2556 Rolls-Royce chassis, with 2445 chassis in the main build sequences, and a further 111 in the two special coachbuilt sequences. Bentleys numbered 1286, including one coachbuilt car.

Chassis Numbers

The chassis number sequences for these cars are set out below, together with delivery dates.

Rolls-Royce chassis numbers for standard steel cars consist of three letters and up to three numbers. The second letter denotes the chassis series. There are no B- or I-series chassis. Cars with left-hand drive have an L prefix. The letter C after the chassis number denotes a coachbuilt car in the SGT, SHS, SJR or SKP series. All CSC series cars were coachbuilt. All Rolls-Royce sequences used odd numbers only and always excepted 13.

Bentley chassis numbers used even numbers only and all start with B followed by up to three digits and two suffix letters, the first of which denotes the chassis series. There are no B- or I-series chassis and left-hand-drive cars have an L before the suffix letters.

Rolls-Royce Silver Cloud III

SAZ1 to SAZ61	October 1962

SCX1 to SCX877	September 1962 to May 1963
SDW1 to SDW601	May to October 1963
SEV1 to SEV495	September 1963 to January 1964
SFU1 to SFU803	December 1963 to July 1964
SGT1 to SGT659	June to November 1964
SHS1 to SHS357	October 1964 to February 1965
SJR1 to SJR623	December 1964 to April 1965
SKP1 to SKP423	April to September 1965
CSC1B to CSC141B	April to December 1965
CSC1C to CSC83C[1]	September 1965 to February 1966

[1] LCSC83C was originally built as Bentley Continental S3 BC56LXE, converted by Rolls-Royce and re-numbered (see the Continental S3 chassis lists for further details).

Bentley S3

B2AV to B26AV	October 1962
B2CN to B828CN	September 1962 to October 1963
B2DF to B198DF	September to December 1963
B2EC to B530EC	November 1963 to June 1964
B2FG to B350FG	May to November 1964
B2GJ to B200GJ	October 1964 to January 1965
B2HN to B400HN	January to July 1965
B2JP to B40JP	July to August 1965

Engine Numbers

Engine numbers are stamped on the rear of the crankcase (just below the air cleaner trunking) on the left-hand side

of the engine. The numbering sequences are consecutive and include 13. There were no B-series sequences for standard steel cars.

Rolls-Royce Silver Cloud III

SZ1A to SZ30A	A-series chassis
SX1C to SX438C	C-series chassis
SW1D to SW300D	D-series chassis
SV1E to SV247E	E-series chassis
SU1F to SU401F	F-series chassis
ST1G to ST329G	G-series chassis
SS1H to SS178H	H-series chassis
SR1J to SR311J	J-series chassis
SP1K to SP211K	K-series chassis
B1CS to B70CS	B-series coachbuilt chassis
C1CS to C40CS	C-series coachbuilt chassis

Bentley S3

BAV1 to BAV13	A-series chassis
BCN1 to BCN414	C-series chassis
BDF1 to BDF99	D-series chassis
BEC1 to BEC265	E-series chassis
BFG1 to BFG175	F-series chassis
BGJ1 to BGJ100	G-series chassis
BHN1 to BHN200	H-series chassis
BJP1 to BJP20	J-series chassis

Long-Wheelbase Silver Cloud III & S3, 1962-65

Not all long-wheelbase cars wore Rolls-Royce badges. This is 1963 chassis BAL10, one of the 24 Bentleys with the Park Ward-converted body that were built on the S3 long-wheelbase chassis. It is also a rare saloon version without a division.

The long-wheelbase Rolls-Royce Silver Cloud III and Bentley S3 have the same 127in wheelbase as their earlier equivalents. Their bodies were converted from standard shells by Park Ward in exactly the same way.

The cars are identical in every respect to their standard-wheelbase sisters, except where noted in the text which follows. Brief details of production changeover points are also given here; see the relevant sections on the standard-wheelbase cars for fuller details of these changes.

Chassis

Steering

Two modifications were made during A-series Bentley chassis production, and three more during B-series. At BAL8, the steering box gained an air bleed, and at LBAL14, the PAS hose was re-routed and protected by a heat shield on the steering box mounting arm. These modifications were reflected on Rolls-Royce chassis probably during CAL-series production. At BBL8, the steering box spool valve and its housing were modified, and the head of the power cylinder was also changed. The first of these modifications was reflected on Rolls-Royce production during the CDL series and the second during the CEL series.

The final change was again during CEL-series production and at BBL10, when the hoses on right-hand-drive chassis were re-routed.

Brakes

Three modifications are recorded. The first was the relocation of the brake fluid reservoirs on the crankcase breather system during CAL-series production. This was probably matched on Bentley chassis during the BAL series. The shorter brake linings were fitted to all cars from CCL79 and BAL18 in October 1963. The third change was the introduction of a slotted brake servo pressure plate, at CEL51/LBBL10 in October 1964.

Wheels

The stainless steel wheel trims arrived with BAL8, and during CBL-series production, while the wider rear rims were introduced at BBL4 and during the CDL series.

Fuel Pumps

The additional condenser was first fitted to the fuel pump at chassis numbers CBL41 and BAL6 in May 1963. It was fitted to all subsequent long-wheelbase Bentley chassis, but these five Rolls-Royce chassis were built without it: CBL45, CBL49, CBL51, CBL53 and CBL57.

Flexible fuel pipes came in during CBL-series production and will have been fitted to all Bentleys from the start of the BBL series, if not earlier. The filter was relocated during CDL-series production and at BAL28, and the AUF400 pumps arrived during the CGL series and at BCL18.

Engine

Block, Pistons, Flywheel & Bellhousing

Interference-fit cylinder liners arrived at BCL14 and during the CFL series. The modified scraper rings were also introduced during the CFL series, and probably at the end of the BCL series.

The modified starter ring with hardened tips for its teeth came in during the CAL series and probably during the BAL series as well. The two bellhousing modifications were the addition of an underpan at BBL2 and during the CDL series, and the provision of ventilation holes at BCL2 and during the CEL series.

Camshaft & Valvegear

The camshaft bushes were deleted during the CBL series and were probably absent from the start of BBL-series production. The camshaft itself was modified at BCL2 and during the CEL series, and the heat-treated chilled-iron tappets came in during the CFL series and were probably on the later BCL series cars as well. The new castings for the tappets and tappet block assemblies were fitted from BBL10 and during the CEL series.

Carburettors & Automatic Choke

From BAL28 and somewhere during the CDL series, the carburettor float chambers were fitted with larger-bore vent pipes. The modified float chamber lids came in at chassis CCL3 and BAL10, and the modified automatic choke stove pipes were fitted at CFL5/BCL12 in July 1965.

Cooling System

New top and bottom hoses were introduced at BAL8 and probably during the CAL series. The wax thermostat was fitted during CBL-series production and was probably on all of the BBL-series Bentleys, if it was not introduced earlier. The 88°C thermostat came in during the CDL series, and probably from the start of the BBL series.

Exhaust System

From BAL18 and probably during the CBL series, a heat shield was fitted to the right-hand manifold.

Transmission

Gearbox

The stronger torus cover springs were fitted at BAL10 and during the CCL series.

Propshaft

The pre-loaded centre bearing was introduced during CDL-series production and was probably fitted from the beginning of the BBL series.

Electrical System

Battery Cable

Copper battery cable was used from BBL8 and some point in the CEL series.

Dynamo & Voltage Regulator

The dynamo bracket was modified at BBL2 and in the CDL series, and the RB340 voltage regulator was fitted from BAL16 and in the CCL series.

Starter Motor

The improved Lucas 26209A starter motor was fitted from chassis numbers CCL61 and BAL16. Earlier motors modified with new brushes were identified by a light blue paint mark on the rear of the solenoid casing. The lengthened starter relay cable was fitted from BAL2 and probably early in the CAL series, and the cable was re-routed during the CCL series and was probably in its new position from the start of BBL-series production. The solenoid cable was replaced by a link strip at BBL8 and during the CDL series.

Sparking Plugs & HT Leads

The N16Y sparking plugs were introduced during the CCL series and were probably fitted from the beginning of the BBL series. High tension leads with resistive cores arrived at BBL10 and during the CEL series.

Lighting

A choke was fitted in the reversing lamp circuit at BAL20 and during the CCL series. The new reversing and number-plate lamp unit arrived during the CDL series and at BBL2, and from BBL8 the relays for the stop and flasher lamps

The absence of the division is evident in this view through BAL10's lengthened rear door window. The opening quarter-light is now part of the rear quarter panel.

were discontinued. This latter change took place during the CDL series on Rolls-Royce production.

Windscreen Wipers
Stops were added to the windscreen wipers at BAL8 and during the CCL series.

Electric Windows
A stop bracket was added to the optional electric window lifts at BBL10 and during CEL-series Rolls-Royce production.

Body

Radiator Grille
Bentley models prior to LBAL14 suffered from radiator shutter vibration. The moaning noise that ensued could be cured by removing a triangular blanking plate behind the grille at the bottom, and by removing some metal in that area.

Doors
Improved door seals were introduced during the CCL series and were probably fitted to Bentley models from the start of the BBL series.

Rear Wings & Fuel Filler
The 100-octane fuel warning plate in the fuel filler compartment was not fitted to Rolls-Royce models on production before chassis number CAL23, but was a recommended retro-fit in service. It was probably fitted to all the Bentleys.

Boot Lid
The chromed boot lid motif was not fitted on production to Rolls-Royce models before CAL23, but the owners of cars without it could have a motif fitted if they so wished from December 1962. The S3 motif was probably supplied from new on all Bentley models.

Rear Window
The wider heated rear window element came at BAL16 and was probably fitted to Rolls-Royce chassis from some point in the CBL series.

Interior

Facia & Instruments
The handbrake-warning lamp was modified during the CAL series, and possibly before Bentley production began. Additional cold air intake controls were provided from BBL4 and during the CDL series.

The improved speedometer cable with the two white wrappings was fitted on production from CBL9/BAL6, although some later cars were also fitted with the earlier type.

The Nemag speedometer with its conventional zero position arrived with BBL8 and during the CEL series.

Handbrake
Right-hand-drive chassis have a pulley-type handbrake from chassis CCL43 and BAL16.

Seats
The standard steel long-wheelbase cars did not have the S3 saloon's improved rear seating and retained the previous S2-type rear seat. Cars with a division also retained the bench front seat but non-division cars could be fitted with the new S3 separate front seats. For the US and Canada, the single-bolt seat belt anchorages arrived during the CCL series, and were probably also available for Bentleys from the beginning of the BBL series.

Heater & Air Conditioning
The air conditioning taps and mounting plates were modified at BAL2 and in the CAL series.

On this Bentley without a division, the normal S3 saloon's separate front seats with picnic tables are combined with the old S2 bench rear seat, which overhangs the heelboard. The 4in of extra legroom are very evident.

PAINT & INTERIOR TRIM

Long-wheelbase cars had the same range of exterior paint colours and interior trim combinations as the standard steel cars.

IDENTIFICATION, DATING & PRODUCTION FIGURES

The chassis identification plate and chassis number on the frame are in the same place on long-wheelbase models as on standard-wheelbase cars.

There were 254 Rolls-Royce Silver Cloud III and 32 Bentley S3 long-wheelbase chassis.

CHASSIS NUMBERS
The chassis number sequences for these cars are set out here, together with delivery dates. Chassis numbers consist of three letters and up to three numbers. All Rolls-Royce sequences began with C, used odd numbers only and always excepted 13. All Bentley chassis series began with B and used even numbers only. The second letter of the prefix denotes the chassis series. Cars with left-hand drive had an L prefix (eg LCAL1).

Rolls-Royce Silver Cloud III Long Wheelbase	
CAL1 to CAL83	October 1962 to January 1963
CBL1 to CBL61	January to June 1963
CCL1 to CCL101	June 1963 to February 1964
CDL1 to CDL95	February to August 1964
CEL1 to CEL105	September 1964 to June 1965
CFL1 to CFL41	June to August 1965
CGL1 to CGL27	August to September 1965

Bentley S3 Long Wheelbase	
BAL2 to BAL30	November 1962 to May 1963
BBL2 to BBL12	June 1964 to January 1965
BCL2 to BCL22	February to September 1965

ENGINE NUMBERS
Engine numbers are stamped on the rear of the crankcase (just below the air cleaner trunking) on the left-hand side of the engine. The numbering sequences are consecutive and include 13.

Rolls-Royce Silver Cloud III Long Wheelbase	
CL1A to CL41A	A-series chassis
CL1B to CL30B	B-series chassis
CL1C to CL50C	C-series chassis
CL1D to CL47D	D-series chassis
CL1E to CL52E	E-series chassis
CL1F to CL20F	F-series chassis
CL1G to CL14G	G-series chassis

Bentley S3 Long Wheelbase	
BL1A to BL15A	A-series chassis
BL1B to BL6B	B-series chassis
BL1C to BL11C	C-series chassis

Bentley Continental S3, 1962-66

The Bentley Continental S3 chassis has neither the higher gearing nor the more powerful engine associated with earlier Continentals. Sales literature described it as a lightweight model with a hand-built body of smaller frontal area than the standard offerings. There were of course a number of different body options, but in all cases the Continentals have more comprehensive instrumentation than the standard cars, a lower radiator grille and a more raked steering column.

Although the last Continental S3 chassis (BC118XE and BC120XE) were delivered to the coachbuilder on 29 November 1965, delivery to the customers did not take place until the end of January 1966.

Chassis

Steering

All chassis from BC152XA have an air bleed on the steering box. The modified spool valve and housing are fitted from BC156XC, and the modified power cylinder head from BC158XC. The hoses were re-routed on left-hand-drive cars at BC12LXB, when a shield was also fitted to the steering box mounting arm, and hoses on right-hand-drive chassis were re-routed at BC182XC.

Brakes

Only the first 82 chassis have the four-shoe front brakes of the earlier V8-engined Continentals,

The Koren-designed Park Ward drophead was joined by a fixed-head derivative for the S3 models, and was available on both Rolls-Royce and Bentley Continental chassis. The single headlamp of the original design was replaced by paired lamps. This car, BC124XC, has the side trim strip which was not on all examples.

James Young built only 20 of their elegant bodies on the Continental S3 chassis and this 1965 four-door saloon is one of the last on chassis BC38XE. It is owned by Alec Norman.

This Park Ward body style was the only drophead coupé offered on the Continental S3 chassis. A power-operated hood was part of the specification.

and the standard type of twin-shoe brakes are fitted from BC166LXA in summer 1963. From BC90LXC in 1964, shorter brake linings were fitted to the rear brakes of the Continentals. Then from BC2XD in October that year, the servo was fitted with a slotted pressure plate.

Wheels & Tyres

Stainless steel wheel covers replaced the chromium-plated type at BC144LXA. The rear wheels always remained the same as the fronts and the wider rear rims were never fitted to Bentley Continental chassis.

Tyres were of 8.00-15 size and the recommended running pressures were 20psi at the front and 25psi at the rear. For high speeds, pressures of 25psi and 30psi respectively were recommended. Drophead coupés had higher rear tyre pressures of 28psi for normal use and 33psi for high-speed motoring. As usual, a variety of tyres could be fitted as original equipment, and all types could be had with white or black sidewalls. The tyre types were: Dunlop Elite C40 (until August 1963, when their availability ceased), Dunlop Road Speed RS5, India Super Speed and Firestone Sports ORB P345. Winter tyres for the rear wheels only were either Dunlop Weathermaster or Firestone Town and Country.

Fuel Pumps

The additional condenser was fitted to the fuel pumps with effect from chassis number BC160XA in May 1963, and the nylon barrier diaphragm was incorporated at BC36XE in May 1965. The AUF400 pumps were fitted from BC68XE.

Engine

Block & Bellhousing

The bellhousing has an underpan from BC152XC, except on BC154XC and on cars destined for dusty or tropical climates. From BC22XD, there are vent holes in the bellhousing. Interference-fit cylinder liners were specified from chassis BC64XE.

Carburettors & Automatic Choke

The modified float chamber lid was introduced at chassis number BC12LXB, and larger-bore carburettor vent pipes are fitted from BC124XC. From chassis number BC42XE in July 1965, there are modified stove pipes for the automatic choke.

Camshaft

Cars from chassis number BC6XE, but not BC8XE, have the modified camshaft.

Cooling System

From BC72LXA there is an improved radiator pressure relief valve, and the new top and bottom hoses are fitted from BC144LXA.

Exhaust System

The right-hand exhaust manifold is fitted with a heat shield from BC116XC.

Transmission

Gearbox

Stronger torus cover springs are fitted from chassis number BC74XB.

Electrical System

Battery Cable

Cars from BC172XC have a copper battery cable.

Ignition System

From BC184XC, HT leads have resistive cores.

Dynamo & Voltage Regulator

The RB340 voltage regulator is on chassis from BC68XC and the modified dynamo bracket is fitted from BC148XC.

Starter Motor

The improved Lucas 26209A starter is fitted from BC48XC. Earlier motors modified with new brushes have a light blue paint mark on the rear of the solenoid casing. From BC24LXA there is a longer starter relay cable, and from BC158XC the solenoid cable is replaced by a link-strip.

Luxurious aircraft-style seats (top) were a feature of the Park Ward saloon. The black knob operates the rake adjustment of the squab. The headrest shown here is special to this car. Rear seats (above) were thickly padded in the Park Ward saloon and more suited to two passengers. The opening rear windows were front hinged and ashtrays were fitted in the veneered dado rail below the windows. Seat belts were an option by the time of this 1964 car (BC124XC).

The rear styling of the Continental S3 Park Ward body, by Vilhelm Koren, is quite distinctive with fins and cowled rear lamps.

On the Park Ward facia the heater and lighting controls were at the outboard edge. This neat chromed outlet was provided for face-level ventilation, controlled by the push-pull knob below.

The handsome aircraft-style facia layout of this 1964 Park Ward-bodied saloon was unchanged from the style used on the S2 Continental chassis.

Lighting
The reversing light circuit is fitted with a choke from BC122XC.

Windscreen Wipers
A more powerful wiper motor is specified for cars fitted with the Park Ward two-door bodies from chassis BC34XE.

Interior

Facia & Instruments
The layout of the Continental instrument panel differs from one body type to the next. However, all of them have the same instruments in common, with a rev counter and speedometer of matching size, and four small round dials instead of the four-in-one instrument of the standard cars.

The improved speedometer cable with the two white wrappings was fitted on production from BC96XA, although some later cars were also fitted with the earlier type. The Nemag speedometer with its conventionally-sited zero was fitted from BC28XD.

Handbrake
A pulley-type handbrake is fitted to right-hand-drive chassis from BC100XC.

Heater & Air Conditioning System
From BC34XE the standard S3 type of demister and blower unit is fitted. Electrically-operated water taps and valves are fitted to Continentals from the same chassis number. Air conditioning was optional at extra cost and most Continentals fitted with it have the Rolls-Royce boot-mounted unit, but the OMC unit was available for cars exported to the US.

Body

Continental bodies were constructed by two main companies, the first being the Rolls-Royce-owned combined H. J. Mulliner, Park Ward concern and the second being James Young. There were four bodies in all. Two were of Park Ward origin, these being the Koren-designed convertible coupé and sports saloon (as they were now called). The third, the Flying Spur, was originally an H. J. Mulliner design, and the fourth was James Young's four-door saloon alternative.

PAINT & INTERIOR TRIM

As the Continental was always seen as a coachbuilt car, which was built to individual order, there were no standard paint finishes or trim colours. Customers could – and did – choose from the range offered on the standard saloons, but also cars were painted or trimmed in other colours to the individual customer's choice.

When the cars were announced in October 1962, the Continental cost exactly the same in Britain with any one of these four bodies: £8495. However, no cars were delivered at that price since in November 1962 the Purchase Tax on new cars was reduced from 45 per cent to 25 per cent and the Bentley Continental's home market price therefore came down to £7860 15s 5d (£7860.77).

Of the 311 Continental S3 chassis, 171 are recorded as having Park Ward bodies, 68 with bodies by H.J. Mulliner, 51 with bodies by the merged H. J. Mulliner, Park Ward company, and 20 by James Young. One chassis was bodied by Swiss coachbuilder Graber.

IDENTIFICATION, DATING & PRODUCTION FIGURES

The chassis identification plate and chassis number on the frame are in the same place on Continental models as on cars with the standard chassis. There were 311 Bentley Continental S3 chassis.

CHASSIS NUMBERS
The chassis number sequences for these cars are set out here, together with delivery dates. All Bentley Continental chassis carry the prefix BC followed by up to three numbers and two letters. The final suffix letter denotes the chassis series. Cars with left-hand drive have an L before the suffix letters (eg BC44LXE). Only even numbers were used in all chassis number sequences.

BC2XA to BC174XA November 1962 to July 1963
BC2XB to BC100XB June to September 1963
BC2XC to BC202XC November 1963 to November 1965
BC2XD to BC28XD February to April 1965
BC2XE to BC120XE[1] March 1965 to January 1966
[1] Chassis BC56XE is omitted. The car was built as a Bentley Continental S3 for the Shah of Iran and exhibited at the 1965 Frankfurt Motor Show. When delivered, however, it was badged as a Rolls-Royce Silver Cloud III and renumbered as LCSC83C.

ENGINE NUMBERS
Engine numbers are stamped on the rear of the crankcase (just below the air cleaner trunking) on the left-hand side of the engine. The numbering sequences are consecutive and include 13.

1ABC to 87ABC	A-series chassis
1BBC to 50BBC	B-series chassis
1CBC to 101CBC	C-series chassis
1DBC to 14DBC	D-series chassis
1EBC to 60EBC[1]	E-series chassis

[1] There was no engine 28EBC. This number was allocated to the engine for chassis number BC56XE (see left).

CONTINENTAL S3 BODIES

PARK WARD
Park Ward's Koren-designed drophead coachwork was renumbered as design 2006 (2041 on Rolls-Royce chassis) after the amalgamation with H. J. Mulliner, and the two-door saloon version became design number 2035 (on Rolls-Royce chassis it is 2045). Cars built into 1963 carry Park Ward sill plates, but later examples have the full H. J. Mulliner, Park Ward coachbuilder's identification plate.

These bodies are the same in all major respects as the popular drophead and two-door saloon styles on the Rolls-Royce chassis; some do not have the side finishing strip. Either the standard S3 overriders or the larger export type may be fitted.

The full list of 171 Continental S3 chassis with Park Ward bodies is:

A series: BC4LXA, BC8LXA, BC14XA, BC22LXA, BC26LXA, BC30LXA, BC34LXA, BC38LXA, BC42XA, BC46XA, BC48LXA, BC50LXA, BC56LXA, BC60XA, BC66XA, BC68LXA, BC70LXA, BC80LXA, BC82LXA, BC86LXA, BC96XA, BC98LXA, BC102LXA, BC106LXA, BC110XA, BC112XA, BC116LXA, BC122XA, BC124XA, BC126XA, BC130LXA, BC132XA, BC136XA, BC138XA, BC142XA, BC146LXA, BC148XA, BC152XA, BC154LXA, BC160XA, BC162XA, BC166LXA, BC170XA and BC174XA.

B series: BC4XB, BC8LXB, BC10XB, BC12LXB, BC16XB, BC18LXB, BC20LXB, BC24LXB, BC26XB, BC28LXB, BC34XB, BC38XB, BC40XB, BC42XB, BC46XB, C48XB, BC50XB, BC56LXB, BC58XB, BC60LXB, BC62LXB, BC64XB, BC72XB, BC76XB, BC78XB, BC80LXB, BC84XB, BC88XB, BC90XB, BC94XB, BC96XB, BC98LXB and BC100LXB.

C series: BC2XC, BC6XC, BC8XC, BC10XC, BC12LXC, BC14XC, BC16XC, BC18LXC, BC20XC, BC26XC, BC28LXC, BC30XC, BC32LXC, BC36XC, BC38XC, BC40XC, BC44XC, BC46LXC, BC48LXC, BC50XC, BC52XC, BC56XC, BC60XC, BC62XC, BC64XC, BC66XC, BC68XC, BC70XC, BC72XC, BC78XC, BC80XC, BC84XC, BC88LXC, BC90XC, BC94XC, BC96XC, BC98LXC, BC102XC, BC104XC, BC110XC, BC112XC, BC114XC, BC116XC, BC120XC, BC124XC, BC126LXC, BC130XC, BC132XC, BC136LXC, BC138XC, BC144XC, BC146XC, BC148XC, BC150XC, BC152XC, BC154XC, BC156XC, BC158XC, BC160XC, BC162XC, BC164XC, BC166XC, BC168XC, BC170XC, BC172XC, BC174XC, BC176XC, BC178LXC, BC180XC, BC182XC, BC184XC, BC186XC, BC188XC, BC190XC, BC192LXC, BC194XC, BC196LXC and BC198XC.

D series: BC2XD, BC6XD, BC8XD, BC10XD, BC14XD, BC18XD, BC20LXD, BC22XD, BC24XD, BC26XD and BC28XD.

E series: BC4XE, BC10XE, BC22XE, BC24XE and BC28XE.

H. J. MULLINER
The most popular Mulliner bodywork on the Continental S3 was the Flying Spur four-door saloon. These cars are generally fitted with the larger, export-type overriders. There is a rare variant with a smaller rear quarter-window. H. J. Mulliner also made a small number of two-door saloons similar to those introduced for the S2 Continental but incorporating the four headlamps and the combined sidelamp-and-indicator units associated with the later S3-series chassis.

The 68 bodies recorded as by H. J. Mulliner, although actually built in the Park Ward factory at Willesden, are on the following chassis:

A series: BC6LXA, BC10XA, BC16XA, BC18XA, BC20XA, BC24LXA, BC28XA, BC32XA, BC36LXA, BC40XA, BC44LXA, BC52LXA, BC54XA, BC58XA, BC62XA, BC72LXA, BC74XA, BC84XA, BC88XA, BC90XA, BC92XA, BC94XA, BC100XA, BC104LXA, BC108XA, BC114XA, BC118LXA, BC120XA, BC128XA, BC140XA, BC144XA, BC150XA, BC156XA, BC164XA, BC168XA and BC172XA.

B series: BC2XB, BC6XB, BC14XB, BC22LXB, BC30LXB, BC36XB, BC44XB, C52XB, BC54LXB, BC66LXB, BC74XB, BC82XB, BC86XB and BC92LXB.

C series: BC4XC, BC22LXC, BC24LXC, BC34XC, BC42XC, BC58XC, BC74XC, BC86XC, BC92XC, BC100XC, BC106XC, BC108XC, BC118XC, BC122XC, BC128LXC, BC134LXC and BC140XC.

E series: BC2XE.

H. J. MULLINER, PARK WARD
There are 51 chassis recorded as carrying coachwork by H. J. Mulliner, Park Ward. The merged company did not produce any new designs during this period, and all the bodies are to former Park Ward or H. J. Mulliner designs. The chassis are:

C & D series: BC82XC, BC142XC and BC16XD.

E series: BC6LXE, BC12XE, BC14XE, BC16XE, BC20XE, BC26XE, BC30XE, BC32LXE, BC34XE, BC36XE, BC40XE, BC42XE, BC48LXE, BC50XE, BC52XE, BC54XE, BC58LXE, BC60XE, BC62XE, BC64LXE, BC66XE, BC68XE, BC70XE, BC72XE, BC74LXE, BC76XE, BC78XE, BC80LXE, BC82XE, BC84XE, BC86XE, BC88XE, BC90XE, BC92XE, BC94XE, BC96XE, BC98XE, BC100XE, BC102XE, BC104LXE, BC106XE, BC108XE, BC110XE, BC112XE, BC114XE, BC116XE, BC118XE and BC120XE.

JAMES YOUNG LTD
James Young's four-door saloon is a four-headlamp version of the SCV100 style, introduced for the S2 Continental chassis, and there were also a couple of two-door variants on BC76XC and BC12XD. Like other bodies on the Continental S3 chassis, they have the standard sidelamp/indicator units in the noses of the front wings. The Continental bodies differ subtly from the bodies on Rolls-Royce chassis in that they do not have the bright trim strip at door handle height.

James Young bodied the following 20 Continental S3 chassis:
BC2XA, BC12XA, BC64XA, BC76XA, BC78XA, BC134XA, BC158XA, BC32XB, BC68XB, BC70XB, BC54XC, BC76XC, BC200XC, BC4XD, BC12XD, BC8XE, BC18XE, BC38XE, BC44LXE and BC46XE.

CARROSSERIE GRABER
One Continental S3 was bodied by the Swiss coachbuilder Graber with a drophead coupé body on chassis BC202LXC. It was not delivered until 1967.

Coachbuilt Bodies

BENTLEY MkVI

The standard saloon body built by Pressed Steel was fitted to the overwhelming majority of MkVI Bentley chassis. Experts disagree about the exact number of coachbuilt cars, but Johnnie Green's standard work on Bentley takes its information from the chassis cards and lists 1002 chassis supplied for coachbuilt bodywork.

Full details of the coachbuilt bodies are beyond the scope of this book, but it is worth noting that Rolls-Royce favoured certain coachbuilders and listed their products in its own sales and service literature. Thus, a January 1951 service bulletin listed the availability of bodies by Park Ward, H. J. Mulliner, James Young, Hooper and Abbott. Nevertheless, a far greater variety of coachbuilders than this actually worked on MkVI chassis. Some were long-established names, both at home and abroad. Others sprang up in the post-war climate where rebodying a pre-war chassis was a popular and economical way of extending its life when new cars were in short supply. Most of these built just one body on the MkVI chassis.

Of the 1002 MkVI chassis supplied without the standard Pressed Steel body, the numbers bodied by the following coachbuilders are:

H. J. Mulliner 299, James Young 212, Park Ward 167, Freestone & Webb 103, Hooper 62, Vanden Plas 21, Abbott 19, Gurney Nutting 19, Harold Radford 17, Graber 17, Facel-Métallon 9, and Franay 8. Graber actually made 18 bodies (one standard steel saloon was rebodied) and as many as 17 bodies by Facel-Métallon have been suggested.

The firms of Farina, David Joel and Rippon each made five bodies, Windovers made four bodies, Ramseier made four (or possibly five) bodies, Simpson & Slater and Seary & Macready each made two bodies.

Sixteen companies made just one body each: Aburnsons, Baker, Beutler, Cooper, Denby, Duncan, Eadon, Figoni, Ghia, J. A. Holland, Ronald Kent, Roos, Saoutchik, Westminster, Van Vooren, and Vincents.

In addition, there are six chassis which have unidentified coachwork.

It is worth noting that the coachbuilders often extended the chassis side-members at the rear so that they could fit boots which were bigger than the standard MkVI saloon type. Once the R-type became available with its lengthened rear chassis, such modifications were no longer necessary.

H. J. MULLINER & CO LTD

H. J. Mulliner built a single four-door, four-light saloon body on the first experimental MkVI chassis, 1BVI, which was later renumbered as B256AK. However, the saloon bodies built in quantity by this firm between 1946 and 1950 were six-light types, to design 7122. This used the standard Bentley bonnet, boot and spare wheel door, and was characterised by slim chromium-plated brass window frames. The front doors were hinged on their leading edges and the rear doors on their trailing edges. Some examples had rear side windows similar to the characteristic Hooper style. In 1951, this design was modified to become number 7220, in which the front wings swept across the doors higher up.

During 1949, H. J. Mulliner announced a new form of construction using extruded Reynolds Metal framing and aluminium panels to create a lighter body. This was pioneered on a two-door saloon with a sloping back and an alligator bonnet, exhibited at the 1949 Earls Court Show and fitted to chassis B9EW. However, quantity production was of design 7243, a modern-looking four-door, six-light saloon, of which the first example was built on B355GT in 1950. Less common was a two-door, four-light, derivative of the same style, and there was also a rare close-coupled coupé variant with a longer boot.

Drophead coupés were not Mulliner's strong suit at this period, and just 13 were built on MkVI chassis. Among them were a three-position sedanca drophead with side-mounted spare wheel, on chassis B382CF, and a four-light design with a metal tonneau cover which gave a fully disappearing hood.

The full list of 299 chassis bodied by H. J. Mulliner is given below. The 13 drophead coupé bodies are indicated with an asterisk.

4¼-LITRE:

A series: B4AK, B22AK, B30AK, B36AK, B42AK*, B44AK, B48AK, B54AK, B56AK, B244AK, B246AK, B248AK, B252AK, B256AK, B5AJ, B19AJ*, B77AJ, B83AJ, B93AJ, B101AJ, B177AJ and B185AJ.

B series: B24BH, B86BH, B88BH, B366BH, B384BH, B83BG, B147BG, B149BG, B153BG, B267BG, B273BG*, B275BG and B319BG.

C series: B6CF, B192CF, B290CF, B292CF, B382CF*, B408CF, B426CF, B428CF, B436CF, B442CF, B444CF, B179CD, B183CD, B315CD, B329CD, B335CD, B441CD and B451CD*.

D series: B122DA, B126DA, B138DA, B238DA, B240DA, B242DA*, B244DA, B250DA, B264DA, B266DA, B366DA, B368DA, B87DZ, B91DZ, B95DZ, B99DZ, B159DZ, B163DZ, B261DZ*, B321DZ, B329DZ, B331DZ*, B339DZ, B371DZ, B387DZ, B393DZ, B395DZ, B399DZ, B409DZ and B477DZ.

E series: B22EY, B64EY, B70EY*, B72EY, B124EY, B130EY, B140EY, B142EY, B216EY*, B254EY*, B260EY, B262EY, B296EY, B378EY, B406EY, B456EY, B458EY, B490EY, B3EW, B7EW, B9EW, B15EW, B43EW, B49EW, B53EW, B87EW*, B139EW, B143EW, B183EW, B187EW, B191EW, B197EW, B299EW, B305EW, B309EW, B311EW, B315EW, B317EW, B359EW, B363EW, B399EW, B401EW, B405EW, B429EW, B433EW, B437EW and B493EW.

F series: B48FV, B80FV, B84FV, B86FV, B120FV, B122FV, B124FV, B158FV, B406FV, B494FV, B496FV, B45FU*, B253FU, B269FU, B271FU, B273FU, B275FU, B281FU, B285FU, B289FU, B295FU, B407FU, B415FU, B419FU, B423FU, B427FU, B543FU and B549FU.

G series: B47GT, B49GT, B51GT, B53GT, B95GT, B97GT, B355GT, B357GT, B359GT and B371GT.

H series: B2HR, B78HR, B82HR, B88HR, B90HR, B156HR, B162HR, B164HR, B59HP, B63HP, B65HP, B67HP, B141HP, B143HP, B147HP, B179HP, B185HP, B187HP, B191HP, B193HP, B197HP, B233HP, B239HP and B241HP.

J series: B122JO, B126JO, B130JO, B132JO, B134JO, B196JO, B204JO, B210JO, B97JN and B99JN.

K series: B94KM, B96KM, B104KM, B186KM, B192KM, B194KM, B73KL, B75KL, B153KL, B157KL, B161KL, B163KL, B173KL and B175KL.

L series: B2LJ, B4LJ, B172LJ, B174LJ, B188LJ, B254LJ, B262LJ, B264LJ, B266LJ, B272LJ, B1LH, B71LH, B75LH, B77LH, B141LH, B143LH, B145LH, B147LH, B215LH, B275LH, B277LH, B279LH, B283LH, B343LH and B345LH.

4½-LITRE:

M series: B4MD, B12MD, B24MD, B28MD, B32MD, B34MD, B36MD, B38MD, B46MD, B50MD, B140MD, B142MD, B194MD, B204MD, B272MD, B322MD, B326MD, B330MD, B388MD, B400MD, B1MB, B135MB, B137MB, B275MB, B279MB, B287MB, B289MB, B291MB, B315MB and B323MB.

N series: B76NZ, B78NZ, B80NZ, B138NZ, B140NZ, B142NZ, B342NZ, B346NZ, B348NZ, B426NZ, B99NY, B105NY, B127NY, B129NY, B133NY, B279NY, B283NY, B285NY, B289NY, B457NY, B459NY, B471NY, B475NY, B479NY, B481NY, B483NY, B485NY and B497NY.

JAMES YOUNG LTD

The 212 bodies by James Young involved a large variety of styles, some of these inherited from Gurney Nutting, which was absorbed shortly after the war.

The very first MkVI chassis, B2AK, carried a James Young foursome coupé body. Young's earliest bodies had razor-edge styling, cutaway rear spats, and slim chromed window frames. Design C10 was a two-door four-light sports saloon of which 62 examples were built. Detail modifications turned this into design C10N in later years. Design C11 had four doors and four lights, and a rear-hinged rear door.

There were some disastrous experiments with slab-sided bodies apparently inspired by the American Hudson. The first was confusingly numbered as design C10M (a 1948 four-door with full rear spats on B495CD and three other chassis) and the second was a two-door with slab sides known as design 3000 on B42FV in 1950. Quantity production concentrated on more rounded styling from 1949, however, exemplified by the C10AM two-door saloon coupé (on B185EW) which gained new front wings in 1950 to become a design C10BM, of which 35 were made. From 1950, James Young bodies featured door handles with the firm's characteristic square push-buttons.

Design C10BM evolved into design C17 when the wing line was raised, and 12 of these two-door bodies were built; the first was seen at the 1951 Earls Court Show on chassis B48MD. Clearly from the same school of thought was a four-door, six-light saloon, although the styling of its wing lines hinted at the contemporary Park Ward designs.

Last but not least, except in terms of numbers, there were two sedanca de ville designs and a drophead coupé. The first of the sedancas was inherited from Gurney Nutting, and was built as James Young's C15 from 1947 to 1949. This is the famous 'teardrop' design, so called for the shape of its rear side window. It was replaced in 1949 by Young's own sedanca de ville, design C16, an altogether less striking style with conventional rear side windows. The drophead was a three-position type with cutaway rear spats, and the only example was built on B491EW in 1950. The body on B263BG was built in conjunction with Bentley Motors.

The full list of chassis bodied by James Young is:

4¼-LITRE:

A series: B2AK, B16AK, B18AK, B20AK, B24AK, B26AK, B28AK, B32AK, B34AK, B38AK, B46AK, B64AK, B68AK, B70AK, B112AK, B228AK, B236AK, B240AK, B250AK, B254AK, B1AJ, B3AJ, B7AJ, B21AJ, B57AJ, B71AJ, B99AJ, B121AJ, B123AJ, B125AJ, B127AJ, B129AJ, B175AJ, B179AJ, B183AJ, B235AJ and B247AJ.

BENTLEY MKVI

B series: B56BH, B58BH, B286BH, B292BH, B356BH, B362BH, B382BH, B386BH, B390BH, B394BH, B141BG, B143BG, B155BG, B161BG, B263BG, B271BG and B393BG.

C series: B104CF, B144CF, B196CF, B298CF, B406CF, B434CF, B327CD, B331CD, B337CD, B339CD, B341CD, B345CD, B377CD, B453CD and B495CD.

D series: B124DA, B128DA, B130DA, B132DA, B134DA, B136DA, B248DA, B268DA, B372DA, B452DA, B458DA, B464DA, B157DZ, B267DZ, B325DZ, B333DZ, B369DZ, B377DZ, B403DZ and B445DZ.

E series: B66EY, B68EY, B118EY, B120EY, B128EY, B134EY, B182EY, B218EY, B222EY, B374EY, B380EY, B5EW, B91EW, B131EW, B185EW, B195EW, B199EW, B201EW, B235EW, B237EW, B239EW, B243EW, B245EW, B267EW, B271EW, B275EW, B277EW, B303EW, B313EW, B361EW, B367EW, B407EW, B431EW, B435EW, B447EW, B491EW and B495EW.

F series: B42FV, B44FV, B139FU, B141FU, B261FU, B263FU, B265FU, B267FU and B431FU.

G series: B347GT, B361GT and B375GT.

H series: B76HR, B84HR, B86HR, B94HR, B152HR, B160HR, B168HR, B61HP, B69HP, B247HP and B249HP.

J series: B128JO, B200JO, B202JO, B206JO and B93JN.

K series: B108KM, B71KL, B77KL, B151KL, B159KL, B165KL and B167KL.

L series: B8LJ, B14LJ, B18LJ, B22LJ, B170LJ, B176LJ, B180LJ, B256LJ, B258LJ, B260LJ, B5LH, B7LH and B281LH.

4½-LITRE:

M series: B42MD, B48MD, B138MD, B144MD, B186MD, B196MD, B198MD, B254MD, B258MD, B260MD, B268MD, B270MD, B3MB, B7MB, B285MB, B293MB, B313MB and B325MB.

N series: B82NZ, B148NZ, B150NZ, B152NZ, B154NZ, B350NZ, B352NZ, B354NZ, B430NZ, B115NY, B121NY, B125NY, B131NY, B275NY, B277NY, B469NY, B487NY, B489NY, B491NY and B493NY.

PARK WARD & CO LTD

Best known for their drophead coupé styles, Park Ward built 167 bodies. Early cars used the standard Bentley front wings and bonnet assembly, and were two-door four-light styles with cutaway rear wheel spats. An attractive new style introduced in 1950 had long flowing wing-lines and spatted rear wheels. This was mainly seen as a two-door, four-light 'foursome' drophead coupé with a power-assisted hood. There was also a fixed-head coupé variant.

Design 230 was a six-light, four-door saloon with similar styling, but only one Bentley (B93GT in 1950) was fitted with this body intended primarily for the Silver Wraith chassis. Design 238 was very similar, with standard bumpers instead of the special ones fitted on design 230; just one example was built, on chassis number B235HP in 1951.

The 167 chassis bodied by Park Ward are:

4¼-LITRE:
DROPHEAD COUPÉS:

A series: B10AK, B107AJ, B109AJ and B119AJ.

B series: B16BH, B132BH, B364BH, B157BG, B279BG and B361BG.

C series: B30CF, B182CF, B282CF, B286CF, B294CF, B430CF, B432CF and B438CF.

D series: B140DA, B142DA, B144DA, B370DA, B378DA, B450DA, B456DA, B462DA, B470DA, B472DA, B89DZ, B97DZ, B155DZ, B161DZ, B323DZ, B335DZ, B373DZ, B375DZ, B397DZ and B401DZ.

E series: B38EY, B62EY, B74EY, B122LEY, B132EY, B138EY, B174EY, B220EY, B256EY, B298EY, B300EY, B404EY, B450EY, B452EY, B486EY, B492EY, B11EW, B51EW, B55EW, B141EW and B233EW.

F series: B160FV, B162FV, B164FV, B410FV, B498FV,

B500FV, B47FU, B95FU, B163FU, B165FU, B167FU, B277FU, B283FU, B413FU, B417FU, B425FU, B429FU and B535FU.

G series: B5GT, B7GT, B345GT and B377GT.

H series: B4HR, B154HR, B158HR, B166HR and B243HP.

J series: B120JO, B136JO, B212JO and B165JN.

K series: B100KM, B188KM, B79KL, B81KL and B171KL.

L series: B6LJ, B20LJ, B186LJ, B268LJ, B347LH and B349LH.

FIXED-HEAD COUPÉS AND SALOONS:

E & F series: B97EW, B196FV, B69FU, B73FU, B97FU, B99FU, B249FU, B251FU, B279FU, B301FU, B421FU and B537FU.

G series: B93GT and B343GT.

H series: B6HR, B80HR, B57HP, B181HP, B235HP and B245HP.

J & K series: B198JO, B169JN, B102KM and B149KL.

L series: B184LJ, B73LH and B337LH.

4½-LITRE:
DROPHEAD COUPÉS:

M series: B14MD, B18MD, B26MD, B328MD, B334MD, B336MD, B340MD, B394LMD, B396MD, B281MB and B319MB.

N series: B72LNZ, B144NZ, B344NZ, B358NZ, B360LNZ, B424NZ, B428LNZ, B95LNY, B117NY, B119NY, B135NY, B453NY, B455NY, B461NY, B463NY, B465NY, B467NY, B499LNY and B501NY.

FIXED-HEAD COUPÉS AND SALOONS:

M series: B16MD, B262MD, B264MD, B398MD, B277MB and B283MB.

N series: B113NY, B123NY and B281NY.

FREESTONE & WEBB LTD

The first post-war offering from Freestone & Webb was a rather old-fashioned looking four-light razor-edge saloon. A six-light saloon became available as well, with more swaging on the wings and a more scalloped waistline. From about 1951, Freestone & Webb followed the trend towards wing lines which swept back across the front doors at a higher point. The company also built two-door, four-light coupés on B281BG and B288BH, and there were five drophead coupés (indicated by an asterisk).

The full list of 103 MkVI chassis bodied by Freestone & Webb is:

4¼-LITRE:

A series: B76AK*, B238AK, B242AK, B63AJ, B97AJ, B103AJ and B239AJ.

B series: B60BH, B80BH, B84BH, B288BH, B358BH, B360BH, B370BH*, B374BH, B392BH, B145BG, B151BG*, B281BG, B381BG, B389BG and B395BG.

C series: B198CF, B202CF, B424CF, B446CF, B181CD, B185CD, B333CD and B445CD.

D series: B252DA, B262DA, B380DA, B474DA, B93DZ, B327DZ, B337DZ, B383DZ, B405DZ and B443DZ.

E series: B180EY, B376EY, B488EY, B45EW, B89EW, B133EW, B189EW, B203EW, B301EW and B497EW.

F series: B46FV, B408FV, B67FU, B143FU, B287FU, B291FU, B293FU, B297FU, B403FU, B411FU and B533FU.

G series: B1GT, B3GT, B91GT, B351GT and B373GT.

H & J series: B139HP, B145HP, B195HP, B237HP and B163JN.

K series: B106KM, B110KM, B196KM and B169KL.

L series: B10LJ, B26LJ, B178LJ, B3LH, B9LH, B79LH, B139LH and B209LH.

4½-LITRE:

M series: B6MD, B8MD, B44MD, B200MD*, B202MD, B256MD, B390MD, B392MD, B133MB and B317MB.

N series: B70NZ, B84NZ, B86NZ, B146NZ, B97NY, B101NY*, B103NY, B107NY, B291NY and B473NY.

HOOPER & CO (COACHBUILDERS) LTD

The first post-war bodies from Hooper, like those of so

many other coachbuilders, came with the razor-edge styling that had been fashionable in the late 1930s. There was a four-door, four-light saloon with cutaway rear wheel spats, and a six-light derivative of it with the characteristic Hooper rear side window. In addition, Hooper built two sedanca coupés, on chassis B1EW and B47EW, and two drophead coupés, on B11AJ and B407DZ. There was a unique van body for B439EW in 1950.

However, the company's biggest success was with its 'New Look' design, number 8294. The front wings of this four-door saloon flowed down with a concave line to terminate behind the rear wheelarch, but there was no separate rear wing feature and a full spat covered the wheel. This design is commonly known as the Empress Line, after its similarity to Hooper's bodywork for the Daimler 2½-litre Empress. There was also a two-door saloon variant.

The 62 Hooper-bodied MkVI chassis were:

4¼-LITRE:

A & B series: B11AJ, B85BG, B137BG and B277BG.

C series: B2CF, B4CF, B102CF, B184CF, B288CF, B342CF, B344CF, B175CD, B325CD, B437CD, B439CD and B501CD.

D series: B118DA, B120DA, B448DA, B460DA, B468DA, B381DZ, B385DZ, B391DZ and B407DZ.

E series: B258EY, B294EY, B336EY, B1EW, B47EW, B135EW, B181EW, B193EW, B241EW, B307EW, B365EW and B439EW.

F & G series: B405FU, B409FU, B547FU and B363GT.

H series: B8HR, B92HR and B183HP.

J & K series: B2JO, B124JO, B208JO and B155KL.

L series: B270LJ, B211LH and B213LH.

4½-LITRE:

B20MD, B22MD, B266MD, B321MB, B88NZ, B156NZ, B109NY, B287NY, B293NY, B477NY and B226PV.

VANDEN PLAS (ENGLAND) 1923 LTD

The Vanden Plas name had been closely associated with Bentley since the 1920s, and the company built a batch of sports saloons, dropheads and coupés for the MkVI in 1946 and 1947. However, the company was bought by Austin during 1946 and the last Bentley body was completed early in 1948. The 21 MkVI chassis bodied by Vanden Plas, with drophead coupés denoted by an asterisk, were:

B8AK, B12AK*, B60AK, B72AK, B78AK*, B110AK*, B114AK, B230AK*, B232AK, B234AK, B17AJ, B241AJ, B243AJ, B245AJ*, B18BH, B62BH, B130BH, B294BH, B388BH, B269BG and B285BG.

E. D. ABBOTT LTD

Their 19 bodies were mostly conventional two-door drophead coupés. There were also at least three closed coupés (on B391BG, B454EY, and B353GT), and there was a solitary utility body on B259FU. The only 4½-litre chassis bodied was B10MD. The full list of chassis is:

B15AJ, B387BG, B391BG, B443CD, B146DA, B265DZ, B319DZ, B389DZ, B454EY, B137EW, B126FV, B71FU, B257FU, B259FU, B539FU, B353GT, B118JO, B177KL and B10MD.

GURNEY NUTTING LTD

The last body under Gurney Nutting's own name was built in 1947, and thereafter the firm and its designs passed to James Young. The most characteristic of the Gurney Nutting bodies was the so-called 'teardrop' sedanca coupé, production of which was later taken over by James Young. There were four drophead bodies (on B283BG, B377BG, B18CF, and B497CD), two saloons (on B449CD and B499CD), and one saloon coupé (B188CF). The body on B368BH was built in conjunction with James Young. The full list of 19 chassis is:

B368BH, B283BG, B287BG, B377BG, B383BG, B18CF, B142CF, B186CF, B188CF, B296CF, B449CD, B497CD, B499CD, B214EY, B334EY, B269EW, B403EW, B320FV and B255FU.

BENTLEY MkVI

HAROLD RADFORD (COACHBUILDERS) LTD

The first Harold Radford Countryman body was a four-door estate car on chassis number B397FG, which was exhibited at the 1948 Earls Court Show. It was built by Seary and McReady under contract to Radford, with timber-faced panelling below the waist which on later examples was available with either walnut or mahogany veneer on aluminium. Eight of these bodies were built in all.

By 1951, Radford had bought Seary and McReady, and the new company introduced a MkII Countryman, which was a four-door saloon with picnic and other items carefully stowed in compartments within the body. However, in 1953 Radford decided that the future lay in conversions of the standard saloon bodywork, and ceased making the fully-coachbuilt Countryman saloons. The conversions introduced on the R-type and later Silver Dawn chassis were also known by the Countryman name.

The 17 Radford Countryman bodies were on the following chassis:

B397BG, B204CF, B343CD, B246DA, B376DA, B341DZ, B379DZ, B441DZ, B190KM, B12LJ, B207LH, B40MD, B5MB, B131MB, B356NZ, B111NY and B495NY.

CARROSSERIE GRABER

Of the 18 bodies built by Graber, 15 were drophead coupés; one chassis number is unidentified. There were also three fixed-head coupés (B146MD, B184MD, and B190MD), and a fourth coupé body replaced the original standard saloon body on B190BH in 1951. (This chassis is not included in the totals for coachbuilt bodies on MkVI chassis.) The 17 known MkVI chassis bodied from new by Graber were:

B86AK, B105AJ, B134BH, B136BH, B190CF, B82FV, B74HR, B189HP, B214JO, B161JN, B146MD, B182MD, B184MD, B188MD, B190MD, B192MD and B74NZ.

FACEL-MÉTALLON

Some sources claim that this French company built as many as 17 bodies on specially-modified Cresta chassis (see the section on R-type Continentals) between 1948 and 1951. However, only nine have been identified for certain, but a tenth may be on chassis B141GT. All but one of these were fastback saloons built under licence from Farina in Italy, whose original design was on B323CD, the 1948 Paris Show car. All the Facel bodies have a traditional upright Bentley grille in place of the wide Farina type; they also carry special wing badging with a double-F in the Farina shield (for Farina/Facel). The final car, on B98KM, has a fixed-head coupé body and was built for Jean Daninos, owner of Facel-Métallon. Despite the chassis number it has a 4½-litre engine, having been returned to the factory for the engine change before completion in 1951.

The nine chassis definitely bodied by Facel-Métallon were:
B447CD, B402LEY, B99LEW, B441LEW, B443LEW, B445EW, B541FU, B167JN and B98KM.

CARROSSERIE FRANAY

Franay's eight bodies were mostly drophead coupés, and ranged from the relatively conventional to the flamboyant. Conventional was the two-door drophead body on B26BH, with full rear spats; instead of door handles, there were press-button releases ahead of the doors on the scuttle sides. Flamboyant was the chrome-laden, pontoon-winged B20BH, possibly one of two cars with this design. Franay also displayed a sedanca de ville at the 1951 Paris Show on B182LJ, with coach lamps on the scuttle and dummy hood irons.

The chassis bodied by Franay were:
B20BH, B26BH, B138BH, B447CD, B136LEY, B341GT, B182LJ and B324LMD.

RIPPON BROS LTD

The first of Rippon's five bodies for the MkVI chassis was a razor-edge four-door saloon on B22EH, and was

exhibited at the Earls Court Show in 1948. There were three further saloon bodies, on B372EY, B349GT and B2MD, at least one of them with sweeping wing lines rather like the Park Ward style introduced in 1950. The fifth chassis, B91FU, had a timber-panelled, two-door, four-light shooting brake body.

DAVID JOEL

The little-known firm of David Joel built bodies on five MkVI chassis. At least four of these were utility or shooting brake types in the contemporary fashion, on chassis numbers B382DA, B263DZ, B340EY and B273EW. The body on the fifth and earliest chassis, B399BG, is still unidentified, but was probably also a shooting brake.

CARROZZERIA FARINA

The Torinese coachbuilder made just five bodies on MkVI chassis, although some bodies built by Facel-Métallon (see above) were to a Farina design. There were four fixed-head coupés and one drophead. The drophead was a two-door car with prominent wings, on chassis B435CD.

Most significant of the closed bodies was the 1948 two-door fastback built as part of the 'Cresta' project, which later was licensed to Facel-Métallon. Farina's original was built on chassis B323CD and had a wide grille quite unlike the standard Bentley item. It was exhibited at the 1948 Paris Motor Show. Two similar bodies were built on B466DA and B476DA, which had been modified to left-hand drive by Rolls-Royce for the project in 1948. This car also had rear wheel spats. The remaining closed body was on 4½-litre chassis number B332MD.

WINDOVERS LTD

Windovers built four bodies on the MkVI chassis. Three were saloons, on B74AK, B95AJ and B313CD, and of these B95AJ was a two-door design. The fourth chassis was B108AK, which had a drophead coupé body with a distinctive waistband in contrasting colour which swept down across the rear wings.

FRITZ RAMSEIER & CO / CARROSSERIE WORBLAUFEN

The Swiss coachbuilder Ramseier (later renamed Worblaufen) built four, or possibly five, bodies on the MkVI chassis. The earliest was a drophead coupé in 1947 on B181AJ, which has sometimes wrongly been attributed to Franay. The other three were both three-position drophead coupés, on B237AJ in 1947, and B88FV and B412FV in 1950. A possible unidentified fifth car is the Worblaufen drophead coupé exhibited at the 1949 Geneva Motor Show.

SEARY & MACREADY

Seary & Macready built the Countryman bodies under contract to Harold Radford and were later bought out by Radford. However, two Countryman bodies are recorded under the Seary and Macready name. These are on chassis B75FU and B95JN.

SIMPSON & SLATER

This otherwise unknown company built two bodies on MkVI chassis. The first was a four-door saloon on B58AK in 1948, and the second a two-seater on B82BH in 1949.

ABURNSONS (COACHBUILDERS) LTD

The single body by Aburnsons was a two-seater shooting brake on B384CF, delivered in 1949.

BAKER

Their only body on the MkVI chassis was a saloon on B200CF, not delivered until 1950.

GEBRÜDER BEUTLER & CO

The Swiss firm of Beutler made a single two-door drophead coupé, on chassis B139BG in 1947.

COOPER MOTOR BODIES

Cooper Motor Bodies of Putney specialised in adapting bodies made by other companies, in some cases second-hand, to new or existing chassis. Their single effort on the MkVI is recorded as a two-door saloon, but it is not clear whether the body which was fitted to B178EY was new or second-hand.

DENBY

Denby built a single shooting brake body on chassis number B93FU in 1950.

DUNCAN INDUSTRIES

Duncan built a single open tourer body on chassis number B385BG in 1948.

EADON ENGINEERING CO

Details of the body built by Eadon on B159BG in 1948 are not known.

FIGONI

This French company, known as Figoni et Falaschi before the war, had specialised in exotic bodywork. Its single effort on the MkVI chassis was recorded as a two-seater cabriolet, and was on chassis number B9AJ in 1947.

CARROZZERIA GHIA SPA

No details are known of the single body built by Ghia of Turin, which was mounted on chassis B299FU in 1950.

J. A. HOLLAND

Mr Holland bought MkVI chassis B289BG in 1947 and then constructed a drophead coupé body for it in his own workshop.

RONALD KENT

Ronald Kent built just one body for the MkVI chassis, a four-door saloon on B290BH, delivered in 1950.

ROOS

Chassis B311CD was delivered to HRH Prince Bernhard and he designed a drophead coupé body, which he had built by the Dutch coachbuilder Roos.

J. SAOUTCHIK ET CIE

There was just one body built by this French coachbuilder, a four-seat tourer with cutaway doors on B440CF in 1948.

CARROSSERIE VAN VOOREN

This French coachbuilder's only MkVI body was a two-door sports saloon with cutaway spats, on chassis number B332LEY in 1949.

VINCENTS OF READING LTD

This Reading coachbuilder was responsible for a single body of unknown type on chassis B379BH. The firm's speciality was formal limousines, and the body may have been of this type.

WESTMINSTER MOTOR SUPPLIES

Westminster made a single saloon body, on B372BH.

UNKNOWN COACHBUILDERS

Only six chassis were bodied by unidentified coachbuilders. One of these (B454DA) was sold in Britain, and some sources claim it was bodied by Mulliner's of Birmingham. All the others went overseas, two to Switzerland, two to France, and one to Belgium. The Swiss chassis were B401BG and B284CF, the first bodied as a coupé and the second as a drophead coupé. It seems probable that one of these chassis carried the 18th Graber body, while the other one may have been the Fritz Ramseier/Worblaufen drophead coupé. However, some sources claim that Walter Köng of Basle built two bodies on MkVI chassis, and these are otherwise unaccounted for. The French chassis were B64CF and B43FU, and the single chassis shipped to Belgium was B374DA.

BENTLEY R-TYPE

There were fewer coachbuilt bodies on the R-type chassis than on the MkVI which preceded it. Only 255 chassis were fitted with bodies other than the standard Pressed Steel-built saloon, which works out at 10.99 per cent of all R-types and compares with 19.26 per cent for the MkVI.

Broadly speaking, the major body styles developed for the MkVI were continued for the R-type with little or no modification. Park Ward was the dominant producer of drophead coupé bodies. The most prolific coachbuilder on the R-type chassis was H. J. Mulliner, which built 60 bodies. Next came James Young with 56, Park Ward with 48, Hooper with 33, and Freestone & Webb with 24. Abbott bodied 13 chassis and Radford ten; seven more were by Graber and two by Franay. Bertone and John Jackson built just one body each.

H. J. MULLINER & CO LTD

All except for three of H. J. Mulliner's 60 bodies were closed types. They included some two-doors and some six-light saloons. The three open bodies were drophead coupés on B52LRT, B73RS and B47SP. The full list of Mulliner-bodied R-types is:

R series: B16LRT, B22RT, B40RT, B52LRT, B58RT, B62RT, B73RS and B87RS.
S series: B84SR, B98SR, B100SR, B326SR, B330SR, B350SR, B354SR, B358SR, B366SR, B370LSR, B386SR, B47SP, B51SP, B63SP, B119SP, B189SP, B195LSP, B199SP, B201SP, B205SP, B255SP, B257SP, B259SP, B261SP, B265SP, B273SP, B323SP, B327SP, B331SP, B337SP, B397SP and B399SP.
T series: B19TO, B397LTO, B136TN, B314TN and B510TN.
U series: B53UL, B55UL and B57UL.
W series: B12WH, B22WH, B30WH and B218WH.
X series: B2LXF, B4XF, B6XF and B112LXF.
Y & Z series: B5YA, B7YA, B5ZX and B215LZX.

JAMES YOUNG LTD

Every one of the 56 bodies by James Young was a closed type. There were two-door and four-door saloons, two-door saloon coupés, and a solitary sedanca coupé on B55LSP. Chassis B364SR was described as a 'two-door sports'. The full list is:

R series: B6RT, B10RT, B30RT, B36RT, B69RS, B71RS, B77RS and B83RS.
S series: B72SR, B80SR, B88SR, B90SR, B92SR, B320SR, B322SR, B328SR, B334SR, B338SR, B348SR, B362SR, B364SR, B368SR, B372SR, B374SR, B376SR, B384SR, B55LSP, B125SP and B391SP.
T series: B1TO, B7TO, B11TO, B15TO, B17TO, B134TN, B152TN, B154TN and B212UM.
U series: B43UL, B45UL, B47UL and B212UM.
W series: B8WH, B10WH, B14WH, B16WH, B20WH, B26WH, B28WH, B212WH, B214WH, B105WG and B107WG.
X & Z series: B114XF, B1ZX and B3ZX.

PARK WARD & CO LTD

Most of Park Ward's 48 bodies were once again drophead coupés. There were six fixed-head coupés (B14RT, B54RT, B59SP, B138TN, B102UM and B18WM), three two-door saloons (B79RS, B85RS and B324SR), and a single six-light saloon (B61SP). The full chassis list is:

R series: B14RT, B26LRT, B38RT, B54RT, B60RT, B79RS, B85RS and B91RS.
S series: B318SR, B324SR, B344LSR, B346SR, B352SR, B356SR, B380SR, B41LSP, B45SP, B53LSP, B57SP, B59SP, B61SP, B65SP, B69LSP, B129SP, B133LSP, B137SP, B187SP, B191LSP, B193SP, B339SP and B341SP.
T series: B3TO, B9TO, B215TO, B219TO, B132LTN, B138TN, B144TN and B146TN.
U & W series: B59UL, B102UM, B208UM, B18WH, B24WH and B202LWH.
Y & Z series: B3YA, B157YA and B69ZX.

HOOPER & CO (COACHBUILDERS) LTD

All 33 Hooper bodies are recorded as saloons, and just one of them (B311LTO) is recorded as having two doors. The full list is:

R series: B24RT, B44RT, B25RS and B75RS.
S series: B74SR, B86SR, B316SR, B378SR, B49SP, B127SP and B335SP.
T series: B213TO, B221TO, B311LTO, B150TN, B156TN, B158TN, B302TN, B320TN and B322TN.
U series: B41UL, B210UM and B216UM.
W series: B206WH, B210WH and B228WH.
X series: B8XF, B10XF, B12XF and B14XF.
Y & Z series: B1YA, B47ZX and B75ZX.

FREESTONE & WEBB LTD

There were 24 bodies by Freestone & Webb on R-type chassis, and 22 of them were four-door saloons. The other two were a two-door utility on B110TN and a drophead coupé on B204WH. The list of chassis is:

R series: B4RT, B12RT, B56RT and B81RS.
S series: B94SR, B382SR, B121SP, B123SP and B333SP.
T series: B5TO, B387TO, B399TO, B110TN, B140TN and B142TN.
U series: B101UL, B104UM, B106UM, B206UM and B214UM.
W series: B2WH, B4WH, B6WH and B204WH.

E. D. ABBOTT LTD

Just one of Abbott's 13 bodies for R-type chassis was a drophead coupé. This was on chassis B18RT. All the others were sleek and stylish two-door saloons, of a style which is sometimes incorrectly associated with the Continental chassis, perhaps because Abbot was allowed to use the lower Continental radiator and steering column. The full list of chassis numbers is:
B2RT, B18RT, B135SP, B263SP, B267LSP, B269SP, B271SP, B325SP, B329SP, B393SP, B395SP, B401SP and B218UM.

HAROLD RADFORD (COACHBUILDERS LTD)

The Radford Countryman saloon was available throughout the production run of the R-type Bentley. A total of 10 chassis had fully coachbuilt bodies by Radford, nine of them confirmed as Countryman saloons and one (on chassis B203SP) described simply as a four-door saloon. The chassis numbers are: B28RT, B78SR, B96SR, B332SR, B336LSR, B360SR, B203SP, B148TN, B49UL and B51UL.

In May 1954 Harold Radford introduced a conversion of the standard saloon to replace his fully-coachbuilt bodies on the R-type chassis. The basic price was around 20 per cent more than that of the standard saloon, although a variety of special fittings could be bought, and the exact combination of these (and therefore the final cost) varied to meet the customer's specific requirements.

These conversions were also known by the Countryman name. They have a divided estate-car type of tailgate let into the boot and rear panel. The upper section includes the rear window and opens upwards, while the lower section opens downwards like the MkVI boot. When opened, the lower lid provides extra luggage space in conjunction with the split-folding rear seats. Its inner cover can also be slid rearwards to provide a picnic table. Compartments containing picnic equipment and a vanity basin are then revealed. The conversion also included a modification which allowed the front seats to be reclined to make a double bed.

The chassis numbers of the 11 Radford conversions are: B268WH, B16XF, B82XF, B31YA, B75YA, B91YA, B133YA, B275YA, B278YD, B85ZX and B139ZX.

CARROSSERIE GRABER

The Swiss coachbuilder Graber built seven bodies on the R-type chassis: Drophead coupés: B42RT, B64RT, B89RS and B342SR. Fixed-head coupés: B82SR, B240SR and B197LSP.

CARROSSERIE FRANAY

The two chassis bodied by Franay in 1954 were B73YA and B321YA. Both were saloons.

CARROZZERIA BERTONE SPA

The single Bertone-bodied car was a four-door saloon built in 1953 for S. H. Arnolt on chassis B43LSP. Bertone had a close relationship with this American entrepreneur, and built the bodies for his Arnolt-MG, Arnolt-Aston Martin and Arnolt-Bristol sports cars. It is of some interest that the car was displayed at an Italian motor show of the time with a plaque describing it as a Bentley MkVII.

JOHN JACKSON

The body built by the otherwise unknown firm of John Jackson on chassis B76SR in late 1952 or early 1953 was a shooting brake or estate car.

ROLLS-ROYCE SILVER DAWN

The 64 coachbuilt Silver Dawns represent 8.41 per cent of the total 761 cars. There were 14 coachbuilt cars on the A- to D-series (short-boot) Silver Dawn chassis, and a further 50 on E- to J-series (big-boot) chassis. Four of the coachbuilt cars were on the 4¼-litre chassis, and the remaining 60 on 4½-litre chassis.

The largest number of bodies (28) was produced by Park Ward. Hooper and James Young came next with 12 and 11 bodies respectively, Freestone & Webb built six, and H. J. Mulliner three. Outside Britain, Chapron, Ghia and Farina all built one body each, and there was one Silver Dawn chassis sent out to Montevideo for which no coachbuilder's details are known.

One additional car, built with a standard steel body on chassis STH73, has been fitted with the Hooper body believed to have been taken from a Bentley.

PARK WARD & CO LTD

The distinctive Park Ward bodies began to appear on Silver Dawn chassis in 1950, and the last one was delivered in 1954. A total of 28 bodies was built, of which only three (all drophead coupés), were constructed on the 4¼-litre chassis.

There were five different designs, four of them drophead coupés. The majority of Silver Dawn chassis had the four-light drophead style, design 322, which had full spats at the rear. There was also a second very similar design. Design 555 was also a four-light drophead coupé, but with a higher wing line on the doors, and it was available in two-light form as design 465. Some examples of these two designs have cutaway spats, and some have none. All the dropheads came with power-operated hoods.

The fifth style was a two-door, four-light saloon based on design 555. Just two of these were fitted to Silver Dawns, chassis LSKE24 and STH93. The full list of Park Ward-bodied cars is:
LSBA108, LSBA138, LSDB30, LSFC50, LSFC136, LSHD34, LSHD46, LSHD48, LSHD54, LSHD58, LSHD60, LSKE10, LSKE24, LSLE19, LSLE43, LSMF4, LSMF10, LSMF32, LSMF36, LSMF76, LSNF21, LSNF41, SNF45, LSOG54, LSRH2, LSRH72, STH91 and STH93.

ROLLS-ROYCE SILVER DAWN

HOOPER & CO (COACHBUILDERS) LTD

All 12 of Hooper's bodies on the Silver Dawn chassis were built to design number 8401, the so-called Empress style with sweeping wings and full rear spats originally introduced for Bentley MkVI chassis as design 8294. The front doors hinge at their leading edges and the rear doors at their trailing edges, and the rear quarters have Hooper's characteristic pointed rear quarterlight. Standard bumpers are fitted. The bodies were all built in 1953 and 1954 on the 4½-litre chassis. Chassis numbers are:

SNF105, SOG52, SOG98, SRH44, SRH46, SRH48, SRH66, STH59, STH99, STH101, SUJ2 and SUJ4.

Chassis STH73 was fitted retrospectively with the Hooper two-door saloon body from a Bentley (possibly chassis B44RT).

JAMES YOUNG LTD

All 11 James Young bodies were saloons on the 4½-litre chassis, built in 1953 and 1954. Nine were built to design number C20SD, a four-door, four-light body which hints at the later standard steel Silver Cloud, but is more upright and awkward with a rather square boot line. Chassis SOG42 was fitted with a unique variant, design number C20SDB, with more curvaceous rear wings and a more sloping boot. The full list of chassis numbers is:

SNF27, SOG42, SOG44, SOG100, SPG101, SRH50, SRH68, SRH70, STH57, STH95 and STH97.

ROLLS-ROYCE SILVER CLOUD

There were 121 coachbuilt bodies on the six-cylinder Silver Cloud chassis. The major suppliers were H. J. Mulliner (43), James Young (33), and Hooper (27). Freestone & Webb built 15 bodies, Park Ward and Radford two each, and Graber made one.

H. J. MULLINER & CO LTD

The most popular of the H. J. Mulliner bodies was the two-door drophead coupé, design 7410, of which 21 examples were built on the six-cylinder Silver Cloud chassis. A two-light version of the 7410 design was fitted to LSGE466, and LSED91 had a fixed-head version of this style, known as design 7458.

The next most popular style on these chassis was what the coachbuilder termed a 'convertible coupé', converted from a standard saloon shell and carrying design number 7504. It was introduced at the New York Show in April 1959 and replaced Mulliner's fully-coachbuilt drophead, design 7410. Interestingly, the first such conversion was actually carried out in March 1958 by Park Ward on a Bentley S-series (B568FA), but that company concluded that the conversion was too costly to continue with! Thirteen of these Mulliner bodies were built on the six-cylinder Silver Cloud chassis.

The shells were 'beheaded' and converted to two-door configuration by welding on additional metal to lengthen the original front doors, removing the B-post and welding up the rear door aperture. H. J. Mulliner did this work at Chiswick as a first stage. The converted bodyshells then returned to Crewe for mounting on the chassis (using special solid mounts rather than the usual flexible ones), and for wiring, painting, and interior trimming. The hood and mechanism were added afterwards at Chiswick. Power-operated hoods, operated via electrically-actuated hydraulic rams, were optional throughout this period. The windscreen is of ¼in Triplex laminated glass but the hood has a PVC backlight. The door windows and wind-down rear quarter windows are of Triplex toughened safety glass. The front seats are the standard saloon types, with a bench cushion and divided backrest, although separate bucket seats were an optional extra. The desirability of the design has persuaded some owners to have standard saloons professionally converted in more recent years.

FREESTONE & WEBB LTD

All six bodies by Freestone &Webb were saloons, built in 1953-1954. Five were to design number 3163, a six-light style with sweeping wing lines and rear spats which was announced at the 1952 Earls Court Motor Show and is clearly derived from Hooper's offering of the time. The Freestone & Webb body has both doors hinged at their leading edges, and has special bumpers which are broader and flatter than the standard style, with the number plate incorporated within the rear bumper. The sixth body, on chassis SOG46, was design 3082/C. It borrowed the lines of the company's 1953 Earls Court Show car on a Bentley R-type chassis, and had more pronounced rear wings with cutaway spats. Freestone & Webb bodies were on the following chassis: SNF107, SOG46, SOG48, SOG50, STH53 and STH55.

H. J. MULLINER & CO LTD

The styling of the three bodies by H. J. Mulliner on Silver Dawn chassis was derived from the lightweight saloon style originally designed for the R-type Bentley chassis. Two of the three were drophead coupés, the 1952 car (SHD50) having the two-light design 7296 with Jensen-style rear window, and the 1953 car (LSLE31) having the four-light version, design 7297. The third body was a four-door lightweight saloon, and was fitted to the very last Silver Dawn chassis, LSVJ133.

HENRI CHAPRON

Chapron's single body on the Silver Dawn was a two-door, two-light drophead coupé built during 1954 on chassis LSTH79. It is broadly similar in appearance to the H. J. Mulliner style 7296.

CARROZZERIA GHIA SPA

The unusual Ghia body was on chassis LSHD22 in 1952 and was a four-door limousine with rear-hinged rear doors and an alligator bonnet. The radiator shell was reduced in height by 3¼in and was mounted 6in ahead of its standard position. The bodywork contains no wood at all, but the metal facia is painted in imitation woodgrain. The car was built for the Contessa Ida Matarazzo but was not, as it was once thought, the model exhibited at the 1952 Turin Motor Show (that was a Silver Wraith).

CARROZZERIA FARINA

Farina's only bodywork for the Silver Dawn was a two-door fastback saloon on chassis SCA43. It was displayed at the 1951 Turin Motor Show.

UNKNOWN

Chassis number SMF72 was exported to Montevideo in early 1953. No further details are known except the name of the first owner, J. L. R. Tellechea.

HAROLD RADFORD (COACHBUILDERS) LTD

When production of the Countryman coachbuilt bodies on Bentley chassis ceased, Radford offered conversions on the 4½-litre Silver Dawn chassis in exactly the same way as on the contemporary Bentley. Just three were made, on chassis SOG30, SRH84 and STH29.

H. J. Mulliner also built one example of a curious style with externally-mounted spare wheel, probably on LSWA62. In addition, H. J. Mulliner did the bodywork conversion for the Radford Safari estates (see below).

The full list of chassis bodied by H. J. Mulliner is:

FULLY COACHBUILT BODIES:
LSWA62, SWA76, SWA94, LSWA104, LSWA106, SYB30, SYB162, LSZB247, SBC118, SCC95, LSED91, LSDD146, SDD194, LSDD302, LSED193, SED257, SED345, LSED451, LSFE449, LSFE451, LSFE483, SGE40, LSGE210, SGE310, LSGE466, SGE482, LSGE492, LSJF204, SKG31 and SKG33.

'CONVERTIBLE COUPÉ' CONVERSIONS:
LSJF60, LSLG110, LSLG114, LSMH21, LSMH57, SMH129, LSMH169, LSMH195, LSMH207, LSMH245, SNH14, LSNH40 and SNH106.

JAMES YOUNG LTD

The first James Young style for the Silver Cloud was a four-door saloon, design SC10. The second example, on SWA52, was exhibited at the 1955 Earls Court Show. There were 17 chassis bodied with this design; earlier examples have fins on the rear wings, but later examples do not. SXA129 had a modified version of the styling with protruding headlamps on the wing fronts.

The same basic styling was also used for a two-door sports saloon, of which five examples were built, on chassis SZB203, SZB205, SDD308, SDD310 and LSHF111.

Design SCV100 was available in either four-door saloon or two-door saloon coupé style. It is broadly similar to the SC10 design, but has a longer rear quarterlight and flatter tops to the rear wings. Just one two-door saloon coupé was built on the six-cylinder Silver Cloud chassis, this being on LSDD44.

James Young also built two drophead coupés (SC20), on LSGE448 and LSHF162, and a single two-seater drophead coupé on LSJF202. In addition, there were two examples of a two-door sedanca coupé, also known as design number SC20, on LSFE99 and LSJF112.

The list of chassis bodied by James Young is:

SWA50, SWA52, SWA54, SWA60, SWA66, SWA88, SWA90, SWA96, SWA110, SXA47, SXA119, SXA121, SXA129, SXA133, SXA135, LSXA137, LSYB114, SZB41, SZB43, SZB203, SZB205, LSBC98, LSDD44, SDD306,

SDD308, SDD310, LSFE99, SGE248, LSGE448, LSHF111, LSHF162, LSJF112 and LSJF202.

HOOPER & CO (COACHBUILDERS) LTD

Hooper's earliest design was also its most popular. This carried number 8435 and was known as the Empress Line body, a four-door sports saloon with sweeping wing line, spatted rear wheels and hooded headlamps in the noses of the wings. Nine of these bodies were built. There was also a touring limousine variant, design 8444, with a shaped cut-out in the rear spats. A third variant, design 8523, was broadly similar but had the headlamps conventionally located inboard of the wing noses.

Hooper also made an unusual two-door drophead body on LSGE252 to design number 8530, and there was a single fixed-head coupé on LSLG78, built in conjunction with Rolls-Royce.

The full list of 27 chassis bodied by Hooper is:

SWA44, SWA46, SWA58, SWA64, SWA72, SWA92, SWA98, SWA100, SWA102, SXA43, SXA45, SXA125, SXA127, SXA131, SYB18, SYB22, SZB25, SZB27, SZB91, SZB93, SZB245, SBC24, SDD148, SED97, SED251, LSGE252 and LSLG78.

FREESTONE & WEBB LTD

The earliest design from this coachbuilder was 3193, a two-door, four-light saloon with sweeping, Hooper-like wing lines and full rear spats. The same overall styling was also adopted for a four-door, six-light saloon, design 3206. Completely different in style was design 3224SC, a four-door, six-light body with hooded headlamps and a rather straight-cut rear wing line. In 1957 a one-off two-seater drophead coupé with prominent fins on the rear wings, design 3243 known as the Honeymoon Express, was built and exhibited at the London Motor Show.

The 15 Silver Cloud chassis bodied by Freestone & Webb were:

SWA42, SWA48, SWA56, SWA74, SWA108, SXA49, SXA117, SXA123, SYB20, SYB24, SZB95, SZB149, SED179, SED337 and SGE270.

CARROSSERIE GRABER

The single body was a drophead coupé on chassis SWA30.

ROLLS-ROYCE SILVER CLOUD

HAROLD RADFORD (COACHBUILDERS) LTD

The Radford Countryman conversions followed the same principles as the Radford conversions on the earlier R-type chassis. They were based on the standard steel saloon, and each one was individually specified with a choice from Radford's list of 38 options. These included: a modified boot lid (raised by 3in), fully-reclining front seats, split-folding rear seat backs, a Tudor Webasto folding fabric sunroof, fine lines painted along the wings, an expanding sunglasses pouch for either sunvisor, a folding wire mesh dog's cage, an extending picnic table (sliding out from the boot floor), a picnic kit of kettle and washbasin in the boot, 'toadstool' cushions for the rear overriders, and a fishing rod container carried below the doors. In addition, glasses, decanters and flasks could be carried in compartments let into the front doors or fitted behind the front seats.

The Harold Radford name is also associated with two Safari Town and Country estate-car bodies, both on left-hand-drive six-cylinder Silver Cloud chassis. These are LSLG112 and LSMH65. The cars were converted from standard saloons, and the metalwork of the body conversion was actually carried out by H. J. Mulliner to their design number 7501. Radford carried out interior trimming, which included a split folding rear seat in each case. (Two similar bodies were also built on long-wheelbase Silver Cloud chassis.)

BENTLEY S-SERIES

Of the 3072 Bentley S-series chassis, just 135 (4.39%) were fitted with coachbuilt bodies. Hooper was the most popular coachbuilder, with 44 bodies. There were 41 by H. J. Mulliner, 34 by James Young, 23 by Freestone & Webb, two by Graber, one by Park Ward and one by Harold Radford.

HOOPER & CO (COACHBUILDERS) LTD

All of the 44 Hooper bodies are recorded as saloons, except for two (B424CK and B172EG) where the bodywork type is unknown. The majority of these bodies probably had the Empress Line styling of design 8435.

The six-cylinder S-series chassis bodied by Hooper were: B50AN, B182AN, B184AN, B208AN, B210AN, B214AN, B460AN, B466AN, B476AN, B5AP, B17AP, B19AP, B25AP, B27AP, B85AP, B123AP, B159AP, B193AP, B287AP, B293AP, B301AP, B10BA, B16BA, B28BA, B40BA, B46BA, B154LBA, B51BC, B53BC, B300CK, B302CK, B356CK, B358CK, B424CK, B172EG, B174EG, B176EG, B500EG, B502EG, B504EG, B17EK, B375EK, B286LFA and B556FA.

H. J. MULLINER & CO LTD

Among the 41 bodies built by H. J. Mulliner on these chassis were 13 fully-coachbuilt drophead coupés. In addition one chassis (B357FD) had the standard saloon body converted to design 7492. The chassis were:

SALOONS:
B216AN, B450AN, B472AN, B11AP, B15AP, B21AP, B195AP, B277AP, B285AP, B295AP, B12BA, B18BA, B22BA, B24BA, B32BA, B34BA, B36BA, B38BA, B42BA, B142BA, B146BA, B150BA, B156BA, B59BC, B345CM, B100DB, B214LEG and B332LEG.

COACHBUILT DROPHEAD COUPÉS:
B1AP, B155AP, B291AP, B299AP, B8BA, B20BA, B48LBA, B52BA, B152LBA, B610LEG, B122LFA, B212LFA and B357FD.

JAMES YOUNG LTD

All 34 James Young bodies on the six-cylinder S-series were closed types. Their chassis numbers were: B452AN, B454AN, B456AN, B470AN, B480AN, B482AN, B484AN, B488AN, B490AN, B9AP, B81AP, B119AP, B157AP, B275AP, B279AP, B283AP, B303LAP, B6BA, B14BA, B26BA, B30BA, B44BA, B50BA, B140BA, B148BA, B55BC, B57BC, B61BC, B63BC, B350CK, B352CK, B207CM, B209CM and B120EG.

FREESTONE & WEBB LTD

All Freestone & Webb's 23 bodies on these chassis were saloons except for one drophead coupé (B377EK). The chassis numbers were: B202LAN, B204AN, B212AN, B458AN, B464AN, B474AN, B486AN, B3AP, B7AP, B23AP, B83AP, B121AP, B281AP, B289AP, B297AP, B138BA, B144BA, B354CK, B53CM, B286LEG, B532EG, B377EK and B402FA.

CARROSSERIE GRABER

The Swiss coachbuilder Graber built just two bodies on the S-series Bentley chassis. Both were drophead coupés on B462LAN and B478AN.

PARK WARD & CO LTD

The only body by Park Ward on the six-cylinder S-series Bentley was the prototype of the drophead conversion later offered by H. J. Mulliner as their design 7504. This body was on chassis B568FA.

HAROLD RADFORD (COACHBUILDERS) LTD

The single body by Radford is recorded as a conversion of the standard car, and was probably therefore a prototype for the Countryman conversions. It was on chassis number B236AN. Radford Countryman conversions of the standard coachwork were available on Bentley chassis in exactly the same way as on Rolls-Royce chassis, and with the same range of optional fittings.

ROLLS-ROYCE SILVER CLOUD & BENTLEY S-SERIES LONG WHEELBASE

Just 50 long-wheelbase chassis were supplied to coach-builders for special bodywork. Of these, 38 were on Rolls-Royce chassis and 12 on Bentley. There were 22 bodies by James Young (five Bentleys), 20 by Hooper (seven Bentleys), three from Park Ward, two from Freestone & Webb, two from Harold Radford and one from Henri Chapron.

JAMES YOUNG LTD

The James Young bodies were mainly to the company's elegant SCT100 touring limousine design, known as the 'mini-Phantom'. However, there were also several cars bodied with design SC12, a four-door, six-light body, which was really a lengthened version of the company's SC10 body for standard-wheelbase chassis. The 22 chassis were:
Rolls-Royce chassis: ALC2, ALC3, ALC4, ALC6, ALC7, ALC8, ALC20, ALC22, ALC23, LALC26, BLC14, BLC15, BLC44, LCLC4, LCLC6, CLC7 and CLC14.
Bentley chassis: ALB8, LALB12, ALB19, ALB20 and ALB25.

HOOPER & CO (COACHBUILDERS) LTD

Hooper built bodies to three designs on the long-wheelbase chassis, but all 20 of them shared instantly-recognisable common styling. The front wing swept down across both doors to meet the leading edge of the cut-out in the rear wheel spat, and the headlamp was cowled within the nose of each wing. Design 8444 was a six-light touring limousine, design 8504 was essentially the same but with a division, and design 8570 was a four-light saloon variant.
Rolls-Royce chassis: ALC5, ALC9, ALC11, ALC12, ALC14, ALC21, BLC2, BLC31, BLC32, BLC35, BLC39, LCLC1 and LCLC5.
Bentley chassis: ALB3, ALB5, ALB6, ALB17, ALB18, LALB28 and LALB29.

PARK WARD & CO LTD

All three bodies by Park Ward were on the Rolls-Royce chassis: ALC1X (prototype of the standard long-wheelbase body), BLC10 and LBLC11.

FREESTONE & WEBB LTD

Both bodies were six-light limousines built on Rolls-Royce chassis to design 3191. The first was on chassis ALC1, exhibited at the 1957 London Motor Show. It had cowled headlamps similar to those favoured by Hooper and an unusual kicked-up styling line on the rear wings, which were separated from the boot. The second similar body was on chassis ALC10.

HAROLD RADFORD (COACHBUILDERS) LTD

The two Radford bodies were Safari Town and Country estate cars, generally similar to the two of the same name built on the standard-wheelbase chassis. H. J. Mulliner did the metalwork of both to their design 7503. They were built on Rolls-Royce chassis LCLC38 and LCLC42 in August 1959.

HENRI CHAPRON

Chapron's single body was a limousine on Rolls-Royce chassis LBLC22.

ROLLS-ROYCE SILVER CLOUD II & BENTLEY S2

There were 107 coachbuilt bodies on Rolls-Royce Silver Cloud II chassis and 18 on Bentley S2 chassis. All were two-door 'convertible coupé' conversions by H. J. Mulliner of the standard saloon body. The design numbers were 7492 (Bentley) and 7504 (Rolls-Royce), but became 2007 under the merged Mulliner, Park Ward concern. Despite the merger with Park Ward, all these cars are thought to have carried sill treadplates bearing only the H. J. Mulliner name. A power-operated hood, with hydraulic rams actuated by an electric motor, was optional on these bodies. The chassis numbers were:

ROLLS-ROYCE SILVER CLOUD II:
A series: SPA108, LSPA258, LSPA260, LSRA19, LSRA139, LSRA245, LSRA295 and LSRA309.
B series: STB28, STB88, LSTB172, STB190, LSTB278, LSTB298, LSTB324, LSTB366, STB410, STB444, LSVB27, SVB63, SVB99, SVB143, LSVB269, LSVB319, LSVB369 and LSVB451.
C series: LSWC68, SWC122, LSWC148, SWC178, LSWC230, LSWC278, LSWC418, LSWC510, LSWC524, LSWC596, LSWC680, LSWC730, LSXC67, LSXC123, LSXC173, SXC277, LSXC323, LSXC359, SXC465, SXC521, LSXC605 and SXC637.
D series: SYD8, LSYD46, LSYD78, SYD118, LSYD150, SYD188, LSYD218, LSYD260, SYD288, SYD310, LSYD334, LSYD366, LSYD390, LSYD428, LSYD456, SYD486, LSZD11, SZD43, LSZD53, LSZD67, SZD79, SZD101, LSZD115, LSZD135, LSZD161, SZD311, LSZD355, SZD373, LSZD381, LSZD395, SZD405, SZD415, LSZD423, LSZD443, SZD475, LSZD483, LSZD493, LSZD519, LSZD539 and SZD549.
E series: LSAE9, LSAE19, LSAE53, LSAE67, SAE79, LSAE89, LSAE105, SAE113, LSAE127, LSAE281,

ROLLS-ROYCE SILVER CLOUD II

LSAE289, SAE293, LSAE347, LSAE497, LSAE499, LSAE561, LSAE583, LSAE637 and LSAE639.

BENTLEY S2:
B169AA, B75LBR, B78BS, B206BS, B328BS, B127CT, B221CT, B323LCT, B28CU, B178CU, B300CU, B360CU, B402CU, B554CU, B277DV, B423LDV, B2LDW and B68LDW.

HAROLD RADFORD (COACHBUILDERS) LTD
The Radford Countryman conversions of the Rolls-Royce Silver Cloud II and S2 Bentley standard saloons were available in exactly the same way as they had been on the previous six-cylinder models. Extra equipment offered included a removable division with sliding glass windows, and divided rear seat squabs which folded singly or together to provide extra luggage space. This could also be increased by a boot lid giving 3in more depth. Interior fittings ranged from vanity sets to flasks and glasses.

ROLLS-ROYCE SILVER CLOUD II & BENTLEY S2 LONG WHEELBASE

There were 41 coachbuilt bodies on the long-wheelbase Rolls-Royce Silver Cloud II chassis, and a further six on the Bentley equivalent. Most were James Young touring limousines; two chassis had Park Ward bodies, and Hooper, H. J. Mulliner and Wendler built one each.

JAMES YOUNG LTD
James Young built 37 bodies on the long-wheelbase Silver Cloud II chassis and a further five on the Bentley equivalent, making the company the most prolific on these chassis with a total of 42 bodies. The majority were touring limousines to design SCT100. However, there were two four-door saloons (LCB81 and LCD19) and one body (on LCB49) was built in conjunction with the London company FLM Panelcraft. James Young also fitted a Park Ward body to LCA39, a chassis ex-stock at Rolls-Royce's Lillie Hall depot in London.

ROLLS-ROYCE CHASSIS:
LCA2, LCA3, LLCA4, LCA23, LCA25, LCA26, LCA27, LLCA38, LLCA43; LCB6, LCB7, LCB8, LCB24, LCB25, LCB38, LCB39, LCB49, LCB68, LCB69, LCB81, LCB101, LLCC2, LLCC3, LCC8, LCC23, LCC39, LCC40, LCC45, LCC46, LCC47, LLCC65, LCC66, LCC68, LCC76, LCC101, LCD1 and LCD19.

BENTLEY CHASSIS:
LBA8, LBA20, LBB7, LBB10 and LBB21.

HOOPER & CO (COACHBUILDERS) LTD
The single body was a saloon with division, on Bentley chassis LLCA1, shown at Earls Court in 1959.

H. J. MULLINER & CO LTD
This was a one-off coachbuilt four-door cabriolet to design 7484 on Rolls-Royce chassis LLCB16. The rear doors were front hinged and the windows wound down completely but there were no rear quarter windows. A special fitting was a handrail across the backs of the front seats.

PARK WARD & CO LTD
Rolls-Royce chassis LLCA12 was bodied as a saloon with division. They also built the body fitted by James Young to Rolls-Royce chassis LCA39 (see left).

WENDLER
This company built a single shooting brake (estate car) on Rolls-Royce chassis LLBA9 for an American customer.

ROLLS-ROYCE SILVER CLOUD III & BENTLEY S3

The variety of body styles available from the coachbuilders was much more limited in this period, and the practice of offering what was essentially the same body on the standard and on the Continental chassis led to the almost total extinction of the coachbuilt Bentley. Just one Bentley S3 standard chassis was given a coachbuilt body, and that was in January 1963.

So for the last three years of chassis production, customers who wanted a coachbuilt body could choose between the Bentley Continental and the standard Rolls-Royce chassis. Even here, the distinction was not what it had been. The Continental no longer offered significantly higher performance, and from mid-1963, the Continental's more steeply raked steering column came as standard on those Rolls-Royce chassis intended for coachbuilt bodywork.

There were 328 coachbuilt bodies on Silver Cloud III chassis. Of these, 217 were bodied before mainstream production ended in mid-1965. Just before then, a new numbering sequence was started for coachbuilt chassis, and these remained available for the coachbuilders until early 1966, when the new H. J. Mulliner, Park Ward two-door saloon version of the Silver Shadow went on sale. A further 111 coachbuilt bodies were delivered on these specially-designated chassis, 103 of them bodied by H. J. Mulliner, Park Ward and the remaining eight by James Young of Bromley.

H. J. MULLINER, PARK WARD LTD
The merged coachbuilding concern of H. J. Mulliner, Park Ward Ltd offered four different body styles on the Silver Cloud III chassis: a drophead coupé, a 'convertible coupé' and two- and four-door saloons.

The 'convertible coupé' design was the Mulliner conversion of the standard saloon body, now renumbered as design 2007. A total of 38 Silver Cloud III models was turned into convertibles with this body style between October 1962 and September 1963. From that date, however, the design was replaced by a derivative of the Koren style, which had been introduced by Park Ward for the Bentley S2 Continental. This drophead coupé was design 2045, and the first Rolls-Royce chassis to be fitted with it (SEV111) was exhibited at the 1963 Earls Court Motor Show.

The Koren style was modified to accept twin head-lamps, and is generally similar to its equivalent on the S3 Continental chassis, except that the taller Rolls-Royce grille is accompanied by different panelwork for the bonnet and nose. The 98 Silver Cloud III chassis to which it is fitted have the more steeply raked steering column of the Bentley Continental chassis, but they have simpler Rolls-Royce instrumentation, grouped in a panel directly ahead of the driver. Cars built into 1963 carry Park Ward sill plates, but later examples have the full H. J. Mulliner, Park Ward coachbuilder's identification. The Rolls-Royce bodies usually have a chromed side strip, which is not usually present on the Bentley version, and most Rolls-Royce chassis with this design also carry the older style of large overriders.

There is also a two-door saloon version of this body, design 2041, which follows the lines of the drophead cars but has a fixed roof with a slightly hooded rear window. H. J. Mulliner, Park Ward built 114 of these Rolls-Royce saloons. The two Koren designs account for the majority (212) of special bodies on the standard-wheelbase Silver Cloud III chassis.

From the 1963 Earls Court Motor Show, the H. J. Mulliner Flying Spur body (now MPW design 2042) was also made available for the Silver Cloud III chassis and 52 were built. Once again the instrumentation was simpler, without the rev counter of the Continental chassis. These bodies were actually built in the Park Ward factory at High Road, Willesden.

The full list of 302 Silver Cloud III chassis with bodies by H. J. Mulliner, Park Ward is:

'CONVERTIBLE COUPÉ' CONVERSIONS (2007):
C series: SCX1, LSCX3, LSCX189, LSCX231, LSCX257, LSCX283, LSCX309, LSCX361, LSCX387, LSCX389, LSCX437, SCX439, LSCX447, LSCX547, LSCX629, LSCX659, SCX723, LSCX789 and LSCX843.

D series: LSDW33, SDW63, SDW87, SDW111, LSDW167, SDW189, LSDW221, SDW247, LSDW297, LSDW429, SDW445, LSDW481 and LSDW573.

E series: SEV11, SEV63, LSEV93, LSEV169, LSEV193 and SEV337.

TWO-DOOR SALOONS (DESIGN 2041):
E series: LSEV113, LSEV115, SEV117, SEV287, LSEV325, LSEV415 and LSEV481.

F series: SFU17, LSFU121, LSFU123, LSFU161, LSFU175, SFU177, LSFU217, LSFU255, SFU257, SFU401, SFU403, SFU407, SFU517, SFU579, SFU581, SFU583, SFU585, SFU587, LSFU617, SFU623, LSFU781, SFU793, SFU795 and SFU797.

G series: SGT555, LSGT557, LSGT559, LSGT561, SGT569, SGT573C, LSGT579C, SGT581C, SGT585C, SGT595C, SGT597C, SGT603C, LSGT605C, SGT613C, SGT615C, SGT619C, LSGT625C, LSGT629C, LSGT639C, LSGT641C, LSGT649C, SGT653C and LSGT659C.

H series: SHS303C, LSHS307C, SHS309C, LSHS315C, SHS317C, SHS319C, SHS325C, SHS327C, SHS331C, SHS337C, SHS339C, SHS345C and SHS355C.

J series: SJR565C, SJR573C, SJR575C, SJR577C, SJR583C, SJR587C, SJR591C, SJR593C, SJR599C, SJR601C, LSJR605C, SJR613C, LSJR619C and LSJR623C.

Coachbuilt B series: CSC1B, LCSC5B, CSC7B, CSC15B, LCSC23B, LCSC37B, LCSC41B, LCSC47B, CSC49B, LCSC57B, LCSC59B, CSC65B, CSC69B, CSC71B, CSC79B, CSC83B, LCSC85B, CSC87B, LCSC89B, LCSC93B, CSC95B, LCSC105B, CSC109B, CSC119B, LCSC123B, CSC131B and CSC133B.

Coachbuilt C series: CSC9C, CSC15C, CSC17C, CSC21C, CSC25C and CSC31C.

FOUR-DOOR SALOONS (FLYING SPUR, 2042):
E series: LSEV119, SEV323 and SEV417.

F series: LSFU119, LSFU215, SFU261, SFU409, LSFU519, SFU621, LSFU783, SFU787 and SFU799 and SFU801.

G series: SGT553, SGT563, LSGT575C, SGT583C, SGT591C, SGT599C, SGT617C, LSGT627C, LSGT631C and LSGT637C.

H series: SHS311C, SHS321C, SHS341C, SHS347C and LSHS353C.

J series: SJR567C, SJR579C, SJR585C and SJR615C.

Coachbuilt B series: LCSC3B, LCSC9B, LCSC19B, LCSC25B, CSC33B, CSC43B, CSC51B, CSC67B, CSC73B, CSC111B and CSC135B.

Coachbuilt C series: LCSC1C, CSC3C, CSC23C, CSC29C, LCSC45C, CSC51C, LCSC61C, CSC69C and CSC71C.

DROPHEAD COUPÉS (DESIGN 2045):
E & F series: SEV111, LSEV253, LSFU83, LSFU117, LSFU125, SFU213, LSFU253, SFU259, LSFU405, LSFU515, LSFU785, SFU789, LSFU791 and SFU803.

G series: SGT565C, LSGT571C, LSGT577C, SGT587C, SGT589C, SGT593C, SGT601C, SGT611C, LSGT621C, SGT623C, LSGT633C, LSGT643C, LSGT645C, LSGT647C, LSGT651C, LSGT655C and LSGT657C.

H series: LSHS323C, LSHS329C, SHS333C, SHS335C, SHS349C, SHS351C and SHS357C.

J series: SJR563C, LSJR571C, LSJR581C, LSJR595C,

ROLLS-ROYCE SILVER CLOUD III

SJR597C, LSJR603C, SJR607C, SJR609C, LSJR611C and SJR617C.

Coachbuilt B series: CSC11B, CSC21B, CSC27B, CSC29B, LCSC35B, LCSC39B, CSC45B, LCSC53B, LCSC55B, CSC61B, CSC63B, LCSC75B, CSC77B, LCSC81B, CSC97B, LCSC107B, LCSC113B, LCSC121B, LCSC125B, CSC127B, LCSC129B, CSC137B, CSC139B and CSC141B.

Coachbuilt C series: CSC5C, LCSC7C, LCSC11C, LCSC19C, CSC27C, LCSC33C, LCSC35C, LCSC37C, LCSC39C, CSC41C, LCSC43C, CSC47C, CSC49C, CSC53C, CSC55C, CSC57C, CSC59C, CSC63C, LCSC65C, CSC67C, CSC73C, LCSC75C, LCSC77C, LCSC79C, CSC81C and LCSC83C.

JAMES YOUNG LTD

James Young bodied 26 Silver Cloud III chassis, and of these 20 had the four-door SCV100 saloon body also offered on the Bentley Continental S3 chassis. The Rolls-Royce variant carries a bright trim strip on the doors at the level of the door handles, and its instrumentation is simpler than on the Continental, with the Rolls-Royce four-in-one combined instrument instead of a rev counter and four smaller dials.

Six examples of a two-door variant of this body were built, on chassis numbers LSGT607C, LSGT609C, CSC31B, CSC91B, CSC99B and CSC101B. The two-door design carries the same SCV100 design number as the four-door from which it is derived.

The full list of chassis bodied by James Young is: SEV121, SFU81, SFU127, SFU265, SFU411, SFU513, SFU619, SFU651, SGT567C, LSGT607C, LSGT609C, LSGT635C, SHS305C, SHS313C, SHS343C, SJR569C, SJR589C, SJR621C, CSC17B, CSC31B, CSC91B, CSC99B, CSC101B, CSC103B, CSC115B and CSC117B.

HAROLD RADFORD (COACHBUILDERS) LTD

Harold Radford continued to offer a variety of modifications for the standard saloon bodies on Silver Cloud III and Bentley S3 chassis. A selection from the company's catalogue includes: removable division, lockable container under the facia, electric aerial on the front wing, rubber overmats for the passenger compartment and boot, wing mirrors, flasher repeater light units on the B/C posts (doubling as parking lamps), picnic table with Formica top in the boot (doubling as a grandstand) and Remington electric razor.

ROLLS-ROYCE SILVER CLOUD III & BENTLEY S3 LONG WHEELBASE

A total of 55 long-wheelbase chassis was fitted with coachbuilt bodywork. Of these, 47 were Rolls-Royce models and eight were Bentleys.

JAMES YOUNG LTD

Most of the special coachwork on the long-wheelbase Silver Cloud III and Bentley S3 chassis was by James Young; the most popular design was the SCT100 touring limousine. This was first introduced for the Silver Cloud II and Bentley S2 chassis, and was similar in many respects to the James Young styling for the Phantom V. For this reason, the cars are often known as 'mini-Phantoms'.

There were also two cars on the Rolls-Royce chassis with a two-door version of the design, known as SCT200: LCDL1 was built for King Hassan II of Morocco, and

CEL19 features different rear quarter-lights in the more angular Hooper style.

The 42 long-wheelbase Silver Cloud III chassis with James Young bodywork are:
LCAL1, CAL3, CAL5, LCAL17, CAL49, CAL55, CAL57, CAL83, CBL15, CBL17, CBL29, CBL31, CBL51, CBL57, LCCL1, CCL5, CCL17, CCL27, CCL33, CCL35, CCL47, CCL57, CCL61, CCL69, CCL73, CCL83, CCL97, LCDL1, LCDL15, CDL53, CDL79, LCDL81, CEL11, CEL19, CEL41, CEL47, LCEL59, CEL71, CEL101, LCFL3, CFL15 and LCFL39.

The eight long-wheelbase Bentley S3 chassis bodied by James Young are:
LBAL4, BAL26, BBL6, BCL4, BCL6, BCL12, BCL16 and LBCL22.

H. J. MULLINER, PARK WARD LTD

Just five bodies on the long-wheelbase Silver Cloud III chassis were built by the combined firm of H. J. Mulliner, Park Ward. All were four-door cabriolets to design 2033, and all have the single headlamps, wing-top sidelamps and taller radiators associated with the six-cylinder and earlier V8-engined cars.

The special bodies on Rolls-Royce chassis CAL37 and CAL39 were built for the Australian Government in 1962, and both have elevating split rear seats for processional purposes. Handrails can be fitted to the tops of both front seats. These cars also have the early type of rear lamps.

The three later cars have the larger rear lamps of the standard Silver Cloud III. They are on chassis numbers CCL9, CDL3, and CEL87.

Rolls-Royce & Bentley Clubs

Even though the UK-based Rolls-Royce Enthusiasts' Club is generally seen as the principal enthusiasts' club, it is by no means the oldest one. Founded in 1957, it was preceded by both its American (1951) and Australian (1956) counterparts, as well as by the Bentley Drivers' Club in Britain.

Rolls-Royce Enthusiasts' Club, The Hunt House, High Street, Paulerspury, Northampton NN12 7NA (tel 01327 811788). The RREC covers the UK and Europe, and it shares its headquarters with the Sir Henry Royce Memorial Foundation. The Club was founded in 1957 and caters for the owners of both Rolls-Royce and post-1931 Bentley cars, right through to the current models. The RREC operates at regional level through 20 sections in the UK and a further 16 in European countries, South Africa, Hong Kong and Canada. These sections arrange social gatherings, rallies, road runs and trips, and the RREC centrally also organises some

outstandingly good technical seminars to assist owners in the maintenance of their own cars. There is an Annual Rally and Concours, and the Club publishes an excellent bi-monthly magazine, called the *Bulletin*.

Bentley Drivers' Club, W. O. Bentley Memorial Building, 16 Chearsley Road, Long Crendon, Aylesbury, Buckinghamshire HP189AW (tel 01844 208233). The BDC was established more than 60 years ago, originally to cater for the owners of pre-1931 Bentleys (those built before Rolls-Royce bought the company). While it would be true to say that the Club's primary orientation has not changed, it does welcome the owners of the Bentley models covered in this book. In particular, owners of the R-type Continentals often have an allegiance towards this club.

Rolls-Royce Owners' Club, 191 Hempt Road, Mechanicsburg, Pennsylvania

17055, USA. The hugely enthusiastic North American club for Rolls-Royce and Bentley owners was founded in 1951 and is the oldest all-model Rolls-Royce club in the world. Like the RREC, it operates at regional level through its sections, of which there are 33 spread right across the United States and Canada. Activities at local level include meetings, rallies and tours, while at national level there are technical seminars and the Annual Meet. The RROC's magazine is a bi-monthly publication called *The Flying Lady*.

Rolls-Royce Owners' Club of Australia, Malcolm Johns & Company, Level 12, Skygarden, 77 Castlereagh Street, Sydney, New South Wales 2000. This club was founded in 1956 and has local branches in six states or territories of Australia, and these take turns to host the annual Federal Rally. In addition, there are activities at a more local level, and the Club publishes a bi-monthly magazine called *Praeclarum*.